MCSE Exam Notes™:
SQL Server 6.5
Administration

Rick Sawtell
Lance Mortensen

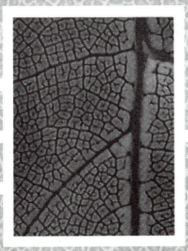

San Francisco • Paris • Düsseldorf • Soest

Associate Publisher: Guy Hart-Davis
Contracts and Licensing Manager: Kristine Plachy
Acquisitions & Developmental Editor: Neil Edde
Editor: Kathy Grider-Carlyle
Project Editor: Lisa Duran
Technical Editor: Doug Smith
Book Designer: Bill Gibson
Graphic Illustrator: Tony Jonick
Electronic Publishing Specialist: Cyndy Johnsen
Production Coordinator: Charles Mathews
Indexer: Nancy Guenther
Cover Designer: Archer Design
Cover Illustrator/Photographer: FPG International

Screen reproductions produced with Collage Complete.

Collage Complete is a trademark of Inner Media Inc.

SYBEX, Network Press, and the Network Press logo are registered trademarks of SYBEX Inc.

TRADEMARKS: SYBEX has attempted throughout this book to distinguish proprietary trademarks from descriptive terms by following the capitalization style used by the manufacturer.

Microsoft, the Microsoft Internet Explorer logo, Windows, Windows NT, and the Windows logo are either registered trademarks or trademarks of Microsoft Corporation in the United States and/or other countries.

Library of Congress Card Number: 98-86620
ISBN: 0-7821-2306-6

Manufactured in the United States of America

10 9 8 7 6 5 4 3 2 1

November 1, 1997

Dear SYBEX Customer:

Microsoft is pleased to inform you that SYBEX is a participant in the Microsoft®
Independent Courseware Vendor (ICV) program. Microsoft ICVs design, develop,
and market self-paced courseware, books, and other products that support Microsoft
software and the Microsoft Certified Professional (MCP) program.

To be accepted into the Microsoft ICV program, an ICV must meet set criteria. In
addition, Microsoft reviews and approves each ICV training product before
permission is granted to use the Microsoft Certified Professional Approved Study
Guide logo on that product. This logo assures the consumer that the product has
passed the following Microsoft standards:

- The course contains accurate product information.
- The course includes labs and activities during which the student can apply
  knowledge and skills learned from the course.
- The course teaches skills that help prepare the student to take corresponding
  MCP exams.

Microsoft ICVs continually develop and release new MCP Approved Study Guides.
To prepare for a particular Microsoft certification exam, a student may choose one or
more single, self-paced training courses or a series of training courses.

You will be pleased with the quality and effectiveness of the MCP Approved Study
Guides available from SYBEX.

Sincerely,

Holly Heath
ICV Account Manager
Microsoft Training & Certification

MICROSOFT INDEPENDENT COURSEWARE VENDOR PROGRAM

To all the MCSE students and their families; and to all the time, energy, and expense spent in pursuit of the MCSE. We hope you will agree that it was worth it.

And to family and friends:

Melissa

Mom

Dad

Rick

Lance

Luann

Bryce

Jessany

Devin

Logan

* Kenya

Acknowledgments

Thanks to all of the great people at Sybex. You've made the mountains of work involved with putting together a book a pleasurable experience.

As always, thanks to Melissa for all of the support and understanding that you gave while I spent long evenings and weekends putting this book together. Your love and companionship made the difficult work easier and the fun work more enjoyable. Of course, I have to send a special bit of gratitude to my neurotic cat Kenya, whose close attention to detail made sure that my computer equipment was running at peak performance.

Finally, thanks Mom and Dad for steering me into the computer industry. Your guidance and love is something that is always cherished.

Rick

Thanks to the Sybex team who are as good as ever. It is always fun to do a project with you.

As always, thanks to Luann—you have great patience. More than once you had to take care of the kids while I was downstairs writing (or taking a break by playing computer games).

Bryce, thanks for playing computer games with your Dad; Jessany, thanks for being your Daddy's Princess; Devin, thanks for being such a livewire; and Logan, thanks for being a mellow baby.

Lance

Table of Contents

Introduction

If you've purchased this book, you are probably chasing one of the Microsoft professional certifications: MCP, MCSE, or MCT. All of these are great goals, and they are also great career builders. Glance through any newspaper, and you'll find employment opportunities for people with these certifications. The ads are there because finding qualified employees is a challenge in today's market. The certification means you know something about the product; but more importantly, it means you have the ability, determination, and focus to learn—the greatest skill any employee can have!

You've probably also heard all the rumors about how hard the Microsoft tests are—the rumors are true! Microsoft has designed a series of exams that truly test your knowledge of their products. Each test not only covers the materials presented in a particular class, it also covers the prerequisite knowledge for that course. This means two things for you—that first test can be a real hurdle, and each test *should* get easier because you've studied the basics over and over.

This book has been developed in alliance with the Microsoft Corporation to give you the knowledge and skills you need to prepare for one of the key exams of the MCSE certification program: 70-026 System Administration for Microsoft SQL Server 6.5. Reviewed and approved by Microsoft, this book provides a solid introduction to Microsoft networking technologies and will help you on your way to MCSE certification.

Is This Book for You?

The MCSE Exam Notes books were designed to be succinct, portable exam review guides that can be used either in conjunction with a more complete study program (book, CBT courseware, classroom/lab environment) or as an exam review for those who don't feel the need for more extensive test preparation. Our goal isn't to "give the answers away," but rather to identify those topics on which you can expect to be tested and to provide sufficient coverage of these topics.

Perhaps you've been working with Microsoft networking technologies for years now. The thought of paying lots of money for a specialized MCSE exam preparation course probably doesn't sound too appealing. What can they teach you that you don't already know, right? Be careful, though. Many experienced network administrators have walked confidently into test centers only to walk sheepishly out of them after failing an MCSE exam. As they discovered, there's the Microsoft of the real world and the Microsoft of the MCSE exams. Our goal with these Exam Notes books is to show you where the two converge and where they diverge. After you've finished reading through this book, you should have a clear idea of how your understanding of the technologies involved matches up with the expectations of the MCSE test makers in Redmond.

Or perhaps you're relatively new to the world of Microsoft networking, drawn to it by the promise of challenging work and higher salaries. You've just waded through an 800-page MCSE study guide or taken a class at a local training center. Lots of information to keep track of, isn't it? Well, by organizing the Exam Notes books according to the Microsoft exam objectives, and by breaking up the information into concise manageable pieces, we've created what we think is the handiest exam review guide available. Throw it in your briefcase and carry it to work with you. As you read through the book, you'll be able to identify quickly those areas you know best and those that require more in-depth review.

NOTE The goal of the Exam Notes series is to help MCSE candidates familiarize themselves with the subjects on which they can expect to be tested in the MCSE exams. For complete, in-depth coverage of the technologies and topics involved, we recommend the MCSE Study Guide series from Sybex.

How Is This Book Organized?

As previously mentioned, this book is organized according to the official exam objectives list prepared by Microsoft for the 70-026 exam. The chapters coincide to the broad objectives groupings, such as Planning, Installation and Configuration, Monitoring and Optimization, and Troubleshooting. These groupings are also reflected in the organization of the MCSE exams themselves.

Within each chapter, the individual exam objectives are addressed in turn. The objectives sections are further divided according to the type of information presented.

Critical Information

This section presents the greatest level of detail on information that is relevant to the objective. This is the place to start if you're unfamiliar with or uncertain about the technical issues related to the objective.

Necessary Procedures

Here you'll find instructions for procedures that require a lab computer to be completed. From installing operating systems to modifying configuration defaults, the information in these sections addresses the hands-on requirements for the MCSE exams.

NOTE Not every objective has procedures associated with it. For such objectives, the "Necessary Procedures" section has been left out.

Exam Essentials

In this section, we've put together a concise list of the most crucial topics of subject areas that you'll need to comprehend fully prior to taking the MCSE exam. This section can help you identify those topics that might require more study on your part.

Key Terms and Concepts

Here we've compiled a mini-glossary of the most important terms and concepts related to the specific objective. You'll understand what all those technical words mean within the context of the related subject matter.

Sample Questions

For each objective, we've included a selection of questions similar to those you'll encounter on the actual MCSE exam. Answers and explanations are provided so you can gain some insight into the test-taking process.

NOTE For a more comprehensive collection of exam review questions, check out the MCSE Test Success series, also published by Sybex.

How Do You Become an MCSE?

Attaining Microsoft Certified Systems Engineer (MCSE) status is a challenge. The exams cover a wide range of topics and require dedicated study and expertise. This is, however, why the MCSE certificate is so valuable. If achieving the MCSE were too easy, the market would be quickly flooded by MCSEs and the certification would become meaningless. Microsoft, keenly aware of this fact, has taken steps to ensure that the certification means its holder is truly knowledgeable and skilled.

To become an MCSE, you must pass four core requirements and two electives. Most people select the following exam combination for the MCSE core requirements for the most current track:

Client Requirement
70-073: Implementing and Supporting Windows NT Workstation 4.0

or

70-064: Implementing and Supporting Microsoft Windows 95.

Networking Requirement

70-058: Networking Essentials

Windows NT Server 4.0 Requirement

70-067: Implementing and Supporting Windows NT Server 4.0

Windows NT Server 4.0 in the Enterprise Requirement

70-068: Implementing and Supporting Windows NT Server 4.0 in the Enterprise

Electives

Some of the more popular electives include:

70-059: Internetworking Microsoft TCP/IP on Microsoft Windows NT 4.0

70-087: Implementing and Supporting Microsoft Internet Information Server 4.0

70-081: Implementing and Supporting Microsoft Exchange Server 5.5

70-026: System Administration for Microsoft SQL Server 6.5

70-027: Implementing a Database Design on Microsoft SQL Server 6.5

70-088: Implementing and Supporting Microsoft Proxy Server 2.0

70-079: Implementing and Supporting Microsoft Internet Explorer 4.0 by Using the Internet Explorer Administration Kit

---

TIP This book is a part of a series of MCSE Exam Notes books, published by Network Press (Sybex), that covers four core requirements and your choice of several electives—the entire MCSE track!

Where Do You Take the Exams?

You may take the exams at any one of more than 800 Sylvan Prometric Authorized Testing Centers around the world. For the location of a testing center near you, call (800) 755-EXAM (755-3926). Outside the United States and Canada, contact your local Sylvan Prometric Registration Center. You can also register for an exam with Sylvan Prometric via the Internet. The Sylvan site can be reached through the Microsoft Training and Certification site or at: http://www.slspro.com/msreg/microsoft.asp.

To register for a Microsoft Certified Professional exam:

1. Determine the number of the exam you want to take.

2. Register with Sylvan Prometric. At this point you will be asked for advance payment for the exam. At this writing, the exams are $100 each. Exams must be taken within one year of payment. You can schedule exams up to six weeks in advance or as late as one working day prior to the date of the exam. You can cancel or reschedule your exam if you contact Sylvan Prometric at least two working days prior to the exam. Same-day registration is available in some locations, although this is subject to space availability. Where same-day registration is available, you must register a minimum of two hours before test time.

3. After you receive a registration and payment confirmation letter from Sylvan Prometric, call a nearby Sylvan Prometric Testing Center to schedule your exam.

When you schedule the exam, you'll be provided with instructions regarding appointment and cancellation procedures, ID requirements, and information about the testing center location.

What the 70-026: System Administration for Microsoft SQL Server 6.5 Exam Measures

The System Administration for Microsoft SQL Server 6.5 Certification Exam covers concepts and skills required for the support of SQL Server 6.5. It emphasizes the following areas:

- SQL Server hardware and software requirements
- Installing SQL Server
- Configuring SQL Server
- Creating databases and their devices
- Creating and managing transaction logs
- Backing up databases
- Backing up transaction logs
- Creating SQL Server users
- Managing database security
- Tuning SQL Server
- Data replication
- Troubleshooting

How Microsoft Develops the Exam Questions

Microsoft's exam development process consists of eight mandatory phases. The process takes an average of seven months and contains more than 150 specific steps. The phases of Microsoft Certified Professional exam development are listed here.

Phase 1: Job Analysis

Phase 1 is an analysis of all the tasks that make up the specific job function based on tasks performed by people who are currently performing the job function. This phase also identifies the knowledge, skills, and abilities that relate specifically to the certification for that performance area.

Phase 2: Objective Domain Definition

The results of the job analysis provide the framework used to develop exam objectives. The development of objectives involves translating the job function tasks into a comprehensive set of more specific and measurable knowledge, skills, and abilities. The resulting list of objectives, or the objective domain, is the basis for the development of both the certification exams and the training materials.

NOTE The outline of all Exam Notes books is based upon the official exam objectives lists published by Microsoft. Objectives are subject to change without notification. Check the Microsoft Training & Certification Web site (`www.microsoft.com\train_cert\`) for the most current objectives list.

Phase 3: Blueprint Survey

The final objective domain is transformed into a blueprint survey in which contributors—technology professionals who are performing the applicable job function—are asked to rate each objective. Based on the contributors' input, the objectives are prioritized and weighted. The actual exam items are written according to the prioritized objectives. The blueprint survey phase helps determine which objectives to measure, as well as the appropriate number and types of items to include on the exam.

Phase 4: Item Development

A pool of items is developed to measure the blueprinted objective domain. The number and types of items to be written are based on the results of the blueprint survey. During this phase, items are reviewed and revised to ensure that they are:

- Technically accurate

- Clear, unambiguous, and plausible

- Not biased toward any population, subgroup, or culture

- Not misleading or tricky

- Testing at the correct level of Bloom's Taxonomy

- Testing for useful knowledge, not obscure or trivial facts

Items that meet these criteria are included in the initial item pool.

Phase 5: Alpha Review and Item Revision

During this phase, a panel of technical and job function experts reviews each item for technical accuracy, then answers each item, reaching consensus on all technical issues. Once the items have been verified as technically accurate, they are edited to ensure that they are expressed in the clearest language possible.

Phase 6: Beta Exam

The reviewed and edited items are collected into a beta exam pool. During the beta exam, each participant has the opportunity to respond to all the items in this beta exam pool. Based on the responses of all beta participants, Microsoft performs a statistical analysis to verify the validity of the exam items and to determine which items will be used in the certification exam. Once the analysis has been completed, the items are distributed into multiple parallel forms, or versions, of the final certification exam.

Phase 7: Item Selection and Cut-Score Setting

The results of the beta exam are analyzed to determine which items should be included in the certification exam based on many factors, including item difficulty and relevance. Generally, the desired items are answered correctly by 25 percent to 90 percent of the beta exam candidates. This helps ensure that the exam consists of a variety of difficulty levels, from somewhat easy to extremely difficult.

Also during this phase, a panel of job function experts determines the cut score (minimum passing score) for the exam. The cut score differs from exam to exam because it is based on an item-by-item determination of the percentage of candidates who would be expected to answer the item correctly. The experts determine the cut score in a group session to increase the reliability.

Phase 8: Live Exam

Once all the other phases are complete, the exam is ready. Microsoft Certified Professional exams are administered by Sylvan Prometric.

Tips for Taking Your 70-026: System Administration for Microsoft SQL Server 6.5 Exam

Here are some general tips for taking your exam successfully:

- Arrive early at the exam center so you can relax and review your study materials, particularly tables and lists of exam-related information.

- Read the questions carefully. Don't be tempted to jump to an early conclusion. Make sure you know *exactly* what the question is asking.

- Don't leave any unanswered questions. They count against you.

- When answering multiple-choice questions you're not sure about, use a process of elimination to get rid of the obviously incorrect questions first. This will improve your odds if you need to make an educated guess.

- Because the hard questions will eat up the most time, save them for last. You can move forward and backward through the exam.

- This test has several exhibits (pictures). It can be difficult, if not impossible, to view both the questions and the exhibit simulation on the 14- and 15-inch screens usually found at the testing centers. Call around to each center and see if they have 17-inch monitors available. If they don't, perhaps you can arrange to bring in your own. Failing this, some have found it useful to quickly draw the diagram on the scratch paper provided by the testing center and use the monitor to view just the question.

- Many participants run out of time before they are able to complete the test. If you are unsure of the answer to a question, you may want to choose one of the answers, mark the question, and go on—an unanswered question does not help you. Once your time is up, you cannot go on to another question. However, you can remain on the question you are on indefinitely when the time runs out. Therefore, when you are almost out of time, go to a question you feel you can figure out—given enough time—and work until you feel you have got it (or the night security guard boots you out!).

- You are allowed to use the Windows calculator during your test. However, it may be better to memorize a table of the subnet addresses and to write it down on the scratch paper supplied by the testing center before you start the test.

Once you have completed an exam, you will be given immediate, online notification of your pass or fail status. You will also receive a printed Examination Score Report indicating your pass or fail status and your exam results by section. (The test administrator will give you the printed score report.) Test scores are automatically forwarded to Microsoft within five working days after you take the test. You do not need to send your score to Microsoft. If you pass the exam, you will receive confirmation from Microsoft, typically within two to four weeks.

Contact Information

To find out more about Microsoft Education and Certification materials and programs, to register with Sylvan Prometric, or to get other useful information, check the following resources. Outside the United States or Canada, contact your local Microsoft office or Sylvan Prometric testing center.

Microsoft Certified Professional Program—(800) 636-7544

Call the MCPP number for information about the Microsoft Certified Professional program and exams and to order the latest *Microsoft Roadmap to Education and Certification.*

Sylvan Prometric testing centers—(800) 755-EXAM
Contact Sylvan to register to take a Microsoft Certified Professional exam at any of more than 800 Sylvan Prometric testing centers around the world.

Microsoft Certification Development Team—Web: http://www.microsoft.com/Train_Cert/mcp/examinfo/certsd.htm
Contact the Microsoft Certification Development Team through their Web site to volunteer for participation in one or more exam development phases or to report a problem with an exam. Address written correspondence to: Certification Development Team; Microsoft Education and Certification; One Microsoft Way; Redmond, WA 98052.

Microsoft TechNet Technical Information Network—(800) 344-2121
The is an excellent resource for support professionals and system administrators. Outside the United States and Canada, call your local Microsoft subsidiary for information.

How to Contact the Authors

Lance Mortensen	LMSQL@aol.com
Rick Sawtell	Quickening@email.msn.com

How to Contact the Publisher

Sybex welcomes reader feedback on all of their titles. Visit the Sybex Web site at www.sybex.com for book updates and additional certification information. You'll also find online forms to submit comments or suggestions regarding this or any other Sybex book.

CHAPTER

1

Server Installation and Upgrade

Microsoft Exam Objectives Covered in This Chapter:

Configure Microsoft Windows NT® for SQL Server installations. *(pages 3 – 10)*

Configure SQL Server for various memory scenarios. *(pages 11 – 16)*

Configure SQL Executive to log on as a service. *(pages 16 – 22)*

Install client support for network protocols other than named pipes. *(pages 23 – 28)*

Load multiple Net-Libraries. *(pages 28 – 31)*

Upgrade SQL Server 4.2x to SQL Server 6.5. *(pages 31 – 36)*

Set up a security mode. *(pages 36 – 41)*

The objectives for this portion of the exam are designed to test your ability to install and correctly configure SQL Server 6.5 in the Windows NT environment and your ability to create and configure a login account that will be used by the SQL Executive service. You also need to understand how to install SQL Server Net-Library support for both SQL Server clients and the SQL Server itself. Choosing the appropriate configuration options can greatly affect the performance of SQL Server. You need to know how to initially configure memory options for SQL Server and be able to make appropriate SQL Server login security decisions. You also need to understand the various issues concerning the upgrade of a 4.2x database to version 6.5.

Configure Microsoft Windows NT® for SQL Server installations.

SQL Server will run on any Windows NT (3.51 or later) machine, including Windows NT Workstation and Windows NT Server. Although the exam objective talks about configuring Windows NT for SQL Server installations, what you really need to know is how a particular Windows NT configuration affects SQL Server. For example, how is SQL Server affected when it is installed on a Windows NT Primary Domain Controller (PDC)? How is SQL Server affected by being installed on an NT Server that does not have access to account information through a trust relationship? How does the current hardware and software configuration affect your SQL Server?

The first step in installing SQL Server is to make sure you have the appropriate hardware and software installed on Windows NT. You also need to decide where in a particular enterprise configuration you should install SQL Server.

Critical Information

As with most Microsoft products, the bigger and faster your platform, the better SQL Server will perform. The exam focuses on the x86 platform, but you can apply the information here to installations on other platforms. Table 1.1 lists the minimum hardware and software requirements to run SQL Server 6.5.

T A B L E 1.1: Minimum Hardware and Software Requirements for SQL Server 6.5

Components	Minimum Requirements
Platform	i486 or later, Power PC, MIPS, DEC Alpha-AXP
RAM	16MB, 32MB for replication
Operating System	NT 3.51 or later
File System	FAT or NTFS
Hard Disk	60MB, additional 15MB for Books Online

RAM and Hard Disk Space Requirements

One of the most important decisions you will make is deciding what hardware to use to maximize SQL Server's performance. As a minimum, SQL Server 6.5 requires 16MB of RAM and 60MB of hard disk space. If you plan to replicate information to other SQL Server machines, you must have at least 32MB of RAM installed on the computer which will support the replication distribution database.

SEE ALSO Replication is covered in greater detail in Chapter 11 of *MCSE: SQL Server 6.5 Administration Study Guide* by Sybex (ISBN 0-7821-2172-1).

SQL Server will run on both FAT and NTFS partitions. You should place SQL Server on an NTFS partition for both security and fault tolerance. If you plan to use Windows NT's software implementation of RAID-5 (striping with parity across multiple NTFS partitions), you should create the partitions and stripe sets before you install SQL Server.

Enterprise Configuration Considerations

To get a better idea of where to install SQL Server, you should know a little bit about SQL Server's security options as they directly relate to your Windows NT environment configuration. SQL Server has three security models: standard, integrated, and mixed. Here is an overview of SQL Server login security.

Standard Security

The standard security model forces SQL Server to perform its own account authentication, rather than having the Windows NT Security Accounts Manager (SAM) database (also referred to as the *directory database*) do it. The standard security model does not require any additional network libraries to be loaded, but it does require that you create login IDs and passwords internal to the SQL Server database. These IDs and passwords will be placed into the SQL Server system table *syslogins*, to be used for authentication.

The standard security model is useful for Windows NT configurations where Windows NT is not used for authentication or environments where SQL Server does not have access to domain accounts through trust relationships.

A domain is a lot like a workgroup. The primary difference is that there is a PDC (Primary Domain Controller) that keeps track of all of the NT user accounts. When users log in, they are authenticated by the PDC. If you have a large number of computers in the domain, the PDC may become very busy authenticating. You can set up Windows NT to replicate the user accounts to other servers called Backup Domain Controllers (BDCs). If the PDC is busy, a user may be routed to the BDC for authentication. Authentication, replication, and file server services can consume a lot of the resources of an NT Server. For this reason, PDCs and BDCs are not the best choices for a SQL Server installation.

Trust relationships work between separate domains. Let's say that Domain A has a list of user accounts and our SQL Server database. Users who are members of Domain B would like access to information and resources in Domain A. In order to gain that access, Domain A can *trust* the accounts that are authenticated in Domain B. This is a trust relationship.

Standard security is also useful in environments where there are no NT Server authenticating logins. For example, if you are working in a Novell NetWare environment, all the network security is handled by NetWare; therefore, you must use standard security for SQL Server because there is no Windows NT domain to authenticate users logging in.

TIP In a Novell NetWare environment, you could create local accounts for all of your users on the Windows NT Server machine that is running SQL Server. However, this causes problems because users now have multiple network user IDs. A workaround is to use the DSMN (Directory Service Manager for NetWare) software, which will synchronize accounts between the NetWare bindery and the Windows NT SAM database. If you do this, then you are not forced into using standard security for SQL Server.

The default security that is installed with SQL Server is standard security. Once you have successfully installed SQL Server, you can change your security mode.

Integrated Security
When your environment is configured with a Windows NT machine performing authentication, you can use the integrated security model. This can greatly simplify administration by using NT's SAM database for validation of SQL Server logins. SQL Server can use NT security either locally (if SQL Server is installed on a domain controller) or through trust relationships with a domain controller. There are a couple of requirements for using integrated security:

- You must install either the SQL Server named pipes and/or multi-protocol network libraries on both the clients and the SQL Server machine.

- The SQL Server machine must have access to the Windows NT SAM database, either locally or through a trust relationship.

To implement integrated security, you (or the network administrator) simply add the user accounts to the SAM database (directory database) through the Windows NT User Manager for Domains tool and assign the appropriate rights, privileges, and groups. You (as the SQL administrator) could then use the SQL Security Manager tool to "map" those Windows NT SAM accounts into the SQL Server *syslogins* database table. When users who have a mapping into SQL Server log in to Windows NT, they are automatically logged in to both Windows NT and SQL Server.

Mixed Security

Mixed security is useful for environments where you have a mixed group of clients. For example, suppose that your organization uses a single SQL Server machine to support databases for both the accounting department and sales department. The accounting department personnel are being validated by a Novell NetWare Server, and the sales department personnel are being validated by a Windows NT Server machine in a trusted domain. In this type of setup, you can use either mixed security or standard security.

Mixed security allows logins to SQL Server to be authenticated by either the Windows NT SAM database or directly by the SQL Server. If you are in a trusted domain and are using either named pipes or multi-protocol network libraries on both the client and the SQL Server machine, then SQL Server will look for a valid Windows NT ID that has been mapped into SQL Server. If there is one, you will be logged in with it. If SQL Server can't find a Windows NT ID, SQL Server will attempt to log you in with the ID you supplied in the Connect Server dialog box.

Choosing an Installation Server

After reviewing all of this information, you need to decide where you should install SQL Server. PDCs and BDCs are not the best choices for installation because they use valuable CPU cycles, memory resources, and network bandwidth to conduct authentication, replication, and file server services for the domain.

Although you can install SQL Server on a domain controller, a better solution is to install SQL Server on a machine that is not busy with these operations. The more system resources you dedicate to SQL Server, the better it will perform.

Finally, if you are running SQL Server in a multidomain environment, you should place SQL Server on an NT Server that has access to domain accounts through trust relationships. This allows you to take advantage of integrated security.

Necessary Procedures

NOTE Necessary procedures are lists of steps to take in order to complete some portion of the implementation of a test objective. This particular test objective does not have any procedures related to it. In future objective sections, if an objective does not have any procedures, the "Necessary Procedures" section will be omitted.

Exam Essentials

You should keep these points in mind when you are preparing for the exam. To pass the exam, you must understand them and how the information in them was derived.

Understand how different Windows NT hardware and software configurations affect the installation of SQL Server 6.5. Windows NT must be configured with at least 16MB of memory and 60MB of hard disk space for SQL Server to be installed successfully. If you plan to use replication, you must have at least 32MB of RAM on the NT Server which will support the replication distribution database.

Given an NT Server domain configuration, know where you should install SQL Server. SQL Server can be installed anywhere in the domain model. The best choice for a SQL Server installation is on a nondomain controller. In addition, you should install SQL Server on an NT Server that has access to domain accounts through trust relationships.

Key Terms and Concepts

BDC: A Backup Domain Controller is used to perform many of the same tasks as the PDC. Authentication jobs can be routed to the BDC, taking some heat off of the PDC. The BDC has a replicated copy of the accounts database stored on the PDC.

PDC: A Primary Domain Controller is an NT Server that controls the login accounts database. It performs login validation for all computers in its domain.

Security: SQL Server has three different types of security: standard, integrated, and mixed. Standard security (the default) forces SQL Server to perform all SQL Server login validation. With integrated security, SQL Server allows Windows NT to do all SQL Server login validation. With mixed security, some accounts are validated by NT and some are validated by SQL Server.

Trust relationship: An administrative link that joins two or more domains. With a trust relationship, users can access resources in another domain if they have rights, even if they do not have a user account in the resource domain. For example, if Domain A has resources that users who are validated in Domain B would like to access, Domain A can trust Domain B to perform authentication for the Domain B accounts. Once Domain A trusts Domain B, users in Domain B can gain access to resources stored in Domain A.

Sample Questions

1. Where *should* you install SQL Server?

   A. Onto a PDC or BDC. The server will have direct access to domain accounts and will, therefore, run much more quickly.

   B. Onto any machine in the enterprise with access to the domain accounts directly or through a trust relationship (preferably not a PDC or BDC).

   C. Onto any machine in the enterprise that is running TCP/IP. This is the default protocol for most machines.

   D. Onto any machine that is not a member of a domain. Because the machine is not involved in any domain related activities, it will run much more efficiently.

   Answer: B is the *best* choice. Answer A is true to a degree, but the domain controller uses up valuable CPU time and memory for its domain functionality. Choice C is false. TCP/IP is not the default protocol that is set up in Windows. Answer D is true, but your SQL Server will not have access to domain accounts through trust relationships; therefore, integrated and portions of mixed security will not be available options.

2. What is the minimum amount of RAM needed to install and run SQL Server?

   A. 12MB; 24MB for replication

   B. 16MB; 32MB for replication

   C. 24MB; 32MB for replication

   D. 32MB; 48MB for replication

   Answer: B is correct. Windows NT with SQL Server requires 16MB of RAM. If you are using replication, then SQL Server must have 16MB of RAM dedicated for it and a total of 32MB installed on the NT Server.

Configure SQL Server for various memory scenarios.

This test objective describes the balance between the amount of memory you should give to SQL Server and the amount of memory you should give to Windows NT. This particular configuration option can make or break a SQL Server as far as performance is concerned. If you give too much memory to Windows NT, SQL Server will not perform optimally. If you give too little memory to Windows NT, then Windows NT and, consequently, SQL Server will perform poorly.

Critical Information

The question really comes down to: I've got *n* megabytes of RAM on this machine. How much should I give to NT, and how much should I give to SQL Server? This question can be a bit tricky, but the answer is always "It depends." You will hear this a lot in the world of data-bases. Proper configuration depends on many factors, including what other services (besides SQL Server) are running on Windows NT. How much memory do those services require to perform well? How many users are going to be working with SQL Server? How big are the databases and queries that will be processing on SQL Server? Are you using SQL Server replication?

For Windows NT to perform optimally, it needs memory. This is true for SQL Server as well. The memory option in the SQL Server con-figuration screen shown in Figure 1.1 allows you to make changes to the amount of memory configured for use by SQL Server. You need to be careful here because Windows NT needs to have a minimum of 12MB of memory for its own use.

FIGURE 1.1: The Server Configuration/Options dialog box

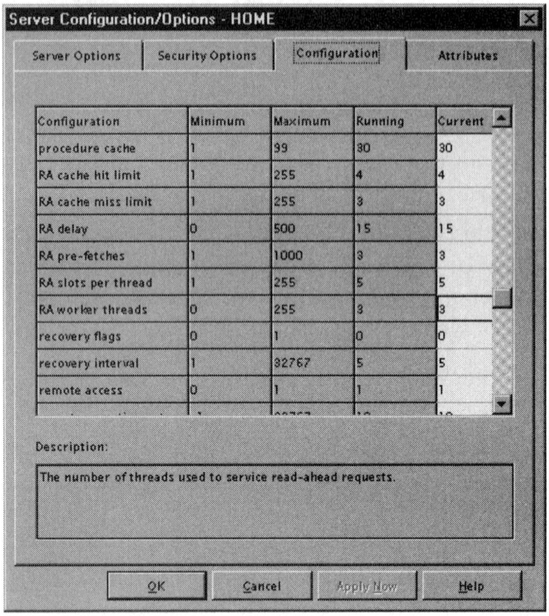

Configuration	Minimum	Maximum	Running	Current
procedure cache	1	99	30	30
RA cache hit limit	1	255	4	4
RA cache miss limit	1	255	3	3
RA delay	0	500	15	15
RA pre-fetches	1	1000	3	3
RA slots per thread	1	255	5	5
RA worker threads	0	255	3	3
recovery flags	0	1	0	0
recovery interval	1	32767	5	5
remote access	0	1	1	1

Description:
The number of threads used to service read-ahead requests.

SQL Server performance is also tied to the performance of the Windows NT Server on which it is installed. As NT performs better, so does SQL Server. Table 1.2 lists the suggested memory configurations for SQL Server and Windows NT.

When you configure memory for SQL Server, you must specify the amount in 2KB data pages. For example, to configure SQL Server to use 16MB of RAM, you must specify 8,192 data pages.

There are two methods for configuring memory in SQL Server. You can do it through the Enterprise Manager's Server Configuration Options screen shown in Figure 1.1, or you can use the *sp_configure* stored procedure.

TABLE 1.2: SQL Server Memory Configurations

Total RAM	Configuration for SQL Server
16MB	4MB/2,048 pages
24MB	8MB/4,096 pages
32MB	16MB/8,192 pages
48MB	28MB/14,336 pages
64MB	40MB/20,480 pages
128MB	100MB/51,200 pages
256MB	216MB/110,592 pages

NOTE The exam focuses on knowledge of what to do given a particular scenario. Although you can accomplish most of these tasks in SQL Server using the SQL Enterprise Manager, the exam focuses on your knowledge of how to accomplish that task using stored procedures. In other words, know which stored procedure to use, when to use it, and why you are using it.

Necessary Procedures

You should be familiar with using the Enterprise Manager to modify database properties and using the sp_configure stored procedure.

Modifying Memory Settings Using the Enterprise Manager

1. Start Enterprise Manager. Select Start ➤ Program Files ➤ Microsoft SQL Server 6.5 ➤ SQL Enterprise Manager.

2. Right-click your server and choose Configure from the Context menu. You can accomplish this by selecting your server and selecting Configure from the Server menu as well.

3. From the Server Configuration/Options dialog box, click the Configuration tab.

4. Locate the memory parameter and make your modifications.

5. Remember that you must stop and restart SQL Server before this modification will take place. (Not all configuration changes will require you to stop and restart SQL Server.) To accomplish this, simply close the Configuration/Options dialog box. Right-click on your server and choose Stop from the context menu. Once your server has stopped, right-click your server again and choose Start from the context menu.

Modifying Memory Settings Using the ISQL/W Tool

1. Start the ISQL/W utility.

2. You can run the following line of code to set SQL Server's memory configuration option to 16MB.

```
EXEC sp_configure 'memory', 8192
```

3. Run the procedure.

Exam Essentials

Properly configuring memory in SQL Server is one of the most important optimization tasks you will perform. Keep the following points in mind when you are studying for the exam and working with SQL Server in the real world.

Understand how different memory configurations affect the performance of SQL Server and Windows NT. Windows NT must have at least 12MB of memory to run. When Windows NT performs more efficiently, SQL Server will also perform more efficiently. Balancing the amount of RAM to dedicate to SQL Server versus how much to give NT is crucial to having a system that performs optimally.

Know how to configure the memory option in SQL Server. You can use both the Enterprise Manager and the sp_configure stored procedure to make configuration changes to your SQL Server. Although making these changes using the Enterprise Manager is relatively straightforward, the exam stresses the use of stored procedures.

Key Terms and Concepts

Balancing memory: You should make sure that Windows NT and SQL Server have the right balance of memory. If Windows NT is performing poorly, then SQL Server will perform poorly. Give as much memory as you can to SQL Server after you have optimized NT's performance.

Memory parameters: This general rule of thumb applies when you are working with memory settings: If you are working with a database, the memory parameters are in megabytes. If you are working with database devices, the memory sizes are in 2KB data pages.

sp_configure: This stored procedure is used from ISQL and allows you to modify SQL Server configuration options like memory.

Sample Questions

1. If your NT Server has 64MB of RAM, what is the optimal amount of memory to configure for SQL Server? (Assume that SQL Server is the only application running on this NT Server.)

   A. 16MB

   B. 24MB

   C. 32MB

   D. 40MB

   Answer: D is the best choice. This is just one of those questions for which you will have to memorize Table 1.2 outlined earlier in this section. Remember that you need to strike a balance between NT's performance and SQL Server's performance. .

2. What stored procedure do you use to make configuration changes to SQL Server?

   A. sp_dboption

   B. sp_configure

   C. sp_config_sql

   D. sp_change_sql

   Answer: B is correct. You can use the sp_configure stored procedure to make global changes to SQL Server. This includes modifying memory, user connections, the lock escalation threshold, and many other changes. The sp_dboption is used to set database properties. There are no stored procedures called sp_config_sql and sp_change_sql.

Configure SQL Executive to log on as a service.

The SQL Executive is a suite of utilities that includes replication, task, event, and alert managers. You can use these utilities to streamline the administration of SQL Server and to distribute information throughout your enterprise using replication. For these utilities to interact with SQL Server, you must provide the SQL Executive service (SQLExecutive) with a valid NT logon account and password, and you must possess the appropriate rights.

Critical Information

Configuring the SQL Executive to log on as a service is a two-step process. The first step is to create the SQL Executive account and give it the appropriate rights and permissions. The second step is to assign this newly created account to the SQL Executive service.

The SQL Executive account can be created through the User Manager for Domains. The SQL Executive account should have the following settings:

- Username (for example, SQLExecAcct)

- Password (a difficult one to guess because this account will have Admin rights)

- User cannot change password

- Password never expires

- Member of the local Administrators group

- Log on at all hours (if you would like services to run at night)

- Log on as a service (advanced user right)

Once you have created the account, you must assign it to the SQLExecutive service. During the installation process, the installer will ask you for the logon account that the SQLExecutive service will use. By default, this dialog box will have the account that you are currently logged in with (normally Administrator). You should change that account to the one you created before your setup (SQLExecAcct), as shown in Figure 1.2. If you missed this step, you can always change it later from the Control Panel/Services dialog box.

FIGURE 1.2:   The SQL Executive Log On Account dialog box

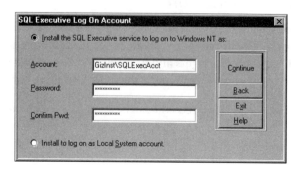

Necessary Procedures

Knowledge of how to properly create and configuring the SQL Executive account is emphasized on the exam. You can follow these steps to create and configure your own SQL Executive account.

Creating and Configuring the SQL Executive Account

1. In Windows NT, start the User Manager or User Manager for Domains tool by choosing Start ➤ Programs ➤ Administrative Tools ➤ User Manager.

2. Select User ➤ New User. The New User dialog box appears.

3. In the Username field, enter **SQLExecAcct**.

4. In the Description field, enter **SQL Executive Service Account**.

5. In the Password field, enter a password (this account will have Administrative privileges).

6. Clear the checkbox for User Must Change Password at Next Logon.

7. Check the Password Never Expires checkbox.

8. Check the User Cannot Change Password checkbox.

9. Click on the Groups button to add your account to the Administrators group.

10. Double-click on the Administrators group entry. Your Group Memberships dialog box should look similar to the one shown here.

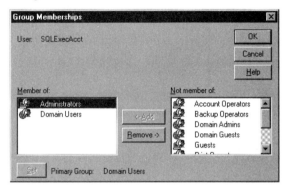

11. Click on OK to return to the New User dialog box.

12. Click on the Add button to add this account.

13. Click on the Close button to close the New User dialog box.

14. To give the account the advanced right "Log on as a Service," select Policies ➤ User Rights.

15. Click on the Show Advanced User Rights checkbox in the lower-left corner.

16. Click on the drop-down listbox and choose the "Log on as a Service" right.

17. You will notice that your SQLExecAcct is not listed in the "Grant To" list. To add this user, click on the Add button to display the Add Users and Groups dialog box.

18. This list currently shows groups only. To add your SQLExecAcct, click the Show Users button. You user accounts should now be displayed.

19. Scroll down through the list of accounts in the top pane and double-click SQLExecAcct. It should now be listed in the lower pane.

20. Click OK to close the Add Users and Groups dialog box.

21. Your account should now be listed in the middle pane of the User Rights Policy dialog box. Click OK to close this dialog box.

22. Close the User Manager for Domains utility.

The second step in these procedures is to assign this account to the SQL Executive service. This is accomplished either through the setup process or after the setup has completed. If you created the account before you began your setup process, then simply add the account name to the SQL Logon Account dialog box as shown in Figure 1.2 earlier.

If you did not assign this account here, follow these steps to configure the SQL Executive account after the installation of SQL Server.

1. Open the Control Panel/Services dialog box.

2. Locate the SQLExecutive service in the Services dialog box.

3. Click Startup. This will open the startup parameters dialog box.

4. In the startup parameters screen, change the login account to **SQLExecAcct.**

5. Type the password for the SQLExecAccount.

6. When you are finished, close this dialog box to return to the Services dialog box.

7. You must stop and restart the service for this new account to be assigned. Click the Stop button and wait for the SQLExecutive service to stop.

8. Click the Start button and wait for the SQLExecutive service to begin running.

9. That is all there is to it. Close the Services dialog box.

Exam Essentials

You should keep these points in mind when you are studying for the exam. The SQL Executive account plays an important role in your SQL Server database operations and administration.

Know why it is important to have a SQL Executive account.   It is important to have a separate account for the SQLExecutive service because it allows the service to log on to Windows NT and SQL Server and perform scheduling, alerting, event tasks, and replication tasks.

Know how to assign the SQLExecutive service with an account. You can assign the SQLExecutive service account either during the SQL Server setup process or through the Control Panel/Services dialog box. If you change the account in the Services area, you must stop and restart the SQL Executive service for this change to take effect.

Know what characteristics should be assigned to the SQL Executive account.   You should assign the SQL Executive account the following characteristics: Log on as a Service (advanced user right), Log on at all hours, Member of the local Administrators group, Password never changes, Password never expires, and Password cannot be changed by user.

Key Terms and Concepts

SQL Executive account: The SQL Executive account is a Windows NT logon account that the SQLExecutive service uses to log on to Windows NT and perform administrative activities in SQL Server.

SQL Executive service: This runs as a Windows NT service. The SQL Executive service allows for the administration of SQL Server through the use of scheduled tasks, events, alert management, and data replication.

Sample Questions

1. The SQL Executive logon account is used:

   A. By the MSDTC to distribute transactions for the Executive service

   B. By the SQLExecutive service to log on to SQL Server and perform automation tasks, alerts processing, event firing, and replication

   C. By the MSSQLServer service to log on to SQL Server and perform automation tasks, alerts processing, event firing, and replication

   D. By Windows NT to log on to SQL Server and place all error messages in the NT Event Viewer

   Answer: B is correct. In addition to giving it the advanced user right of "Log on as a Service," it should also be a member of the local Administrators group, have a password, and have the ability to log on at all hours.

2. How can you assign the SQL Executive account to the SQLExecutive service? (Select all that apply.)

   A. During SQL Server setup

   B. By running the sp_configure stored procedure

   C. From Control Panel/Services

   D. From the User Manager for Domains

   Answer: A and C are correct. You can assign the account during the setup process or through the Control Panel/Services dialog boxes.

Install client support for network protocols other than named pipes.

This test objective focuses on how to install client-side network protocols and where the protocol's driver information is stored. In order for your clients to communicate with SQL Server, they must speak the same language. This is where the client-side network libraries come into play. The client-side network protocols (as well as the driver information) are located in different areas depending on what operating system the client is currently running.

Critical Information

If your SQL Server is configured to use the TCP/IP Net-Library, your client application should also use the TCP/IP Net-Library. The location of the driver information is dependent upon which operating system you are using on the client. For example:

- If you are using 16-bit MS-DOS–based client software, you will be able to install only the 16-bit command-line utilities and network libraries.

- If you are using 16-bit MS Windows (Windows 3.*x*), you will be able to install the 16-bit command-line utilities, as well as the 16-bit GUI utilities and the 16-bit network libraries.

- If you are using a 32-bit Microsoft Windows operating system (Windows 95 or Windows NT), you will be able to install all of the 16-bit utilities plus all of the 32-bit utilities and 32-bit network libraries.

Necessary Procedures

Follow these procedures to install the client utilities and network libraries and to locate the Net-Library information to support your SQL Server clients.

Installing to 16-Bit MS-DOS–Based Operating Systems

If you are going to install to MS-DOS–based systems, you must do all of the work by hand as follows:

1. You should create a \SQL\BIN directory (or any other path that makes sense to you) on your client machine, and then copy all of the files from the \Clients\MSDOS directory on the SQL Server CD-ROM.

2. When you are running MS-DOS, it can have only one Net-Library loaded at a time. You should add lines to your AUTOEXEC.BAT file to run the appropriate client Net-Library. Included on the SQL Server CD are:

   - DBNMPIPE.EXE for use with named pipes

   - DBMSSPX.EXE for use with Novell's IPX/SPX

   - DBMSVINE.EXE for use with Banyan Vines

When using Novell's IPX/SPX, the SQL Server's name is the computer name of the NT Server on which it is running.

NOTE SQL Server has reserved port 1434 for use with TCP/IP sockets.

Installing to 16-Bit Windows Operating Systems

To install the client utilities on a Windows 3.*x* machine:

1. Navigate to the \Clients\Win16 directory on the SQL Server CD-ROM and run the Setup program.

2. The Setup program will create a new directory called \MSSQL\BIN, configure the chosen default Net-Library, create the SQL Server Tools program group, add icons, and then copy all of the necessary files and DLLs to the \MSSQL\BINN directory. Appropriate entries will also be added to your WIN.INI file.

TIP If you are going to use ODBC-based applications, you can install the ODBC drivers that come on the SQL Server CD-ROM. They are located in the \Clients\Win16\ODBC directory. However, these files are dated in general and you should search the Web for the latest and greatest versions. Check out the Microsoft site at `http://www.microsoft.com/odbc/` for the latest ODBC drivers. Also, see Appendix B in *MCSE: SQL Server 6.5 Administration Study Guide* by Sybex, for more information about SQL Server and ODBC.

Installing to 32-Bit Operating Systems

When you have a 32-bit operating system like Windows NT or Windows 95, you can install all of the client software, including the 16-bit and 32-bit utilities. To do this, follow these steps:

1. Navigate to the appropriate directory on your SQL Server CD-ROM (i386 for Intel-based machines) and run the Setup program.

2. The Setup program will create an \MSSQL\BINN directory and an \MSSQL\INSTALL directory if you decided to add SQL Server Books Online to a particular client. The Setup program will also create the SQL Server Tools program group and add the icons for the utilities you've selected. Finally, Setup will

copy the DB-Library and Net-Library DLLs to the appropriate system directory on your machine. New entries will also be added to your Windows NT Registry.

Exam Essentials

You should keep these points in mind when you are working with network client configurations. Problems here can keep your clients from accessing SQL Server.

Know where to find information about the Net-Library configuration on different clients.   Sixteen-bit MS-DOS clients have a single Net-Library loaded in the AUTOEXEC.BAT file. Sixteen-bit Windows 3.*x* clients have their Net-Library configuration information stored in the WIN.INI file. Thirty-two-bit Windows 95 and Windows NT clients have their configuration information stored in the Registry database.

Know which 16-bit MS-DOS–based Net-Library is appropriate for a particular protocol.   DBMSVINE is used by Banyan Vines. DBMSSPX is used by IPX/SPX. DBNMPIPE is used for named pipes.

Know additional information is necessary to connect to SQL Server if you are using a protocol other than named pipes. When you are using Novell's IPX/SPX, you must specify the SQL Server name as the NT Server's computer name. Don't forget that SQL Server has reserved port 1434 for TCP/IP binding.

Key Terms and Concepts

Net-Library: A Net-Library is a set of DLLs that are used to support network connectivity for a client/server.

Port: A port is a logical location in memory where a client and server can exchange information. In SQL Server, the SQL Server machine itself listens for incoming requests on port 1434.

Sample Questions

1. You can have only one Net-Library loaded in an MS-DOS client to SQL Server. If your SQL Server is configured to use named pipes, which of the following should be added to your AUTOEXEC.BAT file?

   A. DBNMPIPE.EXE

   B. DBMSSPX.EXE

   C. NAMEPIPE.EXE

   D. DBMSVINE.EXE

   Answer: A is correct. Answer B would be true if you were running IPX/SPX. There is no such driver called NAMEPIPE.EXE. Answer D is used for networks running the Banyan Vines Street-Talk protocol.

2. Where should you look for Net-Library configuration options in a Windows 3.*x* system?

   A. SYSTEM.INI

   B. NETWORK.INI

   C. WIN.INI

   D. Registry

   Answer: C is correct. In a Windows 95/NT environment, the information is stored in the Registry. In a 16-bit MS-DOS environment, the information is stored in the AUTOEXEC.BAT file.

3. You are currently setting up your client workstation to use TCP/IP to access your SQL Server. To which port will TCP/IP bind?

A. 227

B. 1434

C. 1233

D. Hyannisport

Answer: B is correct. Microsoft SQL Server has reserved port 1434 for TCP/IP communications. Hyannisport is where the Kennedy compound is located.

Load multiple Net-Libraries.

In the previous objective section, we discussed how to install and configure additional client-side network libraries and where the library information is stored. This test objective focuses on how to install additional network library support in SQL Server.

By default, SQL Server uses the named-pipes protocol, but you can install support for TCP/IP, IPX/SPX, Banyan Vines, AppleTalk, and several others. The best way to install these additional protocols is to use the SQL Server Setup program.

Critical Information

SQL Server always has named pipes installed. In fact, you must use named pipes in order to install SQL Server. A named pipe is a bidirectional endpoint through which two machines can exchange information.

You can install additional network support in SQL Server during the initial setup process or at a later time by rerunning the Setup program. In either case, the screen in which you make your changes is the same.

The "Necessary Procedures" will walk you through the process of modifying Net-Libraries on the SQL Server machine.

Necessary Procedures

Earlier in this chapter, you looked at properly configuring your clients to access SQL Server. In this section, you review how to set up SQL Server to support additional network libraries.

Installing the Server-Side Net-Libraries

1. If you are performing an initial installation of SQL Server, you will be presented with an Installation Options dialog box.

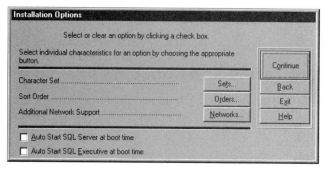

2. When you are presented with this screen, choose the Networks button. This will bring up the Networks screen. Simply select the network protocol that you would like to add.

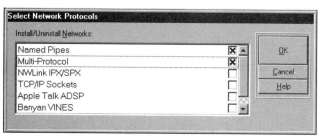

3. If you have already installed SQL Server and want to add network libraries, simply rerun the Setup program. There will be an option to add additional Net-Libraries. Simply choose that option and you will be presented with a window similar to the Networks window. You must stop and restart SQL Server for this change to take effect.

Exam Essentials

Network libraries allow SQL Server to communicate with client workstations. Keep the following in mind when you study for the exam.

Know how to install additional server-side network libraries. Remember that you must have named pipes installed at all times. SQL Server requires named pipes in order to complete an installation. To install additional Net-Libraries, use the SQL Server Setup program.

Key Terms and Concepts

Named pipes: A named pipe is a network protocol that allows for IPC communications.

Sample Questions

1. Which network protocol does SQL Server use to complete an installation?

   A. TCP/IP

   B. NetBEUI

   C. IPX/SPX

   D. Named pipes

   Answer: D is correct. You cannot uninstall named pipes. It is required by SQL Server. Remember, named pipes is one of the protocols that supports integrated security.

2. To install an additional server-side Net-Library, what should you do?

   A. Run the SQL Server NetLib.EXE.

B. Run the SQL Server Setup program.

C. Run AddLib.EXE.

D. Nothing. SQL Server installs with the multi-protocol Net-Library and can, therefore, communicate with any client.

Answer: B is correct. To add additional network libraries, you must run the SQL Server Setup program.

Upgrade SQL Server 4.2*x* to SQL Server 6.5.

This exam objective focuses on the different issues you must be aware of when you attempt to upgrade a 4.2*x* database. You must also know how the upgrade process works.

There are several issues you should be aware of when you attempt to upgrade an existing 4.2*x* database to SQL Server 6.5. This includes dealing with missing information and keyword violations. Dealing with these problems is part of the upgrade process which will be outlined in this section.

Critical Information

There are two different ways in which you can upgrade a 4.2*x* database to a 6.5 database:

- Perform a live upgrade of the SQL Server 4.2*x* engine to 6.5. If SQL Setup detects an earlier installation of 4.2*x* installed on the server, it will default to an upgrade of the old server to the latest version. This includes upgrading your databases as well.

- Leave a SQL Server 4.2*x* engine intact, install SQL Server 6.5 on a separate computer and then transfer the databases using Transfer Manager, or backup and restore.

In either case, for your databases to be upgraded successfully, they must meet certain criteria:

- The old database must have comments in the *syscomments* tables. The *syscomments* tables store the SQL statements that were used to generate your database objects (stored procedures, triggers, etc.).

- Comments in *syscomments* do not use SQL Server 6.5 reserved words. If reserved words are found, then the object in the 4.2*x* database must be dropped and re-created using nonreserved words.

NOTE   You cannot restore a 4.2*x* database from one platform to another. For example, you cannot upgrade a SQL Server 4.2*x* database from an Alpha platform to a SQL Server 6.5 database on an Intel platform. You must use Transfer Manager to do this.

To determine whether or not there are comment violations or reserved word violations, you can use the CHECKUPG65.EXE program. This tool will go through your 4.2*x* databases and search for these violations. If it finds any, it will add information to a report that it generates.

The "Necessary Procedures" section describes the process of upgrading a database using the backup/restore method. You can also use the Transfer Manager to move data from an old 4.2*x* database to a new 6.5 database. The Transfer Manager will be discussed in Chapter 8.

NOTE   Character sets and sort orders must match for an upgrade using backup and restore to be successful.

Necessary Procedures

The preferred method of upgrading your databases is to restore 4.2*x* backups into your 6.5 database. When you upgrade using the backup and restore method, you should first run the CHECKUPG65.EXE program. This program will determine if you have any keyword violations in the old database. In addition to this, it will verify that you have comments in the *syscomments* tables in your database. The comments are T-SQL commands needed to create the objects in your database.

Running CHECKUPG65

1. Open a Windows NT Command Prompt window.

2. Go to the C:\Temp folder.

3. Run the following command on a single line:

```
chkupg65 /S<sqlserver> /Usa /P<sa password>
/oc:\temp\chkupg65.out
```

4. To examine the output, issue the following command:

   notepad chkupg65.out

   Here is an example of the output:

```
===============================
Database: master

Status: 8
<No problem>

Missing objects in Syscomments
None

Keyword conflicts
None

===============================
```

Database: msdb

Status: 8

. . .

5. Check for any errors and make corrections as necessary. This includes dropping objects and re-creating them if there are reserved word conflicts or missing syscomments.

Exam Essentials

You need to know many different things in order to successfully upgrade from an earlier version of SQL Server to a later version. Those steps are summarized here.

Understand the various issues concerning upgrading to SQL Server 6.5.   The recommended way to upgrade 4.2x databases is to back them up in 4.2x and then restore them in 6.5. Before you restore them, you should run the CHKUPG65.EXE utility to verify that all database objects have comments in the syscomments table and that there are no keyword violations.

Key Terms and Concepts

CHKUPG65.EXE: A utility that verifies that there are comments in the syscomments tables and that those comments do not use any SQL Server reserved words. You will normally use the CHKUPG65 utility before you perform an upgrade of a SQL Server database.

syscomments: Every database in SQL Server has a syscomments table. The syscomments table stores the T-SQL statements needed to create database objects like views and stored procedures.

Transfer Manager: The Transfer Manager Interface can be used to move both data and database objects from one database to another. One advantage of TMI is that it supports transfers from one platform to another and one character set and sort order to another.

Sample Questions

1. What is the recommended method for upgrading a 4.2*x* database to a 6.5 database?

   A. Transfer Manager

   B. Backup/Restore

   C. BCP

   D. Use Microsoft Access to port your data.

   Answer: B is correct. However, Transfer Manager can be useful when you are upgrading from one platform to another because backup and restores are not supported across multiple platforms. This means that you cannot back up a database on an Intel platform and then restore it on an Alpha platform.

2. What program should you run before you restore a 4.2*x* backup into a 6.5 database?

   A. CHECKBKP65.EXE

   B. CHECKREST.EXE

   C. CHKUPG65.EXE

   D. You do not have to run any programs.

   Answer: C is correct. You should run the CHKUPG65.EXE utility to verify that there are no reserved word conflicts and that there are T-SQL statements in the syscomments table.

3. To upgrade an Alpha 4.2*x* database to an Intel 6.5 database using backup and restore, which of the following methods could you use? (Select all that apply.)

   A. Transfer Manager

B. Backup/Restore

C. BCP

D. CHKUPG65.EXE

Answer: A is correct. You should run the CHKUPG65.EXE utility to verify that there are no reserved word conflicts and that there are T-SQL statements in the syscomments table, but this does not perform the upgrade. You cannot back up and restore databases from different platforms. BCP can be used to copy raw data from one database to another; however, database objects like stored procedures and views will not be transferred.

Set up a security mode.

This exam topic focuses on not only setting a security mode in SQL Server, but what the ramifications are and what is required to make these changes. As described earlier, the security options are standard (the default), integrated, and mixed. To change your security configuration, you must make changes to the Security Options tab in the Server Configuration/Options dialog box. In addition to the security option, there is a section on the Security tab that references login ID mappings. You should be aware of how these work.

Critical Information

The Security Options tab of the Server Configuration/Options dialog box (see Figure 1.3) is where you can make security changes and set up login ID mapping.

FIGURE 1.3: The Security Options tab

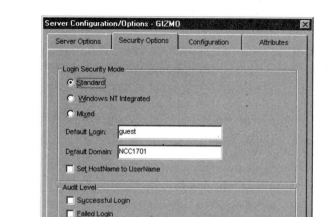

Security Options

Standard security means that every user must have a valid login ID in the SQL Server database. SQL Server will do all authentication. This is also called a *nontrusted connection*.

WARNING   Do not confuse a *nontrusted connection* with a Windows NT Domain Trust Relationship. Trusted connections exist between SQL Server and a Windows NT accounts database.

If you choose the Windows NT Integrated option, you must have either named pipes and/or mixed security as your server-side Net-Library. With integrated security, you must map Windows NT logins into the SQL Server database. Use the SQL Server Security Manager to accomplish this task. In this fashion, Windows NT is performing the login validation rather than SQL Server. These are also known as *trusted connections*.

NOTE To use integrated security, you must have either named pipes and/or multi-protocol Net-Libraries installed on SQL Server.

In a mixed security environment, you must still map NT login IDs, but SQL Server will still perform validation. If you have a mapped ID *and* you log in to SQL Server using your mapped login ID, you will be logged in as a trusted connection. If you specify a login ID to SQL Server other than the one with which you logged in to Windows NT and that ID exists in the SQL Server *syslogins* table, then you will be logged in as that user in a nontrusted connection.

Login ID Mappings

The mappings section is interesting and important for the exam. If you have NT login IDs that have characters that are not valid in SQL Server, the invalid characters will be mapped to these valid login characters. For example:

- Backslashes "\" are mapped as underscores "_".

- Hyphens are mapped as octothorpes "#".

- Spaces are mapped as dollar signs "$".

To test this example, you can create a Windows NT account called Obi-wan Kenobi in the StarWars domain. In Windows NT, your login ID would look like this:

\\StarWars\Obi-wan Kenobi

Your SQL Server login ID would be:

StarWars_Obi#wan$Kenobi

Necessary Procedures

You should be familiar with the process used to alter your security options. You should also be comfortable using the SQL Security Manager to map NT login IDs and user groups into SQL Server.

Changing Security Options

To change your security options:

1. Right-click on your server in Enterprise Manager, and choose Configure from the context menu.

2. Select the Security Options tab, and then make your changes.

NOTE   Your changes will not take effect until you restart SQL Server.

Exam Essentials

You should be familiar with these SQL Server security issues. Mappings, security context, and which network libraries support which type of security are all important test topics.

Remember the login ID mappings.   Remember how SQL Server maps NT login IDs with invalid SQL Server characters.

- Backslashes are mapped as an underscore "_".

- Hyphens are mapped as an octothorpe "#".

- Spaces are mapped as dollar signs "$".

Know the difference between standard, mixed, and integrated security and how the connections are referenced. Standard security is also referred to as using nontrusted connections. Integrated security is also referred to as using trusted connections. Mixed security can have both trusted and nontrusted connections.

Know what network libraries must be loaded to support integrated security. You must have either named pipes and/or multiprotocol Net-Libraries loaded on the SQL Server to support integrated security.

Key Terms and Concepts

Nontrusted connections: These are SQL Server connections under standard security mode. They are called nontrusted because SQL Server performs the authentication rather than Windows NT.

Syslogins: This is the table in the master database that stores SQL Server login information.

Trusted connections: These are SQL Server connections under integrated security mode. They are called trusted connections because NT performs the authentication, not SQL Server.

Sample Questions

1. What protocols support integrated security? (Select all that apply.)

   A. Named pipes

   B. Multi-protocol

   C. TCP/IP

   D. IPX/SPX

   Answers: A and B are correct.

2. If your Windows NT login ID is \\Sonora\Juan de La-Rocha, what would your SQL Server login ID be?

A. Sonora_Juan_de_La-Rocha

B. Sonora_Juan

C. Sonora_Juan#de#La$Rocha

D. Sonora_JuandeLa#Rocha

Answer: D is correct. Backslashes map to the underscore character "_"; spaces map to a dollar sign "$"; and hyphens map to octothorpes "#".

CHAPTER

2

Integration of SQL Server

Microsoft Exam Objectives Covered in This Chapter:

▶ **Identify the impact on SQL Server of integrated security.** *(pages 44 – 51)*

▶ **Locate where Windows NT Registry entries for SQL Server are stored.** *(pages 51 – 55)*

▶ **Identify how SQL Server is integrated with Windows NT.** *(pages 55 – 67)*

▶ **Identify capabilities of SQL Server when used with MAPI.** *(pages 68 – 77)*

The objectives for this portion of the exam cover your ability to recognize how and where SQL Server is integrated in the Windows NT environment. You must understand the impact of integrated security, Registry entries, application integration, and messaging through the Messaging Application Program Interface (MAPI).

Identify the impact on SQL Server of integrated security.

This test objective examines your understanding of how to configure SQL Server to use integrated security with Windows NT. SQL Server has three different security models: standard, integrated, and mixed. SQL Server performs all SQL login validation in standard security. Windows NT does all the SQL login validation in integrated security. Mixed security is a mixture of the two. In the mixed environment, valid NT login IDs that have been mapped into SQL Server will use the integrated portion of mixed security. IDs that haven't been mapped, or that force a SQL login that is different than their NT logon, will use the standard portion of SQL login security.

Critical Information

The exam stresses the configuration required to support integrated security with Windows NT. SQL Server must have the following configuration:

- SQL Server must be running named pipes and/or multi-protocol Net-Libraries.

- The integrated security option must be set in SQL Server.

- You must map valid Windows NT user accounts and groups into SQL Server. You can use the Security Manager to do this.

Once you have configured SQL Server with these options, you can use integrated security with Windows NT. Let's look at some of the steps you need to take in order to properly configure your SQL Server for integrated security.

Necessary Procedures

You need to be able to set up named pipes and multi-protocol Net-Libraries, configure the security option, and use the SQL Security Manager to map valid Window NT users and groups into your SQL Server database.

Installing Named Pipes and Multi-Protocol Libraries

Before you can use integrated security, SQL Server must first be running named pipes and/or multi-protocol. Named pipes is always installed on SQL Server and cannot be uninstalled. Named pipes uses an open IPC (Interprocess Communications Channel) along with ODS (Open Data Services) to communicate with other applications on the same machine or across the network. It is fast and efficient and does not require any proprietary API. Multi-protocol allows for multiple protocols to be used. When SQL Server uses multi-protocol, it is able to communicate through any open IPC mechanism. Multi-protocol uses RPCs (Remote Procedure Calls) to accomplish its tasks and is, therefore, not as efficient as a named pipe. To add the multi-protocol Net-Library to your SQL Server, follow these steps:

1. Start the SQL Server Setup utility. Start ➤ Programs ➤ Microsoft SQL Server 6.5 ➤ SQL Setup.

2. You will be presented with a Welcome screen. Click Continue.

3. You will next be notified that SQL Server is already installed. Click Continue.

4. You will now be presented with an options screen. Select the "Change Network Support" option, and click Continue.

5. You will now be presented with the Select Network Protocols dialog box. Make sure that Named Pipes is selected. If you would like to install support for Multi-Protocol, simply put a check in its box.

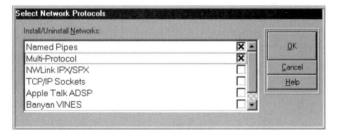

6. Click OK to continue.

7. SQL Server will let you know what name it will use for the named pipe. Click Continue to continue.

8. You will be asked if you would like to enable Multi-Protocol Encryption. This can be useful for security because you will be communicating over any open IPC mechanism, rather than your own private named pipe. Click Continue.

9. SQL Server will make the necessary modifications and then present you with an "Exit to Windows NT" screen. Click the Exit button.

10. For this change to take effect, you must also stop and restart SQL Server.

Changing Security Options

Now that you have installed the named pipes and multi-protocol network libraries, it is time to change your security setting from the default standard security to integrated security. Follow these steps:

1. Start the SQL Enterprise Manager. Start ➢ Programs ➢ Microsoft SQL Server 6.5 ➢ SQL Enterprise Manager.

2. Right-click your server and choose Configure from the context menu. You will now be presented with the Server Configuration Options dialog box.

3. Select the Security Options tab.

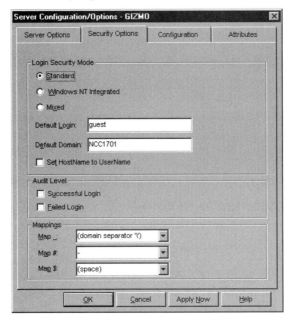

4. Change the login security mode to Windows NT Integrated. You can specify a default login (normally guest) and a default domain. The Set Hostname to UserName option will display the domain name for users who are not members of the default domain.

5. When you are finished making changes, click OK.

6. As with most changes that affect SQL Server as a whole, you must stop and restart SQL Server.

TIP You can stop and restart SQL Server from the Enterprise Manager. Right-click your server and choose Stop. Wait for a second, right-click again, and choose Start.

Mapping NT Users and Groups with SQL Security Manager

Now that you have both the correct network library and the right security configuration, you must map Windows NT users and groups into SQL Server. To do this, you will use the SQL Security Manager shown here:

1. Create your Windows NT users and groups. You can add your SQL Server users into their own NT group. For example, you can create two Windows NT groups: one called SQLUsers and one called SQLAdmins. You can then place some users into each of these groups.

2. Open the SQL Security Manager. Start ➢ Programs ➢ Microsoft SQL Server 6.5 ➢ SQL Security Manager.

3. Enter your server name login ID. In this case, it will be **SA**.

4. Select View ➢ SA Privilege. You should now see that the Administrators group has been granted SA authority.

5. Select Security ➢ Grant New.

6. Choose the SQLAdmins group from the list of groups and click Grant. Click OK to acknowledge your change. Click Done. You have just granted SA authority to the users in the SQLAdmins group.

7. To add non-SAs, select View ➢ User Privilege. Notice that there are no Windows NT users or groups currently set up.

8. Select Security ➢ Grant New and then choose the SQLUsers group from the list. Notice that the option for adding login IDs for the members of the group is checked. Leave this option selected. The second checkbox gives you the option of adding usernames in a database for members of this group. (Leave this option cleared.)

9. Click Grant to grant these members access. This will now add those users in the SQLUsers group from Windows NT to the SQL Server *syslogins* table. This includes both the login IDs and encrypted passwords.

10. You should now see a report that specifies how many new login IDs were added to SQL Server and how many new usernames were added to a particular database. Click Done when you are finished.

11. Close any additional windows that are open, and close the Security Manager.

Exam Essentials

There are only a couple of things to remember when dealing with integrated security in SQL Server. The following point is stressed on the exam.

Understand the necessary requirements to use integrated security.   To use integrated security in SQL Server, you must be running named pipes and/or multi-protocol Net-Libraries. In addition to this, your Windows NT users and groups must be mapped into SQL Server. You can use the Security Manager in SQL Server to accomplish this task.

Key Terms and Concepts

Multi-protocol: A network library available with SQL Server 6.5. Multi-protocol allows SQL Server to communicate over any inter-process communication mechanism. It also provides support for integrated security. Multi-protocol takes advantage of remote procedure calls to pass information between the client and server. It is less efficient than a named pipe.

Named pipes: An interprocess communication mechanism that is implemented as a file system service, allowing programs to be modified to run on it without using a proprietary API. Named pipes was developed to support more robust client/server communications than those allowed by the simpler NetBIOS interface. Named pipes is the default SQL Server protocol and is required to run SQL Server. Named pipes support integrated security.

SQL Security Manager: The SQL Security Manager is a utility that can map Windows NT user and group accounts into a SQL Server which has been configured to use integrated or mixed security.

Sample Questions

1. Which of the following Net-Libraries support integrated security? (Select two.)

A. Named pipes

B. TCP/IP

C. IPX/SPX

D. Multi-protocol

Answer: A and D are correct. Both named pipes and multi-protocol support integrated security.

2. You have configured SQL Server to use integrated security. You have stopped and restarted SQL Server. You have created Windows NT users and groups. After doing all of this, you still cannot log in to SQL Server. What else should you do?

A. You should add login IDs and passwords to SQL Server using Enterprise Manager.

B. You should add login IDs and passwords to SQL Server using the sp_NTLogin_Add stored procedure.

C. You should map login IDs and passwords to SQL Server using the sp_NTLogin_Add stored procedure.

D. You should map login IDs and passwords to SQL Server using the SQL Security Manager.

Answer: D is correct. A is used for standard security, or the standard portion of mixed security. There is no stored procedure called sp_NTLogin_Add.

Locate where Windows NT Registry entries for SQL Server are stored.

SQL Server is integrated into the Windows NT environment in many ways, including via the Registry database. SQL Server uses the Registry to store pertinent information about itself. Windows NT also adds entries to the Registry concerning SQL Server. This exam objective is useful for troubleshooting because knowing where to look in the Registry can help you track down errors.

Critical Information

The Registry is a database integrated with the Windows NT operating system. Programs use it to store all kinds of information about themselves. Programs may store information about their startup parameters, user preferences, service information, and anything else under the sun. SQL Server adds entries to the Registry in two different places. Because you are installing Microsoft software, most of the default startup options for SQL Server will be added to this key:

```
HKEY_LOCAL_MACHINE\SOFTWARE\Microsoft\MSSQLServer
```

Because SQL Server and the SQL Executive run as services, they will also have entries under the Services section of your Registry. You can check on those entries in these keys:

```
HKEY_LOCAL_MACHINE\SYSTEM\CurrentControlSet\Services\
MSSQLServer
```

```
HKEY_LOCAL_MACHINE\System\CurrentControlSet\Services\
SQLExecutive
```

You may note that the entries are for MSSQLServer and SQLExecutive (the two services that are started when SQL Server is running). MSSQLServer is the database engine and SQLExecutive is the suite of management utilities that are responsible for event monitoring, task management, alerts firing, and replication of data.

NOTE Because both the MSSQLServer and SQLExecutive are services, you can start and stop them from the command line using the NET START and NET STOP commands.

Necessary Procedures

These procedures will walk you through the process of using the Registry Editor to navigate the Windows NT Registry and view the different keys where SQL Server information is stored.

Viewing Entries for SQL Server with REGEDT32

Follow these steps to use the Registry Editor utility (REGEDT32.EXE) and view the entries for SQL Server.

1. To start REGEDT32, select Start ➤ Run to display the Run dialog box.

2. In the Open field, type **REGEDT32** to start the Registry Editor utility.

3. Locate the HKEY_LOCAL_MACHINE key. Then drill down through the SOFTWARE key (expand the key by double-clicking on the **+** symbol), then through the Microsoft key, and finally to the MSSQLServer key. You should see something similar to the screen depicted here.

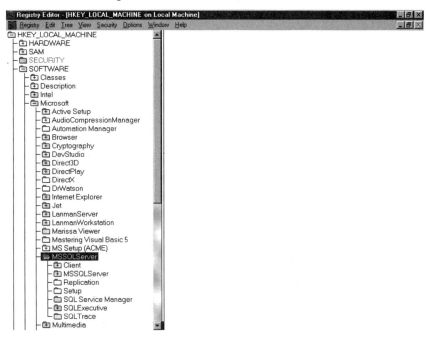

4. Locate the SYSTEM key under the HKEY_LOCAL_MACHINE key. Drill down through the CurrentControlSet, then the Services key. You should see the MSSQLServer (SQL Server service) and SQLExecutive (SQL Executive service) keys.

5. When you are finished, close the Registry Editor.

WARNING Tampering with the Registry is a potentially dangerous activity and could result in a nonfunctioning NT Server if you make improper changes. You should use the utilities in the Control Panel (or other utilities that modify the Registry, such as SQL Enterprise Manager) to make adjustments to your Registry whenever possible.

Exam Essentials

This topic is not stressed heavily on the exam. However, knowing where items are stored in the Registry can be an invaluable tool in your troubleshooting arsenal.

Know where in the Registry SQL Server entries can be found.
Remember the hive keys discussed earlier in this section. The entries are under the HKEY_LOCAL_MACHINE hive and are in both the software and services sections of the Registry.

Key Terms and Concepts

Windows Registry: A database where programs can store information about themselves and their users. The Registry replaces many of the old *.INI files of prior versions of Windows.

REGEDT32.EXE: The program that ships with Windows NT to view and modify the registry database

Sample Questions

1. Where would you look in the Registry to gather information about the SQL Server database? (Assume HKEY_LOCAL_MACHINE\.)

   A. Microsoft\Software\Services\MSSQLServer

   B. Software\Microsoft\MSSQLServer

   C. Microsoft\Software\MSSQLServer

   D. Services\Software\MSSQLServer

   Answer: B is correct. The other Registry entries do not exist. This particular entry will contain information that SQL Server itself uses to store information.

2. Where would you look in the Registry to find out about the current control sets for the SQL Executive service? (Assume HKEY_ LOCAL_MACHINE\SYSTEM\CurrentControlSet\.)

    A. Software\SQLExecutive

    B. Services\SQLExecutive

    C. Microsoft\SQLExecutive

    D. SQLExecutive

Answer: B is correct. The CurrentControlSet is where Windows NT keeps information about the currently running services.

Identify how SQL Server is integrated with Windows NT.

This test objective examines the different areas where Microsoft SQL Server has been integrated into the Windows NT environment. Windows NT has been designed to allow many different entry points for applications to be integrated into the operating system. This includes the Registry database, Windows NT event logging, objects and counters added to the performance monitor utility, Windows NT service integration, Windows NT secure login validation, and access to the Windows NT file systems.

Critical Information

SQL Server is tightly integrated with the Window NT environment. You should be familiar with the various ways this integration is implemented.

Here are NT/SQL integration points:

- SQL Server folders are installed under the Windows NT file management system.

- SQL Server adds entries to the Windows NT Registry.

- SQL Server uses the Windows NT event log for SQL Server event logging.

- With SQL Server installed, you can use the Performance Monitor to watch vital SQL Server statistics.

- With integrated security, you can map a Windows NT login ID into SQL Server.

File System Integration

SQL Server uses the Windows NT file system by placing its own database backup-and-support files there. If you are using NTFS partitions, this can give your database additional file-level security. SQL Server installs its files into the default directory \MSSQL on the drive that you specified during your installation process. Table 2.1 lists the folders that are created and what they contain.

T A B L E 2.1: SQL Server Folders

Folder	Contents
\MSSQL\Backup	Default folder to store backup devices for both databases and transaction logs
\MSSQL\BIN	16-bit utilities and DLLs
\MSSQL\BINN	32-bit utilities and DLLs
\MSSQL\CharSets	All character sets and their associated sort orders
\MSSQL\Data	Default folder to store database devices, as well as the Master device (MASTER.DAT)
\MSSQL\Install	Installation scripts, files needed by the Setup program, and any installation output files (useful for troubleshooting an installation—search for *.OUT files)

TABLE 2.1: SQL Server Folders *(continued)*

Folder	Contents
\MSSQL\Log	Default folder to store SQL Server error logs (up to six error logs may be present in a FIFO rotation)
\MSSQL\ReplData	Working folder for the SQL Server replication process
\MSSQL\SNMP	Working folder for SNMP (Simple Network Management Protocol) files
\MSSQL\SQLOLE\Samples	Sample OLE interfaces into SQL Server
\MSSQL\Symbols	DLLs used for generating stack dumps and traces

Windows NT Registry Integration

As discussed earlier, SQL Server adds entries to the Windows NT Registry in the HKEY_LOCAL_MACHINE hive. This includes entries in the Software section as well as the Services section.

Windows NT Event Log Integration

SQL Server has been configured to send messages to the Windows NT event logs rather than to the screen. You can see the entries in the NT event log by using the NT Event Viewer utility. The Event Viewer tracks three types of information in three different logs:

System log: Lists errors and events originating in the Windows NT kernel and drivers

Security log: Lists security breaches and audits successful and unsuccessful logins

Application log: Lists applications running on Windows NT that write messages to the NT event log

The Application log is the NT event log in which SQL Server events are recorded. The event log can track successful starts and stops of the

SQL Server service as well as the SQL Executive service. It will also track errors that occur within SQL Server.

The Application log itself has three different priority levels:

- Informational messages are denoted with a blue icon with the letter *i* in it.
- Warnings are denoted by a yellow icon with the exclamation symbol (!) in it.
- Critical error messages are denoted by a red stop sign.

The Event Viewer window is shown in Figure 2.1.

FIGURE 2.1: The Windows NT Event Viewer can track SQL Server messages in the Application log.

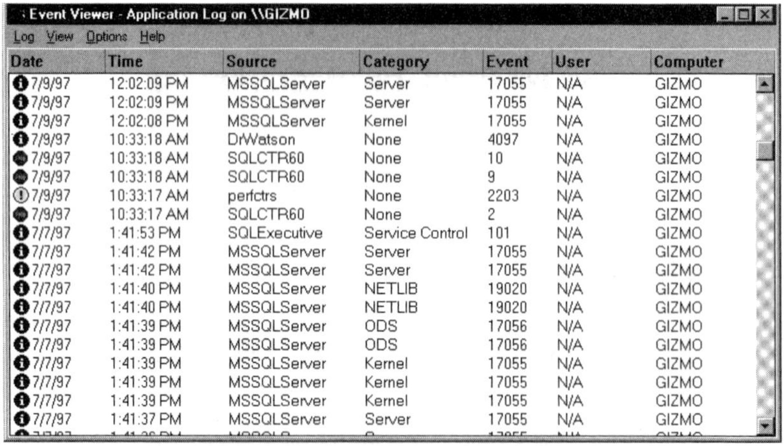

Date	Time	Source	Category	Event	User	Computer
7/9/97	12:02:09 PM	MSSQLServer	Server	17055	N/A	GIZMO
7/9/97	12:02:09 PM	MSSQLServer	Server	17055	N/A	GIZMO
7/9/97	12:02:08 PM	MSSQLServer	Kernel	17055	N/A	GIZMO
7/9/97	10:33:18 AM	DrWatson	None	4097	N/A	GIZMO
7/9/97	10:33:18 AM	SQLCTR60	None	10	N/A	GIZMO
7/9/97	10:33:18 AM	SQLCTR60	None	9	N/A	GIZMO
7/9/97	10:33:17 AM	perfctrs	None	2203	N/A	GIZMO
7/9/97	10:33:17 AM	SQLCTR60	None	2	N/A	GIZMO
7/7/97	1:41:53 PM	SQLExecutive	Service Control	101	N/A	GIZMO
7/7/97	1:41:42 PM	MSSQLServer	Server	17055	N/A	GIZMO
7/7/97	1:41:42 PM	MSSQLServer	Server	17055	N/A	GIZMO
7/7/97	1:41:40 PM	MSSQLServer	NETLIB	19020	N/A	GIZMO
7/7/97	1:41:40 PM	MSSQLServer	NETLIB	19020	N/A	GIZMO
7/7/97	1:41:39 PM	MSSQLServer	ODS	17056	N/A	GIZMO
7/7/97	1:41:39 PM	MSSQLServer	ODS	17056	N/A	GIZMO
7/7/97	1:41:39 PM	MSSQLServer	Kernel	17055	N/A	GIZMO
7/7/97	1:41:39 PM	MSSQLServer	Kernel	17055	N/A	GIZMO
7/7/97	1:41:39 PM	MSSQLServer	Kernel	17055	N/A	GIZMO
7/7/97	1:41:37 PM	MSSQLServer	Server	17055	N/A	GIZMO

NT Scheduling, Threading, and Performance Services for SQL Server

SQL Server is integrated into NT's scheduling and threading services. SQL Server is a multithreaded application. Each thread is scheduled based on its priority level and then given CPU cycles.

Because SQL Server is loaded as a service, its base priority (its lowest thread priority level) is automatically higher than most other applications, therefore allowing it faster access to the CPU more frequently.

Installing SQL Server 6.5 also modifies how NT handles performance for all applications on that particular Windows NT Server machine. SQL Server adjusts the Server Optimization property up one level from "Maximize Throughput for File Sharing" to "Maximize Throughput for Network Applications." (SQL Server is considered a network application.)

You can view the Server Optimization properties on the Services tab of the Network Control Panel (select Start ➤ Settings ➤ Control Panel, and double-click the Network icon), as shown in Figure 2.2.

F I G U R E 2.2:   The Services tab of the Network Control Panel

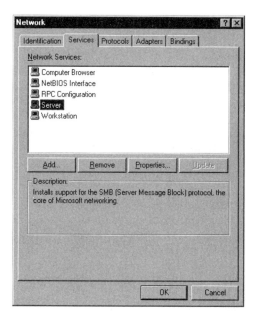

In the Services tab, select Server in the Network Services list, and then click the Properties button. You will now see the Server Optimization properties, as shown in Figure 2.3.

F I G U R E 2.3: The Server Optimization dialog box

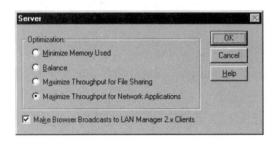

Windows NT Performance Monitor Integration

You can get up-to-the-second information about the performance of SQL Server through the SQL Performance Monitor. The SQL Performance Monitor provides settings for the Windows NT Performance Monitor. This tool can show you statistics on individual data items. These individual data items are called *performance counters*. Performance counters are grouped together into *performance objects*.

When you install SQL Server, the system automatically configures from six to eight performance objects related to SQL Server. These objects are listed in Table 2.2.

T A B L E 2.2: SQL Server Performance Objects

Performance Object	Information Tracked
SQLServer	General information about the performance of the server
SQLServer–Replication-Published DB	Replication transaction information

T A B L E 2.2: SQL Server Performance Objects *(continued)*

Performance Object	Information Tracked
SQLServer–User-Defined Counters	User-defined counters, attached to the currently empty stored procedures sp_user_counter1 through sp_user_counter10
SQLServer–Licensing	Licensing Information
SQLServer–Locks	Information on all locks currently in place
SQLServer–Log	Transaction log information for all open databases
SQLServer–Procedure Cache	Information about the procedure cache
SQLServer–Users	Information about users

When you start the SQL Performance monitor (by selecting Start ➤ Programs ➤ Microsoft SQL Server 6.5 ➤ SQL Performance Monitor) while SQL Server (the MSSQLServer service) is running, you will see the default performance counters, as shown in Figure 2.4.

These default performance counters work as follows:

- The Cache Hit Ratio counter shows the percentage of time that a request was found in the data cache instead of being read from hard disk. This number should be as close to 100% as you can get it. Ideally you'd like to have it be 100%. This is probably not a realistic expectation and could vary with the size of the database, the size of the data cache, the types of queries being executed against the database, etc.

- The I/O Transactions/sec counter shows the number of Transact-SQL commands executed per second. (This is sometimes referred to as *throughput*.)

FIGURE 2.4: The SQL Performance Monitor can be used to track statistical information about SQL Server.

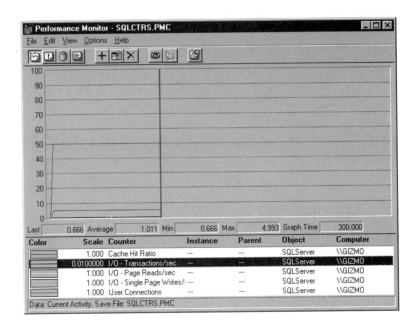

- The I/O Page Reads/sec counter shows the number of physical pages that are read per second. This number should be low for an optimized system.

- The I/O Single Page Writes/sec counter is the number of single page writes performed per second by SQL Server. This number should be low in an optimized system.

- The User Connections counter shows the number of configured user connections.

The most important of these counters is the Cache Hit Ratio. If this figure drops below 85%, you may need to evaluate some configuration options to help increase this value. For example, you might need to give SQL Server more RAM. You may increase this value if you place the tempdb database in RAM. There are other options that you may follow as well. A good performing system will have values consistently in the 90% range for the Cache Hit Ratio.

Integrated Logon to NT and SQL Server

You can use a single Windows NT user account to log in to both Windows NT and SQL Server. This type of logon has the following requirements:

- You must change your SQL Server security mode from its default value of standard security to integrated security.

- To use integrated security, you must have either named pipes and/or multi-protocol installed on the SQL Server as your network libraries.

NOTE   Named pipes is the default protocol and is used to install SQL Server.

- You need to create your Windows NT user accounts and then use the SQL Security Manager to "map" those IDs into SQL Server.

Necessary Procedures

You can use the Windows Event viewer to track messages generated by SQL Server. This includes warnings, errors, and informational messages.

Tracking SQL Messages with Windows Event Viewer

This first procedure will walk you through the process of using the Windows NT Event Viewer to track SQL Server messages.

1. To start the Event Viewer, select Start ➢ Programs ➢ Administrative Tools ➢ Event Viewer.

2. The first time you run Event Viewer, it will display the System log. SQL Server messages are located in the Application log. To view the Application log, select Log ➢ Application.

3. To gather more information about a particular event, double-click on the event to display the Event Detail dialog box. In the example shown here, for a SQL Server event with the Event ID 17055, the Description box indicates that SQL Server message 18109 occurred and that a database with an ID of 5 was successfully checkpointed and recovered.

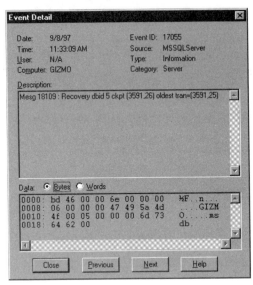

4. After you have reviewed the details, click Close in the Event Detail dialog box.

5. Close the Event Viewer.

Exam Essentials

SQL Server has been integrated into Windows NT in many different areas. You need to be familiar with the different points of integration.

Remember the different ways that SQL Server has been integrated in the Windows NT environment. Remember that SQL Server runs as a service under NT and, therefore, has entries in the

Service section of the Registry. Because it runs as a service, its threads get a boost in priority over normal "applications."

NOTE The most predominant questions on the exam will pertain to SQL Server's integration in the areas of the performance monitor and the integrated login security.

Know the difference between a performance counter and a performance object. Performance objects are simply a group of performance counters.

Key Terms and Concepts

Performance counter: A performance counter tracks an individual element in your system. For example, SQL Server has a performance counter for Cache Hit Ratio.

Performance object: A performance object is a group of performance counters. For example, SQL Server has a performance object called "SQLServer." This object has many counters in it, such as "Cache Hit Ratio," "I/O Transactions/sec," etc.

Thread: Threads are discrete units of executable code (a list of instructions) that are sent to the CPU for processing. A thread has a priority level. When the CPU receives several threads at once (several applications are running simultaneously), the CPU will give time slices to the thread with the highest priority. SQL Server threads get a higher priority than other applications running under Windows NT. For example, if you had the Notepad applet running and a SQL Server query, the threads coming from the query would get preferential treatment over those threads coming from the Notepad application.

SEE ALSO To learn more about threading and scheduling, see *MCSE: NT Server 4 Study Guide*, Second Edition, Sybex, 1998.

Throughput: *Throughput* is a term used widely in the computer industry. In general, it means the number of things that happen in a given period of time. In regard to SQL Server, throughput is generally expressed as the number of transactions processed per second. This statistic can be found in the SQL Performance Monitor utility and is expressed by the I/O Transactions/sec counter.

Sample Questions

1. SQL Server error messages can be viewed in the SQL Server error log and which Windows NT application?

   A. Windows NT Performance Monitor

   B. Windows NT Network Control Panel

   C. Windows NT Network Monitor

   D. Windows NT Event Viewer

   Answer: D is correct. The Performance Monitor is used to track SQL Server performance. The Network Control Panel can be used to alter the login ID for different services and to start and stop those services. The Network Monitor is used to gather information about network activity at this computer.

2. SQL Server is a multithreaded application. The Windows NT scheduler gives the SQL threads CPU time based on the threads priority level. The thread's base priority level is assigned either higher or lower based upon what type of application it is. Which of the following is true about SQL Server threads?

   A. SQL Server threads have a higher priority than the NT Kernel.

   B. SQL Server threads have a higher priority than other applications running under Windows NT.

C. SQL Server threads have the lowest priority in a Windows NT environment.

D. SQL Server threads have the same priority level as other applications running under Windows NT.

Answer: B is correct. SQL Server threads have a higher base priority level than other applications running under Windows NT. The scheduler looks at the priority levels of all processing threads and then assigns them CPU cycles. In addition to this, the scheduler will also boost and lower the priority of threads according to some internal rules. For example, foreground applications will get a priority boost, while long compute bound threads will get their priority level decreased.

SEE ALSO   For more information, refer to *MCSE: NT Server 4 Study Guide*, Second Edition, Sybex, 1998.

---

3. What is the difference between performance counters and performance objects?

A. Performance objects are grouped together into a single performance counter.

B. Performance objects are used to track vital statistics.

C. Performance counters are grouped together into a single performance object.

D. Performance counters are not used to track vital statistics.

Answer: C is correct. Counters like Cache Hit Ratio and I/O Transactions/sec are grouped together into a single performance object called SQLServer. It is also important to note that this is another way in which SQL Server has been integrated with Windows NT.

Identify capabilities of SQL Server when used with MAPI.

This exam objective focuses not so much on how to configure SQL Server to use mail, but more on the capabilities of SQL Server with its MAPI-compliant interface and when and where e-mail messages can be generated. MAPI stands for Messaging Application Programming Interface. Essentially, MAPI allows SQL Server to generate and send e-mail messages. These messages can include query result sets as an attachment.

Critical Information

SQL Server is said to be MAPI enabled. This means that SQL Server can generate and send e-mail messages. MAPI is the messaging application programming interface. This is a .DLL file that can be used by many different applications to generate, send, and retrieve e-mail messages. When an application is said to be MAPI compliant, this means that the application can use e-mail services with any MAPI-compliant post office. Nearly every current e-mail package supports MAPI. This includes MS Mail, MS Exchange, cc:Mail, Profs, DECNet Mail, and many more packages.

SQL Server is designed to allow you to generate e-mail messages in the following situations:

- When an alert is generated
- When a task starts and/or completes
- When a task fails to start and/or complete
- When explicitly invoked with an xp_sendmail extended stored procedure

The most difficult part of working with SQL Server and a mail client is making sure that SQL Server can see the post office. Essentially, you must create an e-mail account that the SQL Server Executive service account will use to send e-mail.

If you are using the MS Mail system:

1. Create the mail account and assign it a password.

2. Configure SQL Server with the same mail account and password.

3. Start MS Mail, then start SQL Server post office. SQL Server Mail will piggyback on MS Mail. If SQLMail is started before the MS Mail, you may encounter problems. Refer to the Microsoft SQL Server Books Online for more information.

NOTE   If the password is changed in the mail account, you must also change the password in SQL Server's Mail setup.

If you are using Microsoft Exchange:

1. Log in to Windows NT with the account that the SQL Server is using. (The SQLExecAcct is normally assigned to both the SQL-Executive service and the MSSQLServer service.)

2. Set up a Messaging Profile for the account.

3. Log off NT and then log back in with an administrator account.

4. Log in to SQL Server as SA.

5. Configure SQL Server to use the new profile for mail services.

Necessary Procedures

You should be familiar with the process of installing MAPI support for SQL Server. This objective is not stressed on the exam; however, this knowledge will make the administration of your SQL Server much more flexible.

Installing MAPI Support for SQL Server

Follow these procedures to install MAPI support for SQL Server running on Windows NT 4.0 with Microsoft Exchange. In this example, you will first create a post office. You will then create a user profile for the SQLExecAcct account. In this fashion, SQL Server will have a valid profile for use when logging on. The ability to use these profiles is an advantage of Exchange of MS Mail. Password and other changes take place at the profile, not both at the profile and in SQL Server.

1. Log in to NT as the user you created for the SQL Executive (SQLExecAcct).

2. Make sure the Exchange client and messaging services are installed by checking in Control Panel. There should be an icon for Mail and Post Office. If messaging services are not installed, install them by going to Control Panel /Add-Remove Programs and choosing the Microsoft Mail and Windows Messaging services as shown here.

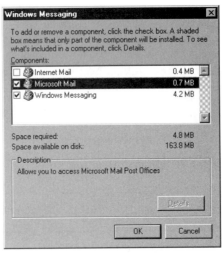

3. Ensure that Service Pack 3 for Windows NT 4.0 is installed by opening Windows NT Diagnostics (located in Administration Tools) and looking at the Version tab as shown. If the service pack

is not installed, install it. You will need to reboot NT after installing the service pack.

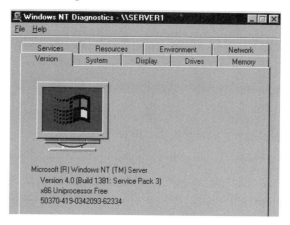

4. Ensure that there is an existing user in an existing post office for you to use. If you need to set up a post office, use the Control Panel/Microsoft Mail Post Office to create it. Create an Admin account named Admin with a mailbox of Admin.

5. Log in to the post office as the Admin and create a post office user for SQL Server to use. We will make one called Server1 with a mailbox of Server1 as shown here.

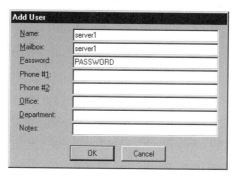

6. Now create a user profile for the SQLExecAcct (your current Windows NT login) by running the Control Panel/Mail applet and

choosing Add for the profile, or double-click the Inbox on your desktop.

7. When the applet starts, choose the Microsoft Mail client as shown here. Choose Next to continue.

8. Enter the postoffice pathname (or browse to it). Choose Next.

9. Choose Server1 as the user of the post office. Choose Next.

10. Enter the password of the mailbox (password is the default password).

11. Choose Next twice to save your personal folders to the local hard drive.

12. Choose Finish. The profile is called "Windows Messaging Settings." Choose Close to close the window.

13. If you have not set the MSSQLServer service account to the SQLExecAcct, do so now. To assign the profile to SQL Server, first go to Control Panel/Services and double-click the MSSQLServer

service. In the Log On As dialog box, choose the This Account option and assign it to use the SQLExecAcct as shown here.

14. Log off of Windows NT and log in as Administrator.

15. Start the SQL Enterprise Manager.

16. Open the mail configuration screen by highlighting the SQL Mail icon, right-clicking, and choosing Configure as shown here.

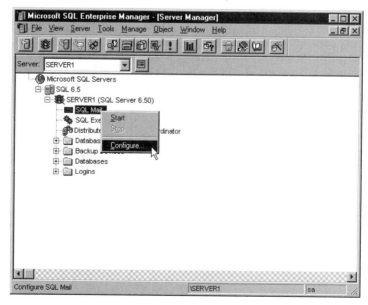

17. Enter the name of the profile you created just a few minutes ago: **Windows Messaging Settings** (as shown on the following screen). Click OK to save your changes.

18. Start the SQL Mail session by highlighting the MS Mail icon, right-clicking, and choosing Start. The icon should turn green, indicating that it successfully started a session with the mail client.

19. To have SQL Mail start automatically every time, right-click your SQL Server and choose Configure from the options menu. From the Server Options tab, check Auto Start Mail Client, as shown here. (Note that you could change the profile settings by clicking the Mail Login button on this screen.)

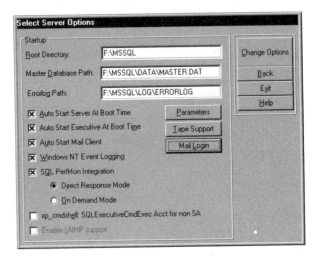

20. To test your mail client, open an ISQL/W window and run the following query:

```
use master
go
EXEC xp_sendmail
@recipients = 'Administrator',
@subject = 'Test',
@message = 'If at first you don't succeed, then
skydiving isn't for you!'
```

You should receive a response that says, "Mail Sent."

Exam Essentials

SQL Server is a MAPI-enabled product and, as such, you should understand the capabilities that this messaging ability lends to SQL Server.

Remember that SQL Server is MAPI enabled. SQL Server can generate e-mail messages to any MAPI-compliant post office. Most modern e-mail systems are MAPI compliant. SQL server can generate e-mail messages when a task starts or completes, when an alert fires, when a task fails, and when used with the xp_sendmail extended stored procedure.

SQL Server can send e-mail messages with attachments and the results of queries. Remember that SQL Server can send e-mail attachments as well as the results of running queries. You can use the xp_sendmail stored procedure to test this.

Remember that MS Mail and Exchange are configured in a different manner. If you are using MS Mail and you change the SQL Server e-mail password in MS Mail, then you must also change the e-mail password stored in SQL Server. This is not a problem if you are using Exchange because you will specify a Windows messaging profile in your SQL Server.

Key Terms and Concepts

MAPI: Messaging Applications Programming Interface. This is an international standard suite of functions stored in a .DLL file. These functions allow any front-end application to take advantage of e-mail services from any MAPI-compliant post office. Nearly every e-mail system today is MAPI compliant.

Messaging profile: A messaging profile is used with Microsoft Exchange to track a user's e-mail settings and preferences.

Sample Questions

1. SQL Server uses which API to support its e-mail functionality?

   A. TAPI

   B. Crypto API

   C. OLE

   D. MAPI

   Answer: D is correct. TAPI is the telephony API, Crypto API is the cryptography API, and OLE is used for Object linking and embedding technologies as well as OLE Automation.

2. Because SQL Server is mail enabled, to which post offices can e-mail be sent? (Choose the best answer.)

   A. Exchange

   B. cc:Mail

   C. Profs

   D. Any MAPI-compliant post office

   Answer: D is correct. SQL Server can send e-mail to any MAPI-compliant post office. Exchange, cc:Mail, and profs are also MAPI-compliant post offices. This question might seem a little unfair in that you can send e-mail to any of the choices, but this is similar to what you might expect on the exam.

3. The xxxxxxx's in the following code should be replaced with which of the following commands to send the results of a query as part of an e-mail message from SQL Server?

```
EXEC xp_sendmail
@recipients = 'Administrator',
@subject = 'Test',
@message = 'Testing 1,2,3',
xxxxxxx = 'SELECT * FROM pubs..authors'
xxxxxxx = 'TRUE'
```

   A. @attach_results, @query

   B. @query, @attach_results

   C. @sql, @attach_results

   D. @query, @attachment

Answer: B is correct. With @attach_results, you could send an attachment to the e-mail message. There is no such thing as an @results or @cursor.

4. If you are using MS Mail as your MAPI post office and you change the password for the SQLExecAcct, what must you do to SQL Server to guarantee that SQLMail will still be able to send e-mail messages?

   A. Nothing because the AutoStart E-mail Client option is set by default

   B. Change the mail password in SQL Server

   C. Change the profile settings in SQL Server

   D. Nothing because the profile settings will always point at the profile and the password in the profile was changed, not your password in SQL Server.

Answer: B is correct. You must make sure that both passwords match up when using MS Mail and SQL Server. If you are using Microsoft Exchange, then answer D would be more appropriate because SQL Server will point at a profile. That profile will hold all changes, but the profile itself will not likely change names.

CHAPTER

3

Enterprise-Wide
Database Administration

Microsoft Exam Objectives Covered in This Chapter:

▶ **Configure servers in the enterprise.** *(pages 80 – 109)*

▶ **Manage servers in the enterprise.** *(pages 109 – 117)*

▶ **Administer servers in the enterprise.** *(pages 109 – 117)*

The objectives for this portion of the exam cover your ability to configure, manage, and administer SQL Servers anywhere in your enterprise. This includes your ability to register servers, set database options, start and stop servers, and gather additional information about servers.

▶ Configure servers in the enterprise.

This test objective covers a wide range of material, from using stored procedures to configure a server, to running some simple Transact-SQL SELECT statements, to making modifications using the Enterprise Manager.

Critical Information

You need to review some of the utilities that come packaged with SQL Server. One of those utilities is the SQL Enterprise Manager. You should focus on creating and managing multiple servers and server groups with SQL Enterprise Manager and the stored procedures necessary to accomplish many of the same tasks. You must know how to modify the server options on any SQL Server that has been registered in SQL Enterprise Manager.

You also need to know about the ISQL and ISQL/W utilities, which are used to execute Transact-SQL statements. Make sure you are familiar with Transact-SQL and some simple SELECT statements that you, as a SQL Server administrator, will find useful. Finally, you need to review some stored procedures and DBCC commands that can be used for administration, management, and configuration.

SQL Server Configuration

After you've registered a server in SQL Enterprise Manager, you can make configuration changes on your local or remote SQL Servers using the Configuration Settings dialog box.

To access the configuration settings in SQL Enterprise manager, right-click on a server that is running SQL Server and choose Configure from the context menu, or choose Server ➤ SQL Server ➤ Configure from the drop-down menus. You'll see the Server Configuration/Options dialog box, as shown in Figure 3.1.

This dialog box has four tabs: Server Options, Security Options, Configuration, and Attributes. The following sections describe the settings available on each of these tabs.

Server Options

The settings on the Server Options tab allow you to specify general server options. The three text boxes at the top of the dialog box allow you to specify paths, as follows:

Root Directory: Specifies the path for the root folder containing the SQL Server files.

Master Database Path: Specifies the path and filename for the Master database device.

Error Log Path: Specifies the path and filename used for the SQL Server error log. SQL Server will keep a history of error logs up to six levels deep. If you do not want to have any SQL Server error logs, delete this entry.

FIGURE 3.1: The Server Options tab of the Server Configuration/
Options dialog box

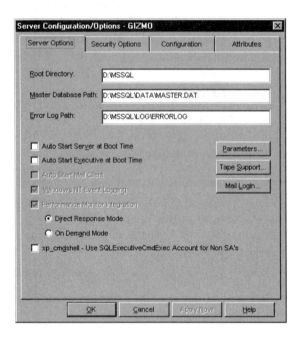

The checkboxes control Auto Start options, Windows NT event logging, and the Performance Monitor mode used for SQL Server. They
also control the security mode of users when they run commands
from the DOS prompt. These checkboxes work as follows:

Auto Start Server at Boot Time: Automatically starts the
MSSQLServer service whenever Windows NT is booted.

Auto Start Executive at Boot Time: Automatically starts the
SQLExecutive service whenever Windows NT is booted.

Auto Start Mail Client: Automatically starts the mail client when
SQL Server is started.

Windows NT Event Logging: Logs SQL Server and SQL Executive events to the NT Application log. If you are going to use alerts, you must select this option. Alerts fire only when an event is recorded in the NT Application log. (See Chapter 7 for more information about alerts.)

Performance Monitor Integration: Makes SQL Performance Monitor statistics available to Windows NT's Performance Monitor utility. With the Direct Response Mode option selected, SQL Server performance statistics are gathered in a batch and then displayed. You will have better performance overall for SQL Server this way; however, you will have a slight information lag for information passed to the Performance Monitor. With the On Demand Mode option selected, SQL Server performance statistics are shown as they happen. You get real-time information about SQL Server, but you lose some performance overall due to the overhead.

xp_cmdshell–Use SQLExecutiveCmdExec Account for Non SA's: Forces the user to run in the security mode of the client (the user that they are logged in to Windows NT as) when the *xp_cmdshell* extended stored procedure is used. If it is not selected, the user will run in the context of the account running the MSSQLServer service, which can be very dangerous as this account normally has Admin rights.

WARNING   The `xp_cmdshell` extended stored procedure is used to run NT Shell commands from within SQL Server batches. If the xp_cmdshell... option is not selected, your server's security is at risk. For example, while working in the security context of the account running the MSSQLServer service (the option is not selected), a user could run the SQL batch command `xp_cmdshell 'DELTREE c:\*.* /y'` successfully. When the xp_cmdshell...option is selected, Windows NT's security prevents users from actually deleting anything for which they did not have permissions. This is not the least of the things users could do. With knowledge of the `NET USER` statements, users could add a new user ID and give that ID administrative privileges.

The Server Options tab also has three command buttons that lead to additional options:

Parameters: Allows you to set SQL Server startup options.

Tape Support: Allows you to specify how long SQL Server will wait before trying to read a tape drive. This gives you enough time to load a tape into a tape drive before SQL Server tries to read it.

Mail Login: Allows you to specify parameters needed for starting the mail client.

Security Options

The settings on the Security Options tab of the Server Configuration/ Options dialog box, shown in Figure 3.2, are grouped in three areas: Login Security Mode, Audit Level, and Mappings.

F I G U R E 3.2: The Security Options tab of the Server Configuration/ Options dialog box

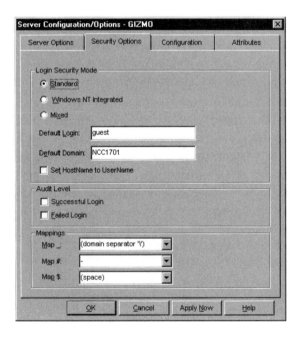

Although these options will be covered in more detail in other chapters, we will examine them here as well.

Login Security Mode   This section specifies what type of security SQL Server will be using. The default security mode is standard in which SQL Server validates all logons. This is known as standard security or nontrusted connections. You can change this to integrated (if you have named pipes and/or multi-protocol installed) and allow Windows NT to validate all logons. This is known as trusted connections. Mixed security is a mixture of both standard and integrated. In this scenario, if you have a valid Windows NT account that has been mapped into SQL Server, then you will have a trusted connection. If you do not have a mapped account, you will have to log in to SQL Server using a nontrusted connection.

You can specify a default login and default domain as well. The default account should be highly restricted as anyone who does not have a valid SQL Server login will use the guest account to gain access.

The option to set the username to hostname is useful when you run the *sp_who* stored procedure. When this option is not set, a user with the same name from one computer will look just like a user from another computer. For example: \\ComputerA\Joe and \\ComputerB\Joe would show up in an sp_who as Joe and Joe. With the option set, the hostname will precede the username.

Audit Level   The audit level can allow you to track how many successful and unsuccessful logins occurred in SQL Server.

Mappings   SQL Server does not allow the use of certain characters as part of a login ID. These invalid characters need to be mapped to other characters. The most common three mappings are "\" to "_", "-" to "#", and spaces to "$". For example, if your NT login ID and domain was: \\StarWars\Obi-Wan Kenobi, then your SQL Server login ID would be mapped as follows: StarWars_Obi#Wan$Kenobi.

Configuration Options
The Configuration tab of the Server Configuration/Options dialog box, shown in Figure 3.3, allows you to make many configuration

changes to SQL Server. If you select a setting from the Current field, the Description box at the bottom of the dialog box will tell you what the option does. For example, in Figure 3.3, the Current field for the Allow Updates option is selected, and the Description box says:

Specifies whether or not direct updates are allowed against system tables. Users with appropriate permissions can update system tables directly if this value is set to 1. Takes effect immediately.

F I G U R E 3.3: The Configuration tab of the Server Configuration/Options dialog box

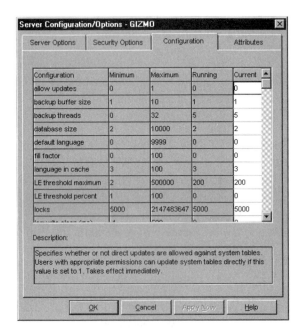

There are options to change the index fill factor settings, memory, locking, and many more settings. There are even advanced options which are listed in their own dialog box. To view the advanced options, scroll down to the Show Advanced options field, change the value to 1, and click OK, which will close the dialog box. Reopen the

Configuration screen to see the advanced options. The first item in the list is no longer Allow Updates; it is Affinity Mask.

The memory option is one of the most important options in SQL Server. The memory option allows you to specify how much memory will be allocated to SQL Server. This option is specified in 2KB data pages. When you work with this option, remember to leave enough memory for Windows NT to run efficiently. (Windows NT requires a minimum of 12MB of RAM.)

Attributes

The Attributes tab of the Server Configuration/Options dialog box is shown in Figure 3.4. This tab lists the values of attributes for this running instance of SQL Server. It is for informational purposes only; you cannot make any changes here.

F I G U R E 3.4: The Attributes tab of the Server Configuration/Options dialog box

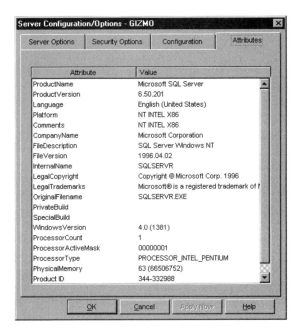

SQL Server Utilities

SQL Server comes with quite a few utilities, some of which we have already discussed. Table 3.1 summarizes the utilities and their functions.

T A B L E 3.1:   The SQL Server Utilities

Utility	Usage
BCP (Bulk Copy)	A command-line utility used for transferring information into and out of SQL Server.
CHKUPG65	A command line utility used to check the compatibility between a current version of SQL Server and older user-defined databases that are being upgraded.
ISQL	A command-line utility that provides a query interface to SQL Server. You can run Transact-SQL statements, as well as stored procedures and DBCC commands. This utility is primarily used by administrators.
ISQL_w	A utility that allows you to run all of the same commands that the ISQL command-line utility does. It has an added advantage of having a Windows graphical user interface. This allows you to run multiple queries and view the results of multiple queries in their own separate windows.
MAKEPIPE and READPIPE	Command-line utilities that can be used to verify that the named pipes protocol is working properly.
Microsoft ODBC SQL Server Driver	A SQL Server ODBC (Open Database Connectivity) driver help file.

T A B L E 3.1: The SQL Server Utilities *(continued)*

Utility	Usage
Microsoft Query	A utility used to graphically create SQL statements for any ODBC-compliant data source.
SQL Client Configuration	A utility used to configure SQL Server client network libraries. It also reports on the DB Library version that is in use for a particular client.
SQL Distributed Management Objects	A help file that displays the SQL-DMO framework, which is particularly useful to SQL Server application developers.
SQL Enterprise Manager	A utility used to graphically manage nearly every aspect of one or more servers in your enterprise.
SQL Performance Monitor	A utility used to capture statistical information about the performance of SQL Server.
SQL Security Manager	A utility used to "map" Windows NT user accounts to SQL Server when SQL Server has been configured to run in integrated, or mixed security mode.
SQL Server Books Online	An electronic version of the SQL Server manuals, which contains a fully cross-referenced search engine.
SQL Server Web Assistant	A utility used to create static Web pages of SQL Server data.
SQL Service Manager	A utility used to start, stop, and pause the SQL Server, SQL Executive, and the Distributed Transaction Coordinator services.

TABLE 3.1:   The SQL Server Utilities *(continued)*

Utility	Usage
SQL Setup	A program used to upgrade SQL Server or to make other modifications to the system.
SQL Trace	A utility used to monitor who is running what on SQL Server.
SQLMaint	A utility used to create tasks that will take care of day-to-day administration of SQL Server. This includes automating backups, updating statistics, and rebuilding indexes. Information generated here can be sent out in a report locally, to a UNC path, or to an e-mail operator.
SQLSERVR	An executable file used to start SQL Server from the command line. It has special options to start your server in a troubleshooting mode.

The SQL Setup Utility

You can use the SQL Setup utility to upgrade your version of SQL Server, change network support, add languages, rebuild the Master database, set server options, set security options, and remove SQL Server.

To run SQL Setup, select Start ➢ Programs ➢ Microsoft SQL Server 6.5 ➢ SQL Setup. You will be presented with a Welcome screen. Click Continue to continue. You will then be presented with a screen notifying you that SQL Server is already installed. Once again, click Continue to move on to the next step. SQL Setup now displays the Microsoft SQL Server 6.5 – Options dialog box, as shown in Figure 3.5.

FIGURE 3.5:   The SQL Setup utility's Options dialog box

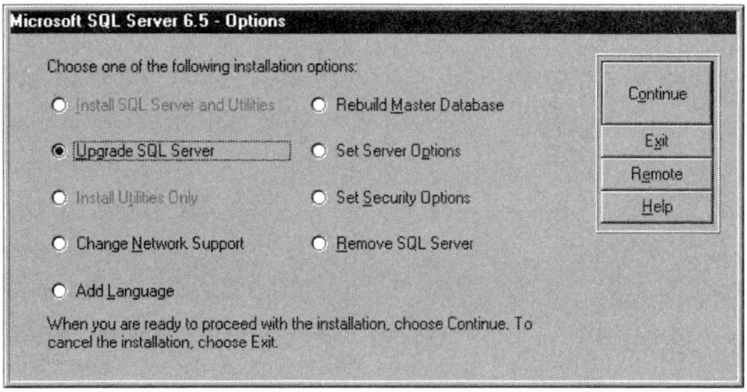

These options work as follows:

Upgrade: Allows you to upgrade from a previous version of SQL Server.

Change Network Support: Allows you to modify the current network clients.

Add Language: Allows you to add a new language to SQL Server. (You must have the SA password to do this.)

Rebuild Master Database: Re-creates the Master database.

NOTE   You should not need to use the Rebuild Master Database option if you have created backups of your Master database. However, there are some instances where a disaster could force you to re-create the Master database using this option. If you re-create the Master database, you will need to recover all of your user-defined databases.

Set Server Options: Allows you to set server options.

Set Security Options: Allows you to set the security used by your SQL Server.

Remove SQL Server: Removes SQL Server from your Windows NT server. It will also remove most of the Registry entries associated with SQL Server.

Choose an option and click Continue. When you're finished, click the Exit button. You will see another dialog box asking you whether or not you want to exit to Windows NT. Click the Exit to Windows NT button.

Transact-SQL and the ISQL Utilities

As explained in previous chapters, SQL Server uses the Transact-SQL version of the SQL language. You can run queries using Transact-SQL to manipulate the information stored in your databases. These queries can be created and run from the ISQL, ISQL/W, and MSQuery utilities, and from program code in third-party programs like Microsoft Access or Microsoft Visual Basic.

Let's take a look at the utilities that come with SQL Server, and then review some basic Transact-SQL statements.

The ISQL Utility

You access the ISQL utility from the command prompt. The command syntax is:

```
isql /U<user id> /P<password> /S<servername>
```

If you do not supply a server name, you will be logged in to the local server. Remember that passwords may be case-sensitive.

To run a query, type it in, and then execute the batch by adding the word GO on a line by itself.

The ISQL/W Utility

You can run all of the same queries in ISQL/W that you can run in the ISQL utility. The ISQL/W utility has the advantage of being an MDI (multiple document interface) application. This allows you to run multiple queries in separate windows, and then view the results in a separate window as well, which allows you to see the entire result set. Within the Results window, you can scroll through the results and use cut, copy, and paste features. Another feature of the ISQL/W utility is its ability to retrieve and store SQL scripts.

There are two ways to start the ISQL/W utility:

- To start it as a stand-alone utility, select Start ≻ Programs ≻ Microsoft SQL Server 6.5 ≻ ISQL_w. When you use this method, you will need to log in by filling out the fields in the Connect Server dialog box. This includes the server to which you are connecting, your login ID, and password.

- To enter through SQL Enterprise Manager, select Tools ≻ SQL Query Tool or click the SQL Query Tool icon (the one that looks like two mini-spreadsheets, one overlapping the other) on the toolbar. You will not need to log in again when you start the Query Tool in SQL Enterprise Manager.

You can type your Transact-SQL statements directly into the Query tab.

Simple SELECT Statements

Now that you know how to use the ISQL utilities, let's take a look at the SELECT statement.

NOTE   Although you will not see questions that are specific to SELECT statements on the MCSE exam, being able to read simple SELECT statements and understand what they do will be beneficial not only when you're taking the exam, but also in your work as a SQL Server system administrator.

The SELECT statement can be used to retrieve specific rows and columns of information from one or more tables in one or more databases. Every SELECT statement has three basic components: SELECT, FROM, and WHERE. (Although the ISQL/W utility is not case-sensitive when you are using Transact-SQL statements, we will show the Transact-SQL keywords in uppercase for clarity.)

The syntax for a simple SELECT statement is:

```
SELECT <column_list>
FROM <table(s)>
WHERE <search_criteria>
```

One of the simplest SELECT statements is to select all columns from a single table. You use the * operator to do this, as in this example:

```
SELECT *
FROM authors
```

These statements select all columns and all rows from the Authors table, which would look something like this (the table has been edited to fit the page):

au_id	au_lname	au_fname	phone
172-32-1176	White	Johnson	555 496-7223
213-46-8915	Green	Marjorie	555 986-7020
238-95-7766	Carson	Cheryl	555 548-7723
267-41-2394	O'Leary	Michael	555 286-2428
274-80-9391	Straight	Dean	555 834-2919
341-22-1782	Smith	Meander	555 843-0462
409-56-7008	Bennet	Abraham	555 658-9932
427-17-2319	Dull	Ann	555 836-7128
472-27-2349	Gringlesby	Burt	555 938-6445
486-29-1786	Locksley	Charlene	555 585-4620
527-72-3246	Greene	Morningstar	555 297-2723
648-92-1872	Blotchet-Halls	Reginald	555 745-6402
672-71-3249	Yokomoto	Akiko	555 935-4228
712-45-1867	del Castillo	Innes	555 996-8275
722-51-5454	DeFrance	Michel	555 547-9982
724-08-9931	Stringer	Dirk	555 843-2991
724-80-9391	MacFeather	Stearns	555 354-7128
756-30-7391	Karsen	Livia	555 534-9219
807-91-6654	Panteley	Sylvia	555 946-8853

au_id	au_lname	au_fname	phone
846-92-7186	Hunter	Sheryl	555 836-7128
893-72-1158	McBadden	Heather	555 448-4982
899-46-2035	Ringer	Anne	555 826-0752
998-72-3567	Ringer	Albert	555 826-0752

(23 row(s) affected)

Specifying Columns   You can specify individual columns in the *column-list* parameter. This is sometimes called *vertical partitioning* because you are selecting only certain columns. For example, if you want to retrieve only the authors' last names and first names, you can run this query:

```
SELECT au_lname, au_fname
FROM authors
```

The result set would look like this:

au_lname	au_fname
White	Johnson
Green	Marjorie
Carson	Cheryl
O'Leary	Michael
....	....
Panteley	Sylvia
Hunter	Sheryl
McBadden	Heather
Ringer	Anne
Ringer	Albert

(23 row(s) affected)

Specifying Rows   The WHERE clause is used to discriminate between rows of information. This is also known as *horizontal partitioning* because you are selecting only certain rows of information. For example, if you want to retrieve information on all authors who have last names that begin with the letter *M,* you can run this query:

```
SELECT *
FROM authors
WHERE au_lname LIKE 'M%'
```

au_id	au_lname	au_fname	phone
724-80-9391	MacFeather	Stearns	555 354-7128
893-72-1158	McBadden	Heather	555 448-4982

```
(2 row(s) affected)
```

Joining Information   For more complex queries, you can join information from two or more tables and then extract the results. For example, to find out which authors publish which titles, you need to join the Authors table, Titleauthor table, and the Titles table, and then display results based on matching title IDs in the Authors and Titles table in a join table called Titleauthor. This query would look like this:

```
SELECT authors.au_lname, authors.au_fname, titles.title
FROM authors, titleauthor, titles
WHERE titleauthor.au_id = authors.au_id
AND titles.title_id = titleauthor.title_id
```

Your results would look like this:

au_lname	au_fname	title
Green	Marjorie	The Busy Executive's Database Guide
Bennet	Abraham	The Busy Executive's Database Guide
O'Leary	Michael	Cooking with Computers: Surreptitious Balance Sheets

au_lname	au_fname	title
MacFeather	Stearns	Cooking with Computers: Surreptitious Balance Sheets
Green	Marjorie	You Can Combat Computer Stress!
Straight	Dean	Straight Talk About Computers
del Castillo	Innes	Silicon Valley Gastronomic Treats
DeFrance	Michel	The Gourmet Microwave
Ringer	Anne	The Gourmet Microwave
....	....	....
O'Leary	Michael	Sushi, Anyone?
Gringlesby	Burt	Sushi, Anyone?
Yokomoto	Akiko	Sushi, Anyone?

```
(25 row(s) affected)
```

Ordering Results   You can also order your result sets in either ascending (the default) or descending order. For example, if you want to list some author information in descending order by last name, you can run this query:

```
SELECT au_fname, au_lname
FROM authors
ORDER BY au_lname DESC
```

Your results would look like this:

au_fname	au_lname
Akiko	Yokomoto
Johnson	White
Dirk	Stringer

au_fname	au_lname
Dean	Straight
....	....
Cheryl	Carson
Reginald	Blotchet-Halls
Abraham	Bennet

(23 row(s) affected)

Stored Procedures

Stored procedures are precompiled Transact-SQL statements that are stored on the SQL Server machine itself. There are three types of stored procedures:

- System stored procedures, which are shipped with SQL Server and are denoted with an *sp_ prefix* and are typically found in the Master database.

- User-defined stored procedures, which you can create yourself (only the SA can register user-defined stored procedures with the system).

- Extended stored procedures, which work outside the context of SQL Server and generally have an xp_ prefix. These are actually calls to DLLs.

Because stored procedures are precompiled, they run much more quickly and efficiently than regular queries do. The compiler doesn't need to figure out what it needs to do in order to run a stored procedure. The query plan, or blueprint, is saved with the stored procedure. All SQL Server has to do is load blueprint information and run it. Regular queries must be compiled and optimized every time they are run.

Some stored procedures require parameters to be passed to them. You can use the *sp_help <procedure name>* to gather more information on a particular stored procedure.

You can run stored procedures from the ISQL utilities. For example, to find out information about all databases, run the following query:

```
EXEC sp_helpdb
```

Your results might look something like this:

name	db_size	owner	dbid	created	status
master	17.00 MB	sa	1	Apr 3 1996	trunc. log on chkpt.
Model	1.00 MB	sa	3	Apr 3 1996	no options set
msdb	8.00 MB	sa	5	Sep 14 1997	trunc. log on chkpt.
Pubs	3.00 MB	sa	4	Apr 3 1996	trunc. log on chkpt.
Tempdb	2.00 MB	sa	2	Sep 15 1997	select into/ bulkcopy
testpubs2	8.00 MB	sa	6	Sep 15 1997	trunc. log on chkpt.

DBCC Commands

The DBCC commands are used to check the logical and physical consistency of your databases. DBCC commands generally report information about the state of your databases. If problems are reported, the DBCC commands are generally not used to fix the problems. You should use stored procedures and Transact-SQL statements to resolve these problems.

As an administrator, you should become familiar with the DBCC commands. These commands can help you to more quickly and efficiently diagnose problems with SQL Server. They can also help you optimize your system and pass the exam.

Here are a few DBCC commands that you should definitely know about:

DBCC CheckCatalog   Checks for consistency between system tables.

DBCC CheckDB   Checks all tables and indexes in a database to see that index pages are correctly linked to their data pages. It will also make sure that the indexes are in sorted order and that the information on each page is reasonable.

DBCC NewAlloc   Makes sure that all pages in a database are correctly allocated and used.

DBCC SQLPerf(LogSpace)   Reports on the currently used amount of transaction log space expressed as a percentage.

DBCC SQLPerf(LRUStats)   Reports on how your procedure and data caches are being utilized.

Necessary Procedures

There are many different ways that you can configure your registered SQL Servers. We will revisit some of the topics that you should be comfortable doing.

Using the ISQL Utilities

ISQL and ISQL/W are used to run queries, stored procedures, and DBCC commands in SQL Server. To use the ISQL utility, try the following:

1. Go to a command prompt: select Start ➤ Programs ➤ Command Prompt.

2. From the command prompt, you must log in to a SQL Server. Type the following command:

```
isql /Usa /P
```

You should now see a command prompt that looks similar to this: 1>

3. To find out the name of your SQL Server machine, enter the following commands:

```
SELECT @@servername
GO
```

You should see the results, which will look similar to:

```
-------------------
Gizmo
(1 row(s) affected)
```

4. Type in the following statements:

```
USE pubs
Go
SELECT * FROM authors
GO
```

You will quickly notice one of the major limitations of using the ISQL utility. Although you retrieved all of the information from the Authors table in the Pubs database, it scrolled past the top of your screen and word-wrapped in such a way that it is difficult to read. For this reason, you will find that working with the ISQL/W utility is much easier.

5. To exit the ISQL utility and return to a command prompt, type the following:

```
Exit
```

6. To exit the command prompt, type the same command:

```
Exit
```

Using the ISQL/W Utility

1. Start the ISQL/W utility: select Start ➤ Programs ➤ Microsoft SQL Server 6.5 ➤ ISQL_w. When you use this method, you will need to log in by filling out the fields in the Connect Server dialog box, as shown here.

2. The following illustration shows you the Query tab of the ISQL/W window. We've added labels to identify the parts of the window. The two other tabs are Results and Statistics I/O.

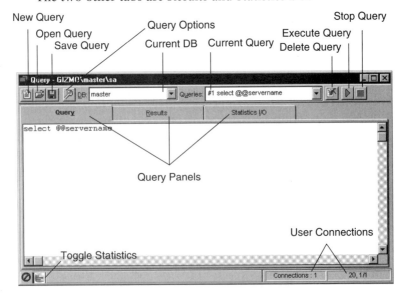

3. You can type your Transact-SQL statements directly into the Query tab. The following example uses the same select statement that was used in the ISQL utility.

4. Now it's your turn. In the Query tab, enter the following:

   ```
   SELECT @@servername
   ```

5. Click on the Execute Query button (with the icon of a green arrow) or press Ctrl+E to execute the query. You should see the results in the Results tab, as shown here.

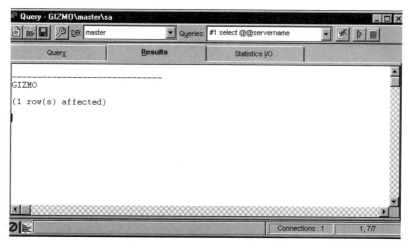

6. Click on the New Query button (on the far right of the toolbar). Notice that the Current Query list box shows that you are now working on Query #2.

7. Enter and execute the following query:

   ```
   SELECT @@version
   ```

   The Results tab should show your current version. You may also notice that the Connections indicator on the status bar shows two connections.

8. Click the Open Query button (the second one from the right on the toolbar) and browse to the \MSSQL\Install folder. From there,

select the InstPubs.SQL script. This is a fairly extensive SQL script, which is used to create or re-create your Pubs database.

9. Before you run this script, make sure that you will be able to see some statistics as they are generated. Check that the Statistics icon on the left side of the status bar shows that toggle is on.

10. Execute the script. This script can take from half a minute to several minutes to run, depending on the hardware. If you look in the Current Query list box, the world icon will be spinning while the query is running. You could stop the processing of this query by clicking on the Stop Query button (on the far-left side of the toolbar).

11. When the query has finished executing, click on the Statistics tab. You will see statistics that were generated during the running of this query, which should look similar to the window shown here.

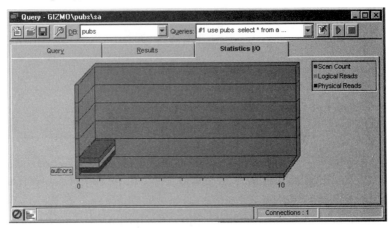

12. From the Current Query list box, select the first query you executed, and click on the Query tab. You will see your original query. You can look at the saved result set by clicking on the Results tab, or you can re-execute the query and view the new results (which in this case will be the same server name as before).

So far, you have been working with the Master database. In the next steps, you will use two different ways of switching to a different database and running a query.

13. Click on the New Query button to start a new query. In the Query window, type the following:

```
USE pubs
SELECT * FROM authors
```

14. Execute this query. You will notice that the current database has been switched to Pubs. The result set should look similar to the window shown here.

15. Click on the New Query button, and in the Current Database list box, select the Pubs database.

16. Enter and execute the following query:

```
SELECT * FROM authors
```

You should see the same result set as you did in Step 13.

17. You can follow these same steps to run both stored procedures and DBCC commands. For example, run the following stored procedure:

```
EXEC sp_who
```

18. Now run the following DBCC statement:

```
USE Pubs
GO
DBCC CheckDB
GO
```

19. Close the ISQL/W utility window or the Query Tool window in SQL Enterprise Manager.

Exam Essentials

This topic discussed all of the different areas where you can make configuration changes to SQL Server.

Know how to get to the configuration options screens and what the major choices are.   Remember that you can pull up the configuration screens by right-clicking on a registered server and choosing Configure from the context menu. There are four tabs in the configuration options screens. You should know what the major features of each these tabs accomplish.

Know what simple SQL queries do.   You should be able to read simple SQL Queries and understand what results they will return. Remember also that you can run stored procedures and DBCC commands in the ISQL utilities.

Know how to start and use both of the ISQL utilities.   Remember that to start the command line version, you must log in as follows:

```
isql /U<login ID> /P<password> /S<servername>
```

Key Terms and Concepts

DBCC commands: Database Consistency Checker commands are used to check the consistency of your databases. In general, these commands report problems rather than fix them. To fix reported problems, you should use stored procedures and T-SQL statements.

Stored procedures: Precompiled SQL statements. The query plan or blueprint for running the procedure is stored in memory. This is a big time saver over regular T-SQL statements as each T-SQL statement must be compiled and optimized and a query plan generated before they can be run. There are three types of stored procedures: system procedures (sp_), extended stored procedures (xp_) which are function calls to .DLL files, and user-defined stored procedures which you create and store in your databases.

T-SQL statements: Transact-SQL is used to query the database. You can use SELECT statements to gather information from database tables. You can use modification statements like INSERT, UPDATE, and DELETE to modify data stored in your database. You can also use T-SQL statements to create all manner of database objects like tables and indexes.

Sample Questions

1. How would you force a user to work in the security context of the client rather than the server?

   A. Set the xp_cmdshell option

   B. Set the sp_client option

   C. Set the xp_client option

   D. Set the sp_server option

   Answer: A is correct. If you do not set this option, it is possible for a user with few rights to do serious damage to your server.

2. The SQL Setup utility can be used to do which of the following? (Choose all that apply.)

   A. Add network libraries

   B. Add database libraries

C. Install languages

D. Rebuild the Master database

Answer: A, C, and D are correct. To add database libraries (DBLibs) you must use the SQL Client configuration utility.

3. Which of the following will start the ISQL command-line utility and log you in?

   A. isql /Login sa /Pwd *****

   B. isql /Lsa /S

   C. isql /Usa /P

   D. sqlservr /Usa /P

   Answer: C is the correct choice. The other choices will give you syntax errors.

4. Which of the following is true about the ISQL/W window?

   A. You can run Transact-SQL, but not DBCC commands

   B. You can run both Transact-SQL and DBCC commands

   C. You can run DBCC, but not Transact-SQL commands

   D. You can run DBCC, Transact-SQL, but not stored procedures

   Answer: B is correct. You can run both T-SQL and DBCC commands from any of the ISQL windows as well as stored procedures.

5. What does the following Transact-SQL script do?

```
SELECT Employee.FirstName, Employee.LastName,
WorkInfo.YearsExp FROM Employees, WorkInfo WHERE
Employee.EmpID = WorkInfo.EmpID
```

   A. Displays all information in an employee record and all associated work information

   B. Displays the first name and last name in an employee record (if the employee has work experience, it will display that too)

    C. Displays all employees' first names and last names and their work experience (if there are records that have a matching employee ID in the WorkInfo table)

    D. Displays all employees' first names and last names and their work experience (whether or not they have a matching employee ID in the WorkInfo table)

Answer: C is correct.

  6. What are the benefits of stored procedures? (Choose all that apply.)

    A. They are precompiled and, therefore, run more efficiently than normal queries.

    B. They can be used in Transact-SQL batches.

    C. They are not precompiled and, therefore, run more efficiently than normal queries because the optimizer can look at the current conditions and make the necessary optimizations in real-time.

    D. They are not used in Transact-SQL batches.

Answer: A and B are correct. Stored procedures are precompiled and can be included in T-SQL batches.

Manage servers in the enterprise.

Administer servers in the enterprise.

These two topics can be grouped together. They are so similar that it is very difficult to distinguish between the two. In fact, much of the configuration section just presented could be part of the manage or administer topics here as well. There is really only one true-blue management/administration topic that we will look at here.

Critical Information

Before you can do any configuring, administration, or management, you must first register your SQL Server and add it to a server group. To be prepared for the exam, you need to take a look at server groups and registering a SQL Server.

Server groups are used to provide logical groupings for administrative purposes. You can set up server groups through SQL Enterprise Manager. You should create your server groups first, and then register your servers and place them in the newly created groups.

There are some rules that apply to creating server groups and registering your servers:

- Server groups can be created at the local server only. If you want the SQL Enterprise Manager utility running on other machines to have the same logical groups, you must go to each of those machines and repeat the same steps that you did with the first server.

- Group names must be unique at each server.

- Registering servers must also take place at each machine that is running SQL Enterprise Manager. You cannot do this remotely.

- SQL Server computer names can consist of only letters, numbers, and these characters: _ (underscore), # (octothorpe), and $ (dollar sign). You should avoid using the punctuation symbols because they have special meanings in the SQL Server environment.

- If you are not using integrated or mixed security, you must provide a valid ID and password for each server registered. You should use the SA account because this will give you the most rights when you are managing remote SQL Servers from within Enterprise Manager.

TIP You can drag-and-drop registered SQL Servers from one server group to another.

Necessary Procedures

There are many different ways that you can administrate your registered SQL Servers. You should be comfortable doing the step-by-step walkthroughs in this section.

Before you can administrate a SQL Server, you must first register it.

Creating Server Groups and Registering Servers

1. Start SQL Enterprise Manager by selecting Start ➤ Programs ➤ Microsoft SQL Server 6.5 ➤ SQL Enterprise Manager.

2. Select Server ➤ Server Groups, or right-click the SQL 6.5 server group and choose New Server Group from the context menu to display the Manage Server Groups dialog box.

3. To add the Accounting server group, in the Name box, enter **Accounting**. Make sure that the Top Level Group option button is selected, as shown here, and then click the Add button.

4. To add the Sales server group, enter **Sales** in the Name box, make sure that the Top Level Group option button is selected, and click Add.

5. To add the Inside subgroup, enter **Inside** in the Name box, click the Sub-Group of option button, and select Sales in the lower box, as shown here. Then click the Add button.

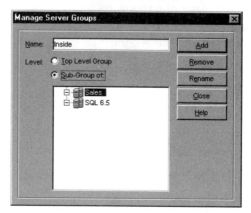

6. To add the Outside subgroup, enter **Outside** in the Name box, click on the Sub-Group of option button, select Sales, and click the Add button.

7. Click the Close button to close the Manage Server Groups dialog box. Your Server Manager window should look similar to the one shown here.

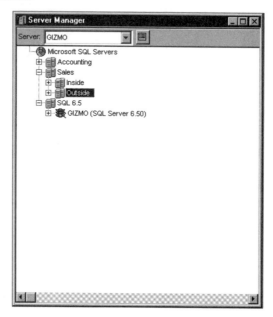

8. To register the server in the Accounting group, select Server ➢ Register Server, or right-click the Accounting group and choose Register Server from the context menu. This brings up the Register Server dialog box. Notice that your server groups are listed in the lower box.

9. In the Server box, type **AcctSvr**. This would be the computer name of the Accounting server, which resides somewhere in the enterprise. Leave the Use Standard Security option button selected, and enter **sa** for the Login ID as shown. You also need to specify the password for the SA account that is on the AcctSvr. (In the example, this field is left blank.) Make sure that the Accounting group is selected in the Server Group list, and click the Register button.

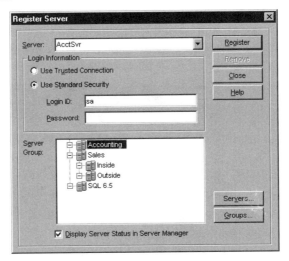

Because the AccSvr server used in this example doesn't really exist, the error message shown in the following graphic appears. You can get this error message for several reasons. If you've entered the name of an existing computer, the most probable reason for this message is that there is a connectivity issue. Make sure that the SA account exists on the computer you named, that you have typed the correct password, and that the computer name is correct. (See

Chapter 12 for more information about troubleshooting networking problems.)

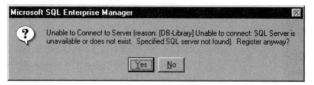

10. Click the Yes button to register anyway.

11. In the Register Server dialog box, repeat the procedure to register a server named **InSales,** placing it in the Inside subgroup of the Sales group. Then register two more servers, named **SalesA** and **SalesB,** placing each of them in the Outside subgroup.

12. Click the Close button in the Register Server dialog box. Your Server Manager window should now look something like the one shown here.

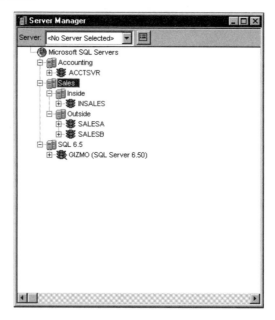

A handy technique that you can use in SQL Enterprise Manager is drag-and-drop. You can easily move servers to different server groups by simply dragging them with your mouse and dropping them into their new place. For our example, let's say that the Sales staff has been reorganized from Inside Sales and Outside Sales groups into a single Sales group. Now we need to rearrange our server groups to match this reorganization.

13. In the Server Manager window, click on the INSALES server and drag-and-drop it onto the Sales group icon. This moves the INSALES computer out of the InSales group to the Sales group.

14. Drag-and-drop the SALESA and SALESB servers onto the Sales group icon. When you are finished, your Server Manager window should look something like the one shown here.

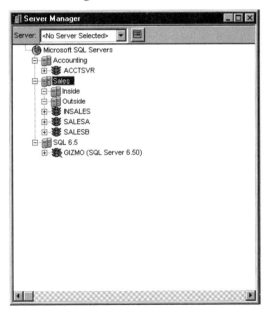

15. To quickly remove the empty Inside server group, right-click it, choose Remove from the context menu, and then verify the deletion. Remove the Outside group in the same way.

Exam Essentials

This topic examined the necessary configuration to administrate and manage your SQL Server.

Know how to create server groups and register servers within them. Remember that once you have registered a server within a server group, you can move that server to another group using drag-and-drop. You can also move a server group to another server group using drag-and-drop. As far as we know, there are no other drag-and-drop features currently supported in SQL Server.

Key Terms and Concepts

Registering a server: Before you can manage or configure a SQL Server, it must first be registered. In addition to registering a server, you must place the server in a server group. You can create your own server groups and then drag-and-drop your servers into these different groups. When you register a server, you must specify a login ID and password. You should use the SA login ID because this will give you the most rights on those local and remote servers. Finally, server groups are local in nature. If you want to create the same server groups in SQL Enterprise Manager on another computer, you must physically go to that computer and create the groups in the same manner.

Sample Questions

1. Which of the following is true regarding server groups. (Choose all that apply.)

    A. You can use drag-and-drop to move registered servers from group to group.

    B. You can use drag-and-drop to move a server group to a subgroup.

    C. You can use drag-and-drop to move server groups in SQL Enterprise Manager on Machine A to SQL Enterprise Manager on Machine B.

    D. You can use the stored procedure sp_movesvrgrp to move server groups from Machine A to Machine B.

Answer: A and B are correct. You can use drag-and-drop to move servers and server groups around in the Enterprise Manager.

2. Before you can administer a SQL Server machine in SQL Enterprise Manager, what must you do?

    A. You must register the server and provide the proper login credentials.

    B. You must go to that other server and register it in your Enterprise Manager.

    C. Nothing. SQL Enterprise Manager will find all servers on your network automatically.

    D. Nothing. You cannot manage multiple servers from one Enterprise Manager.

Answer: A is correct. To work with any servers in the Enterprise Manager, they must be registered. In order to register a server, you must supply valid login credentials for the server you are trying to register.

CHAPTER

4

Managing Database Storage

Microsoft Exam Objectives Covered in This Chapter:

▶ **Create a device.** *(pages 120 – 127)*

▶ **Create a database.** *(pages 128 – 133)*

▶ **Alter a database.** *(pages 133 – 140)*

▶ **Create database objects.** *(pages 141 – 146)*

▶ **Estimate space requirements.** *(pages 147 – 153)*

The objectives for this portion of the exam cover your ability to create and manage your databases and the devices on which they are stored. You need to fully understand the creation of a device, the creation of databases and transaction logs, resizing your database, and moving a transaction log from a "data and log" device fragment to a "log only" fragment. You should also understand the process to create database objects and estimate the amount of storage needed for your database, system tables, and objects.

Create a device.

This exam objective examines your understanding of how to create a device and its uses. Before you can create a database, you must first reserve disk space in which to store it. This reserved disk space is called a database device. You can create your database devices using the DISK INIT statements, or through the SQL Enterprise Manager.

Critical Information

Because nothing can be stored until a device is created, you should begin your review by creating devices. A device is simply preallocated disk space in the form of a file. When you installed SQL Server, three devices were created for you. They include:

Master: Which stores the following databases: Master, Model, Tempdb, and Pubs.

MSDBData: Which stores the MSDB database. The MSDB database is used by the SQL Executive utilities.

MSDBLog: Which stores the transaction logs for the MSDB database.

You can use both the Enterprise Manager and Transact-SQL code to create a device. Although the GUI interface is easy to use, the exam focuses on the DISK INIT statements.

Creating a device is the process of reserving disk space for the exclusive use of SQL Server. Devices can be created as files on an NTFS or FAT partition, or they can be created on raw partitions. When creating a device, you have the choice of using the Enterprise Manager interface or Transact-SQL using the DISK INIT statement. Only the SA has authority to create devices, and this permission cannot be given to any other user.

TIP   Although you can create devices on raw partitions, there is little advantage to doing so. The device creation process will take less time if you use a raw partition, but once the device is created there will be little if any performance benefit. It does, however, eliminate your ability to perform standard file system operations (such as copying and renaming) with the device.

When you create a device, the new information will be added to the *sysdevices* table in the Master database. Devices can hold both data and transaction log fragments. Databases and transaction logs can span multiple devices. Information on these fragments can be found in the *sysusages* table in the Master database.

Necessary Procedures

In this section, you will learn about the different processes involved in successfully creating a device in SQL Server. This includes the use of the DISK INIT statement and its corresponding parameters.

Creating a Device

Use the DISK INIT statements to create a device. This approach allows a little more control over how the device is created, but it also requires you to do a little mathematical conversion and remember some code. Sometimes the added control can really be worth the extra effort.

The syntax of the DISK INIT statement is:

```
DISK INIT
NAME = 'logical_name',
PHYSNAME = 'physical_name',
VDEVNO = virtual_device_number,
SIZE = number_of_2K_blocks
```

The parameters of the DISK INIT statement are used as follows:

Name: This parameter is the logical name of the device or the name by which the device will be known inside the server.

Physname: The Physname parameter is the full path for the physical file location on a local disk drive.

VDEVNO: This parameter is the Virtual Device Number of this device. SQL Server can host up to 256 devices per server. These devices are differentiated by their virtual device number. This number literally translates into the starting virtual page address for this device. Because a device can be up to 32GB in size, these virtual starting addresses are 32GB apart. This value can be any available device number between 1 and 255. The numbers 126 and 127 are taken by the MSDB devices (0 is taken by Master).

Size: The size parameter is expressed in 2KB page units. You will probably think about database sizes in megabytes, so you may have to do a little conversion here. There are 512 2KB pages per megabyte.

In order to use SQL code to create a device, you must first find out which virtual device numbers are free. This information can be obtained with a stored procedure, *sp_helpdevice*.

Once you have obtained a virtual device number, you can create a device. In the following example, we will create a device that is 10MB in size, with the logical name Frogger and the physical name Frogger.Dat.

```
DISK INIT
NAME = 'Frogger',
PHYSNAME = 'C:\MSSQL\DATA\Frogger.dat',
VDEVNO = 2
SIZE = 5120
```

WARNING Be careful when you create your devices. They can be enlarged, but not shrunk.

You can follow these steps in order to secure a free virtual device number and then create a new database device.

1. From the Enterprise Manager menu, select Tools ➢ SQL Query Tool or open ISQL/W from the SQL Server 6.5 program group.

2. Enter and execute the following statements:

```
USE master
EXEC sp_helpdevice
go
```

3. The results will list all of the devices currently installed on your system. Scroll all the way to the right in this window until you see the *device_number* column. This column will list all used virtual device numbers. Make a note of which numbers between 1 and 255 are free. You will need this information to create your device.

4. Close the Query Tool or ISQL/W.

5. Now with a free virtual device number in hand, you are ready to create a device using SQL code.

6. Enter and execute the following statements to create a new device. You may need to change a path or virtual device number if these parameters are not appropriate for you server. (Don't forget the commas!)

```
USE master
DISK INIT
NAME = 'SybexTestLog',
PHYSNAME = 'C:\MSSQL\DATA\SybexTestLog.DAT',
VDEVNO = 2,
SIZE = 1024
go
```

7. The results window should return the following message:

```
This command did not return data, and it did not return
any rows
```

8. Close the Query Tool of ISQL/W utility, and return to the Server Manager window of the Enterprise Manager.

9. Refresh the devices list by clicking the Database Devices folder with your right mouse button. Select Refresh from the pop-up menu.

10. Now see your new device in the Database Devices folder. You could also rerun sp_helpdevice to see your new device information.

Exam Essentials

You will need to have a well-developed understanding of the following points to successfully complete this objective on the exam.

Know who can create devices and where.   Remember that only SA has permission to create a device. This permission cannot be transferred. Database devices must be on a local hard disk. (Dump devices can be created on nonlocal media.) You can create a device on a RAW partition, NTFS partition, or an MS-DOS partition.

Know the DISK INIT statement and its parameters.   The DISK INIT statement has the following parameters: NAME which is the logical name, PHYSNAME which is the physical path and filename, VDEVNO which is a virtual device number, and SIZE which is the device size expressed in 2KB data pages.

Know how to get an unused virtual device number.   You must supply a virtual device number when you create a new device using the DISK INIT statements. Remember that the virtual device numbers are from 0 to 255. (The numbers 0, 126, and 127 are reserved by SQL Server.) Free device numbers can be retrieved using the sp_helpdevice stored procedure.

Remember that device sizes are expressed in terms of 2KB data pages rather than in megabytes.   A good tip to remember is that when you deal with database sizes, you are generally using megabytes. When you refer to database devices, you are generally using 2KB pages.

Remember that devices can be made larger, but they cannot be made smaller.   Unlike a database, a device can only be made larger. You should make sure that you don't create a device that is much too big for your needs because this will eat up valuable disk space which then won't be used.

Key Terms and Concepts

Device: Devices store data and logs. Data and logs can span multiple devices. A single device can store multiple databases. Information on these file fragments is stored in the sysusages table in the Master database.

DISK INIT: The T-SQL command used to create a new device in SQL Server 6.5. It requires a name, physical filename, virtual device number, and a size expressed in 2KB pages.

Sysdatabases: The table in the Master database where database information is stored.

Sysdevices: The table in the Master database where device information is stored.

Sysusages: The table in the Master database where information about which part of a database and transaction log resides.

Sample Questions

1. Which of the following system tables is used to store information about the relationship between databases and devices?

   A. sysdatabases

   B. sysdevices

   C. sysusages

   D. sysfragments

   Answer: C is correct. The sysdatabases table holds information about individual databases. Sysdevices holds information about individual devices. There is no sysfragments table.

2. How large can a device in SQL Server be?

    A. 32MB

    B. 32GB

    C. 32TB

    D. There is no limit to device size

    Answer: B is correct. SQL Server can address up to 32GB per device. This does not mean that the largest database you can work with is 32GB. A database can span multiple devices.

3. What is the unit of measure for the SIZE parameter when using the DISK INIT statement?

    A. Incremental change in 2KB pages

    B. Final Size in 2KB pages

    C. Incremental change in megabytes

    D. Final size in megabytes

    Answer: B is correct. As a general rule, anytime you are referring to a device, you will use 2KB data pages. Normally, when you refer to a database, you will use megabytes.

4. Which stored procedure is used to find out what virtual device numbers are available?

    A. sp_vdevno

    B. sp_virtual_device

    C. sp_helpdb

    D. sp_helpdevice

    Answer: D is correct. You must have a free virtual device number in order to create a new device.

Create a database.

T his exam objective focuses on using T-SQL statements to create a database. You can use the CREATE DATABASE statements, or you can use the Enterprise Manager. Although the Enterprise Manager is easier to use, there are advantages to using the T-SQL statements for database creation. The main advantage is that you can save your T-SQL statements in a script file. If you ever need to re-create your system, all you need to do is load the script file and then run it.

Critical Information

It's time to make a major shift in the way you think about databases. Take the word "file" out of your vocabulary. If you have worked with traditional desktop databases, everything is a file.

So what is a database if it is not a file? A database is a preallocated portion of a device that is available to tables and indexes in that database for extent allocation. You must decide how large to make the database when it is initially created. You have the ability to expand databases after they are initially created, but you will pay a small price for doing so. You can also shrink databases, but there are some specific restrictions on how this can be done.

Creating a database is a process that allocates space for that database on the devices of your choice. A database can be created on a single device, or fragments of a database can be located in multiple devices (up to 32). Every database that is created will record a line in the *sysdatabases* system table. Each fragment of a database will write a line to the sysusages table. Both of these tables are part of the system catalog and are located in the Master database.

When databases are created, it is generally good practice to divide the database into at least two fragments, one for the data and another for the transaction log. There are some advantages to creating the transaction log on a separate device:

- When the transaction log is placed on a separate device, it can be backed up separately from the database. This is not allowed if the database and transaction log are created on one device.

- If the transaction log is placed not only on a separate device but on a separate physical disk, this provides the greatest possible level of fault tolerance. This is not an issue if Raid 5 striping is used on the drives. You will also get better performance because this reduces disk contention.

- When the transaction log is placed on a separate device, the log can be explicitly sized. If the log and data are on the same device, they compete for space and will both fill up at exactly the same point in time.

You can discern what portions of a database are stored on what portions of which devices by running the *sp_helpdb* stored procedure. This procedure will read information from the sysusages table.

Necessary Procedures

In this section, you will walk through the processes needed to create a database. Although you can do this work with the Enterprise Manager, an understanding of the CREATE DATABASE statement is essential knowledge that is tested on the exam.

Creating a Database

The Transact-SQL approach to creating databases uses the same parameters that are used in the GUI. You must provide size and device information. You can even include the For Load parameter if you want. The CREATE DATABASE syntax is:

```
CREATE DATABASE database_name
[ON {DEFAULT | database_device} [= size]
    [, database_device [= size]]...]
[LOG ON database_device [= size]
    [, database_device [= size]]...]
[FOR LOAD]
```

Note the following issues regarding the CREATE DATABASE statement:

- The DEFAULT keyword can be used in place of a specific data device if you want to place the database fragment on a default device. If there are multiple default devices, they are used in alphabetical order.

- A database can be spread across multiple data or log devices by using a comma between device parameters. Up to 32 fragments can be created for any given database.

- All sizes are indicated in MB, not 2KB pages.

- The FOR LOAD parameter is used when you want to create the database, but you do not want to initialize the database fragments. Initialization is similar to formatting your hard drive. It clears any information that might have been stored there before. When you create a database FOR LOAD, you are specifying that you are going to load a backup into it. The FOR LOAD option also marks the database as DBO Use Only.

To create a 12MB database called mydb hosted on a 5MB data device called MyDataDev, another 5MB on a second device called MyData-Dev2, and a 2MB log device on MyLogDev, the statement would be written like this:

```
CREATE DATABASE mydb
ON MyDataDev = 5, MyDataDev2 = 5,
LOG ON MyLogDev = 2
```

Notice that the database size is 12MB. When you are looking at the size of a database, you must include all of the database fragments, including the transaction log.

To create a database that has its data and log residing on the same device, you could use the following statements:

```
CREATE DATABASE mydb
ON MyDataDev = 10
```

In this example, both the data and log are on the same device. This means that you cannot back up the transaction log separately from the database. If you increase the size of the database, you are really just allowing more room for both the database and the transaction log.

The exam will focus on your ability to create a database with specific portions of the database on specific devices. The following example will show you how to create a 100MB database that spans three devices with a log on two devices.

1. Start the ISQL/W utility. Start ➤ Programs ➤ Microsoft SQL Server 6.5 ➤ ISQL/W, or you can use the Query tool from the Enterprise Manager.

2. The following example will not work for you, unless you first create the devices specified in the example:

```
CREATE DATABASE Leap
ON DataDev1 = 40, DataDev2 = 20, DataDev3 = 20,
LOG ON LogDev1 = 10, LogDev2 = 10
GO
```

Exam Essentials

You should keep the following concepts in mind when you are studying for your exam. Creating and managing databases is stressed.

Remember that a database consists of both a data portion and a log portion.   A database is split into two entities, a data portion and a log portion. If you create a database on a single device, then both the log and the data will share that same space and will be in contention for those resources. If you separate the data and the log, you gain several advantages.

Know the advantages of separating your data from your transaction log.   There are advantages to keeping your transaction log separated from your database. They will not compete for the same resources. Writes to the log will not interfere with writes to the data portion. Safety is increased in the event of a disk failure. Your transaction logs can be backed up separately.

Be able to recognize the different parameters of the CREATE DATABASE statement. This includes the size parameters in megabytes and the FOR LOAD option. Remember that the FOR LOAD option will not initialize the database, but it will mark the database as DBO Use Only. You must load a database into it from backup.

Remember that when you refer to the size of a database, you must include the size of the transaction log as well. The total size of the database includes all database fragments and all log fragments.

Knowledge of all stored procedures covered in this book is essential to passing the exam. Remember that

```
sp_helpdb <database name>
```

will give you information about a particular database and where its fragments are stored and what those fragments consist of (i.e., data only, data and log, or log only).

Key Terms and Concepts

Extent: Extents are the 16KB blocks of memory (eight 2KB data pages) that are used to create tables and indexes. They will be discussed in more detail later in this chapter.

sp_helpdb <database_name>:   This stored procedure is used from ISQL and allows you to gather information about the disposition of a database and transaction log.

System catalog: The system catalogs are the system tables stored in the Master database. This includes sysdatabases, sysdevices, and sysusages.

Sample Questions

1. How many fragments can a SQL Server database contain?

    A. 2

    B. 3

C. 32

D. There is no limit to the number of fragments that a SQL Server database can contain.

Answer: C is correct. A database can have up to 32 different storage fragments.

2. What is the unit of measure for the SIZE parameter when using the CREATE DATABASE statement?

A. Final size change in 2KB pages

B. Final size in 16KB extents

C. Final size in allocation units

D. Final size in megabytes

Answer: D is correct. You must specify the size of a database in megabytes, whereas you specify device sizes in 2KB data pages.

3. Which stored procedure is used to find out what portion of a database lives in which device fragment?

A. sp_vdevno

B. sp_virtual_device

C. sp_helpdb

D. sp_helpdevice

Answer: C is correct. There is no stored procedure called sp_vdevno, or sp_virtual_device. Sp_helpdevice is used to gather information about database devices.

Alter a database.

Altering a database is something that you as an administrator may need to do frequently. As such, the exam will definitely focus on your knowledge of the ALTER DATABASE T-SQL statements.

Critical Information

If your database fills to capacity, you will need to expand the database before you will be able to add any more data. You also may need to add more capacity to your transaction log if you find that your transaction log is filling up before your scheduled transaction log backups. To expand either the data or log portions of a database, you will need to add fragments to that database. These fragments can be on existing devices, or you can expand them onto new devices.

When you extend a database, you are actually adding entries to the sysusages system table. This table identifies which pages in the device are used for the database fragment. As stated earlier, a database can contain up to thirty-two fragments. These fragments can be added with either the Enterprise Manager or Transact-SQL code. You must know how to expand a database using the Transact-SQL code for the exam. It is also a good idea to save these T-SQL scripts for recovery purposes. If you ever have to re-create your databases, they must be re-created and expanded in the same order and sizes as you initially created and altered your database.

The process of expanding a database is very much like the process of creating a database. You can explicitly expand the data portion or the log portion of the database depending on your needs as long as they are separated on different devices. If they are not separated, you can force a separation with the sp_logdevice stored procedure. In order to alter a database, you must also be the SA or the DBO with CREATE DATABASE permissions.

Necessary Procedures

You can use the following procedures to alter the size of your databases.

Expanding a Database

The statement used to expand a database is ALTER DATABASE. ALTER DATABASE allows you to expand the data or transaction log portions of your databases by providing the logical name of the device upon which you want to expand. The syntax for the ALTER DATABASE statement is:

```
ALTER DATABASE database_name
[ON {DEFAULT | database_device} [= size]
[, database_device [= size]]...]
[FOR LOAD]
```

You see from the syntax that you can also expand on multiple devices using this method. However, you will clearly see that no distinction is made between data devices and log devices in the ALTER DATABASE syntax. The distinction is made in the device itself. If you expand a database on a device already holding data fragments, then the expansion will result in an increase of storage capacity for the data portion of the database. Likewise, if the expansion takes place on a device already containing transaction log fragments for this database, it will add more room for your transaction log. Finally, if a single database and its log share the same device, then adding more room for the database on that device just adds more room for both the data and the transaction log to fight over.

Remember that the result of the ALTER DATABASE statement will add a new row to the sysusages table.

As an example, assume you want to expand a database called mydb to create an additional 5MB data fragment on a device called MyDataDev. This device currently holds other data fragments of this database. No log expansion is desired. The syntax would be:

```
ALTER DATABASE mydb
ON MyDataDev=5
```

Expanding a Transaction Log

If your transaction log is on a different device than your data, then you can expand it in the same fashion as described in the last section. If, however, your transaction log and data are on the same device, you must split them apart. This is a two-step process. You must first expand the database and log on to a new device. Immediately after the expansion, you must run the sp_logdevice stored procedure. This will separate the data from the log portion.

Here is an example:

```
ALTER DATABASE Frogger
FrogLogDevice = 20
GO
EXEC sp_logdevice Frogger, FrogLogDevice
GO
```

This example first expanded the data and log onto the FrogLogDevice by 20MB. You then separated the log from the data portion by running the sp_logdevice stored procedure.

NOTE To separate a transaction log from a data and log device, you must expand the database and log to a new device and then run the sp_logdevice stored procedure to separate the two.

Shrinking Databases

If you have overstated the size of your database, it is possible to shrink that database by removing some of the unused space. Shrinking a database requires the alteration of the internal allocation structure. For this reason, you don't have a lot of control on what you can shrink and where it will take place. This means that when you shrink a database, SQL Server will determine how much to decrease the data fragments and how much to decrease the log fragments.

Shrinking a database requires the deallocation of internal storage structures, called allocation units. Whenever there is a need to manipulate internal storage structures, a special set of commands will be used. These commands are part of the Database Consistency Checker, and they are called DBCC commands. The DBCC command used to shrink a database is called DBCC SHRINKDB.

The syntax of DBCC SHRINKDB is:

```
DBCC SHRINKDB (database_name [, new_size ])
```

When using this command, the size of the database is an optional parameter. If it is not supplied, the command will take no action on the database, but rather will return the smallest possible size to which the database can be reduced.

When you reduce the size of a database using the Enterprise Manager, you are forced to put the database in single-user mode. This will also be the case when using SQL code. This is done with the sp_dboption stored procedure.

The syntax of the sp_dboption stored procedure is:

```
sp_dboption <database_name>, '<option>', <True|False>
```

In the following example, you will see how to shrink the Frogger database using T-SQL code.

1. Open the Query Tool or ISQL/W utility.

2. To set the database to single-user status, enter and execute the following statements:

```
USE master
EXEC sp_dboption Frogger, 'single user', true
go
```

3. You will be informed that the database has been changed.

4. To find out the smallest possible size for the database, enter and execute the following statement:

```
DBCC SHRINKDB(Frogger)
```

5. The results window will show you, in 2KB pages, the current size of the database and the smallest possible size. Notice that the results also tell you which objects, if any, are preventing further reduction of the database.

6. Shrink the database to 5MB by entering and executing the following statement:

```
DBCC SHRINKDB(Frogger, 2560)
```

7. Notice that the size of the database is in 2KB data pages. This is the only time that you will refer to database sizes in pages rather than in megabytes. Reset the status of the database back from single-user by entering and executing the following statements:

```
USE master
EXEC sp_dboption Frogger, 'single user', false
go
```

8. Verify the new database fragmentation by entering and executing the following statements:

```
USE master
EXEC sp_helpdb Frogger
go
```

9. You should see that the database is back down to two fragments from four, 4MB data and 1MB log.

Exam Essentials

Managing the size of your database is an important task that is stressed on the exam. You should keep the following in mind when you are taking your test.

Know how to use the ALTER DATABASE statements. Remember the following about ALTER DATABASE: you must be an SA or DBO. If you are the DBO, you must have CREATE DATABASE permissions in order to use the ALTER DATABASE statements. The size parameter is in megabytes, not 2KB data pages. Finally, the database must be in single-user mode to make changes to it.

Know how to use the DBCC SHRINKDB command. The DBCC SHRINKDB command (when used without a size parameter) will tell you how much a database can be shrunk. If you specify a size parameter, it will attempt to shrink your database to that size. The size parameter when using the DBCC command is in 2KB pages, not in the usual megabytes.

Know how to set a database to single user only. You can accomplish this task with the sp_dboption stored procedure as follows:

```
EXEC sp_dboption pubs, 'Single User', TRUE
```

Know the process involved in separating a database from its transaction log when the data and log are on the same device. This is a two-step process: first expand the database (and log) onto a separate device and then run the sp_logdevice stored procedure immediately after the expansion to separate the database and the log.

Key Terms and Concepts

ALTER DATABASE: Use this command to expand a database or transaction log onto the same device or to other devices.

DBCC SHRINKDB: Use this command to find out how small you can shrink a database or to actually shrink a database.

sp_dboption: Use this command to change database settings like single-user mode or DBO use only.

sp_logdevice: Use this command to separate a transaction log from the data portion of a database.

Sample Questions

1. What is the unit of measure for the Size parameter when using the ALTER DATABASE statement?

   A. Incremental change in 2KB pages

   B. Final size in 2KB pages

   C. Incremental change in megabytes

   D. Final size in megabytes

   Answer: C is correct. You specify how much larger you want to make a database whether it is an additional 5MB on the same device, or 5 additional megabytes on a new device.

2. Which statement is used immediately after an ALTER DATABASE statement to separate a data and log device to two devices, one with data only and the other with log only?

   A. sp_separatelog

   B. sp_virtual_device

   C. WITH LOG ON

   D. sp_logdevice

   Answer: D is correct. There is no such thing as sp_separatelog, sp_virtual_device, or ALTER DATABASE WITH LOG ON. The WITH LOG ON is used during the CREATE DATABASE statements.

3. Which command is used to shrink a device?

   A. sp_shrinkdevice

   B. sp_changedevice

   C. DBCC ShrinkDevice

   D. You cannot shrink a device.

   Answer: D is correct. You cannot shrink the size of a device. You can, however, shrink a database with the DBCC SHRINKDB statements.

Create database objects.

Although the system administration exam does not cover the creation of some of the more advanced objects (such as stored procedures, views, and triggers), it is very helpful to understand the process of creating tables and indexes. These may be tasks that you are called upon to perform as a DBA.

Critical Information

Although tables and indexes can both be created with Transact-SQL code and the Enterprise Manager, focus on using the Enterprise Manager in this instance. Using this method, you can create your tables and indexes in a "point and click" fashion, eliminating the need to write a lot of code. In this example, you will create a Customer table and a clustered index on that table.

Tables

Tables are created in the Enterprise Manager using the Manage Tables dialog. This dialog allows you to name fields, set data types, and specify field lengths. The Manage Tables dialog is shown in Figure 4.1. This figure shows the structure of the authors table in the Pubs database.

When a table is created, a primary key can be defined and field properties such as nullability can also be configured. You will have a chance to work with this in the "Necessary Procedures" section.

Indexes

Indexes are used to speed up data access. All indexes can be placed into one of two categories:

- **Clustered:** Each table is allowed one clustered index. This index is the actual sort order for the data in the table. In other words, the

FIGURE 4.1: The authors table in the Pubs database

Key	Identity	Column Name	Datatype	Size	Nulls	Default
🔑		au_id	id(varchar)	11		
		au_lname	varchar	40		
		au_fname	varchar	20		
		phone	char	12		(UNKNOWN)
		address	varchar	40	✓	
		city	varchar	20	✓	
		state	char	2	✓	
		zip	char	5	✓	
		contract	bit	1		

Manage Tables - HOME\pubs — Table: authors (dbo)

data in the index is stored in sorted order as part of the data in the table, rather than as a separate index object.

- **Non-clustered:** Non-clustered indexes consist of a list of ordered keys which contain pointers to the data in the data pages. Numerous non-clustered indexes can be created, but they occupy more space than clustered indexes. You can have up to 249 non-clustered indexes per table.

Indexes are created in the Enterprise Manager with the Manage Indexes dialog. In this example, assume that the users select information by state very frequently, so you need to add a clustered index on state to speed the process of extracting the data. You will take a look at this in the "Necessary Procedures" section a little later.

Although you may create indexes as a DBO, one of your more common tasks will be rebuilding existing indexes. When indexes become fragmented or if you need to re-create a fill factor for your indexes, you will have to rebuild the index. This can also be done from the same dialog. After the index has been created, the caption of the Build button changes to Rebuild. Use this to rebuild your indexes when needed.

Necessary Procedures

The following is one method that you can use to create tables in SQL Server. Table creation, however, is not stressed on the exam.

Creating Tables

You can follow these steps to create a new table in the Pubs database.

1. In the Server Manager window, select the Pubs database.

2. From the Enterprise Manager menu, select Manage ➤ Tables. This will open the Manage Tables dialog.

3. Focus should be in the Column Name box. Enter **CustID** as a Column Name. Click in the Datatype box. Select *Int* from the list. Click in the Nulls box. Ensure that there is no blue checkmark in this box. If one is present, click the box again to clear it.

4. Click in the Column Name box on the next line. Enter a field name as **CustName**. Set the type as Char and size at 20. This will allow you to enter twenty characters in this field. Do not allow nulls. Repeat this process until your dialog looks like the one pictured here.

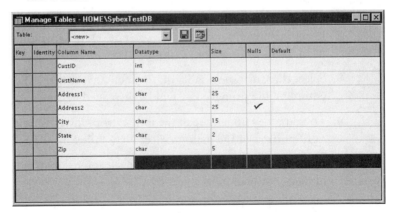

5. To add a primary key, click on the button with the green plus sign at the top of the dialog. This will open the advanced features window. Make sure that the Primary Key / Identity tab is selected. In the primary key section, choose CustID as the primary key and set the option button to Non-Clustered. This will build a unique non-clustered index to enforce the primary key.

6. The advanced features portion of the dialog should look like the one on the graphic here. Press the add button in this section of the dialog when finished. This will put an icon of a key on the field.

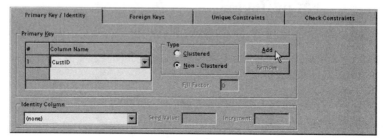

7. Press the Save Table button with the icon picturing the floppy disk at the top of the dialog. When prompted, enter the name **Customers**. Close the dialog.

8. You should now see the Customers table in the list of tables associated with the Pubs database.

Now you can use the Enterprise Manager to create an index.

1. Select the Pubs database from the Server Manager window.

2. From the menu, select Manage ➢ Indexes. This will open the Manage Indexes dialog.

3. Select the Customers table that you created earlier. The index enforcing the primary key will be displayed in the dialog.

4. To add a new index, open the index drop-down list in the upper-right portion of the dialog. Select New Index from the list.

5. In the Index box which now has focus, enter the index name of **idxState**.

6. In the list of available columns, click State and then click the Add button in the center of the dialog which just became active.

7. In the Index Attributes section, click the checkbox for Clustered.

8. Notice the estimate of the size and number of levels of the index based on index specifications and current data in the tables. The completed dialog should resemble the following graphic.

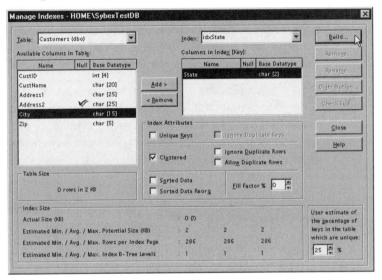

9. Click the Build button to create the index. Choose Execute Now when prompted for a schedule.

10. Close the dialog.

Exam Essentials

Much of the SQL Server exam reads like a vocabulary test. You should remember the following vocabulary words.

Remember what the different types of indexes are and how they operate. There are two types of indexes in SQL Server: clustered and non-clustered. Data is stored in sorted order with the data pages at the leaf level in clustered indexes. You can have one clustered index per table. Data is stored as pointers to rows in the table in non-clustered indexes. The index data is stored in its own separate extents. You can have as many as 249 non-clustered indexes per table.

Key Terms and Concepts

Clustered index: This index is the actual sort order for the data in the table. In other words, the data in the index is stored in sorted order as part of the data in the table, rather than as a separate index object. Each table is allowed one clustered index

Non-clustered index: Non-clustered indexes consist of a list of ordered keys that contain pointers to the data in the data pages. Numerous non-clustered indexes can be created, but they occupy more space than clustered indexes. You can have up to 249 non-clustered indexes per table.

Sample Questions

1. Which of the following is true of indexes? (Select two.)

   A. Clustered indexes store data as pointers to table records.

   B. Non-clustered indexes store data as pointers to table records.

   C. Clustered indexes store data in sorted order with the data pages themselves.

   D. Non-clustered indexes store data in sorted order with the data pages themselves.

   Answer: B and C are correct.

Estimate space requirements.

This objective is geared toward your understanding of how different database objects affect storage space. The biggest objects in any database are the tables and the indexes. Indexes can range greatly in size depending on the size of the fields that make up the index and the index's FILLFACTOR. This topic forces you to ask yourself, "How large should my databases and devices be?"

Your databases and devices need to be large enough to accommodate your data needs without excessive expansion, yet they must not be too large or they will simply become wasted space. When estimating storage requirements, you must go to the basic level of data storage, the table and the index. Let's look at how storage space can be estimated by using these objects.

Critical Information

Tables are really nothing more than templates specifying how data is to be stored. All data stored in a table must adhere to a data type. There is a specific process that you can follow to estimate the space required by a table.

1. Calculate the space used by a single row of the table.

2. Calculate the number of rows that will fit on one 2KB data page.

3. Estimate the number of rows that the table will hold.

4. Calculate the total number of pages that will be required to hold these rows.

Necessary Procedures

The following procedures are not necessary knowledge for an administrator to have, but they can make your life much easier when you must deal with the needs of your database programmers. This topic is not stressed on the exam.

Calculating Row Size

Data types are of various shapes and sizes and allow you incredible control over how your data is stored. Table 4.1 lists some of the most common data types.

T A B L E 4.1: Data Types and Sizes

Data Type Name	Description	Size
TinyInt	Integer from 0 to 255	1 byte
SmallInt	Integer from –32,768 to 32,767	2 bytes
Int	Integer from –2,147,483,648 to 2,147,483,647	4 bytes
Real	1 to 7 Digit Precision Floating Point	4 bytes
Float	8 to 15 Digit Precision Floating Point	8 bytes
Small-datetime	1/1/1900 to 6/6/2079 w/ Accuracy to Minute	4 bytes
Datetime	1/1/100 to 12/31/9999 w/ Accuracy to 3.33 Milliseconds	8 bytes
Smallmoney	4 byte Integer w/ 4 Digit Scale	4 bytes
Money	8 byte integer w/ 4 Digit Scale	8 bytes
Char	Character Data	1 byte per character

When calculating storage requirements for a table, simply add the storage requirements for each data type in the table and add an additional 2 bytes per row of overhead. This will give you the total space that is occupied by a single row. For example, if a table in a database has three fields defined as Char(10), Int, and Money, the storage space required for each row could be calculated as follows:

- Char(10) = 10 bytes

- Int = 4 bytes

- Money = 8 bytes

- Overhead = 2 bytes

- Total = 24 bytes

WARNING   A row is limited to 2 bytes of overhead only when no variable data types have been used and no columns allow nulls. If variable length columns are used or nulls are allowed, additional overhead must be added. The amount will depend on the data type and number of columns.

Calculating Rows per Page

Once you have a number indicating the total bytes used per row, you can easily calculate the number or rows that will fit on a single page. Every page is 2KB in size and has a 32-byte header. This leaves 2,016 bytes free for storing data. The total number of rows per page can be calculated as 2,016 ÷ RowSize. The resulting value is truncated to an integer.

In our example, each row requires 24 bytes of space to store. We can calculate the rows per page as follows:

- 2,016 ÷ 24 = 84

Special Considerations

When calculating rows per page, you will need to consider some additional factors. First, only 256 rows can fit on a single page. If you have some very short rows, you may by necessity have some wasted space in your pages.

Remember that rows can never cross pages. If there is not enough space on a page to complete the row, the row will be placed on the next page. This is why we had to truncate the result of our calculation.

Also, the number of rows that can fit on one page may also be dependent on a fill factor that is used for the clustered index. Fill factor is a way of keeping the page from filling 100% full. If we use a fill factor, this may reduce the amount of space used on a page when the index is built. However, the space will be eventually used because fill factor is not maintained. Fill factor allows faster inserts of new records as the new records have free space to be inserted into. Once the page is full and a new record needs to be added, the page must be split (which takes valuable CPU cycles).

As an example, if a clustered index were built on our table with a fill factor of 75, the data will be reorganized such that the data pages are only 75% full. This means that instead of 2,016 bytes free on each page, you are only allowed to use 1,512. The reason for a fill factor is to provide room inside the data pages for additional insertions. This means that the space may eventually be used.

Estimating the Number of Rows for the Table

There is no magic secret to this. You have to know your data to provide an estimate of how many rows your table will eventually hold. When you make this estimate, try to consider as much as possible how large you expect your table to grow. If the table grows and you have not allowed for this growth in your estimates, then the database and perhaps even the devices will need to be expanded. If this happens, all of your efforts to project storage requirements are a wasted effort.

Calculating the Number of Pages Needed

This calculation will be accurate as long as you have reliable figures of the rows per page and the number of rows you expect the table to hold. The calculation is # Rows in table ÷ # Rows per page. This result will be rounded up to the nearest integer.

In our example, 84 rows would fit in a single page of the table. If you expect this table to eventually hold 100,000 records, the calculation would be:

- 100,000 ÷ 84 = 1,190.476

- Round the value to 1,191 pages

Now extend your calculation to determine the number of extents that must be allocated to this table to hold this data. Because all space is allocated in extents, you again need to round up to the nearest integer. Remember that there are eight 2KB pages per extent. The calculation would be:

- 1,191 ÷ 8 = 148.875

- Round the value to 149 extents

Because a megabyte can store 64 extents, this table would take about 2.4MB of space to store. Add a little bit of extra space "just in case," and you are ready to proceed to the next table.

Estimating Index Storage Requirements

Indexes in SQL Server are stored in a B-Tree format. Think of an index as a large tree. You can also think of an index as a table with a pyramid built on top of it. The ultimate concept here is that for every index, there is a single entry point, the root of the tree or the apex of the pyramid.

When estimating storage requirements, the base of this pyramid can be thought of as a table. You go through the same process in estimating the leaf level of an index that you go through estimating the storage requirements of a table. Although the process is very similar, there are a few issues that are important to consider.

1. You are adding the data types of the index keys, not the data rows.

2. There is no 256 row limit to an index page.

3. Clustered indexes use the data page as the leaf level. There is no need to add additional storage requirements for a clustered index leaf level.

The toughest part of estimating the size of an index is estimating the size and number of levels that you will have in your index. Although there is a fairly long and complex series of calculations to determine this exactly, it is usually sufficient to add an additional 35% of the leaf-level space estimate for the other levels of the index.

Exam Essentials

Although you don't need to know exactly how to calculate storage requirements, you should know how those calculations are affected by the items listed below.

Know what factors into storage requirements. These are mostly common sense things like: how many rows are in your current database (if you are upgrading), how many new rows do you expect to add to this database, how many indexes are there, what fields make up each of these indexes, what is your fill factor, and how many rows of data will fit on a 2KB data page?

Key Terms and Concepts

Data page: SQL Server stores data in 2KB data pages.

Data types: Data types specify what kind of data will be stored in a particular field and how much memory that field will consume.

Fill factor: This is the maximum percentage of page space available for storage of index values at index creation. Tables that have a lot of data modification should use a low fillfactor setting to improve inserts. Tables that have a low amount of modification can use a higher fill factor setting.

Row size: The size of a row cannot span multiple pages. Therefore the maximum row size is 2KB less any overhead associated with the row.

Sample Questions

1. How much space is available for data in a data page?

   A. 1,962 bytes

   B. 2,016 bytes

   C. 2,048 bytes

   D. 2KB

   Answer: B is correct. A data page is 2,048 bytes, but there are 32 bytes of overhead per data page.

2. You are estimating the storage requirements for a table defined with the following fields: Char(15), Int, Float, and Char(10). How many bytes will be used to store each row (assuming no fields allow nulls)?

   A. 33

   B. 35

   C. 37

   D. 39

   Answer: D is correct. Char = 15 + Int = 4 + Float = 8 + Char = 10. This comes out to 15 + 4 + 8 + 10 = 37. Don't forget to add the 2 bytes of overhead per row as well. This will give you a total of 39 bytes.

3. If a row requires 34 bytes of space for storage, how many rows can be placed on a page with a fill factor of 80?

   A. 60

   B. 59

   C. 48

   D. 47

   Answer: D is correct. If you take a 2KB data page and subtract the 32-byte header, you get 2,016 bytes of storage space. If you then apply the fill factor or 80 to this (2,016 * .80), you get a value of 1,612. Now divide 1,612 bytes by 34, and you get 47 rows per page.

CHAPTER

5

Managing User Accounts

Microsoft Exam Objectives Covered in This Chapter:

▸ **Differentiate between a SQL Server login and a SQL Server user.** *(pages 156 – 162)*

▸ **Create a login ID.** *(pages 162 – 169)*

▸ **Add a database user.** *(pages 169 – 181)*

▸ **Add and drop users for a group.** *(pages 181 – 187)*

The objectives for this portion of the exam cover your ability to create, manage, and maintain two out of three levels of SQL Server security. The first level of security is the ability to log in to SQL Server. Once you are in SQL Server, you cannot do anything until you are given access to a database. The third level, which we will examine later, covers your ability to look at, create, and utilize database objects within a particular database to which you have been given access.

Differentiate between a SQL Server login and a SQL Server user.

This topic examines the difference between a SQL Server login ID and a SQL Server database user. Essentially, a login ID gives you access to the SQL Server itself. Once there, you cannot do anything until you have a username in a database that is mapped to your login ID. Let's take a closer look at how all of these pieces fit together.

Critical Information

When a user accesses a SQL Server database, the ultimate goal in most cases is to access a database object (such as a table, view, or stored procedure). Before the user can gain access to the object, the user must be properly authenticated. This authentication happens at three distinct stages: the server, the database, and the database object itself. Let's take a look at the first two stages of authentication.

You can think of access authentication stages as a series of three gates. Before you can get to your ultimate goal, you must pass through each gate. That would be easy enough if the gates were unlocked and unguarded, but this is not the case. Each gate has a gatekeeper whose job it is to keep you out unless you can provide the proper keys to let you through the gate. The first two gates in SQL Server include security at the server and security at the database.

Security at the Server

The first gatekeeper is the SQL Server itself. At this gate you must provide a login ID and a password in order to obtain access to the server. This login information is stored in the *syslogins* system table located in the Master database. Only the SA has authority to add, delete, or modify login information. If you can provide a valid login ID and password to the server, you will be granted access to server resources. As you continue to the next gatekeeper, the database, you will take your login ID with you.

The syslogins system table is part of the system catalog, and it is only found in the Master database. This table holds the Server User IDs, login IDs, encrypted passwords, and other types of information. Every user that gains access to the server can work with the system tables; however, only the SA has the authority to select the password field from the syslogins table. Even though this field is encrypted, this column-level permission provides added protection against intrusion into your SQL Server.

Security at the Database

The second gatekeeper is the database whose resources you want to access. When you come to this second gate, the gatekeeper verifies that your login ID is mapped to a username in the list of usernames that are allowed to access that database. There are two lists to check. One is a list of database users. This is the *sysusers* system table, which is stored in each individual database. The sysusers system table stores the login ID of every user who is allowed access to the database along with a username that the login will be assigned when it passes through the gate. The login ID that each user carries from the first gate is compared against this list. If there is a match, then that login ID is allowed access to the database and is tagged with the username stored in the table. You can have only a single mapped login ID in any single database. In other words, you cannot have a login ID of Max mapped to a username in Database A of Max and login ID Max mapped to another username in the same database.

The other list that can be checked as a login attempts access to a database is the list of aliases. An alias is essentially a mapping of an existing user name to a login ID. This allows multiple logins to access a database under a single username. Aliases are also held in a system table inside each individual database. This table is called *sysalternates*. A login can only access a database under a single username, either as the actual user or a login aliased as that user. For this reason, each login will have at most one entry in either the sysusers or sysalternates system tables and will never have an entry in both.

TIP The login name for the server and a username for a database may be the same. This is not a requirement but is often the case for simplicity of maintenance.

Figure 5.1 illustrates several SQL Server login IDs that have been mapped into the Pubs database. Take a minute to look over the different mappings.

FIGURE 5.1: Mapping login IDs to usernames

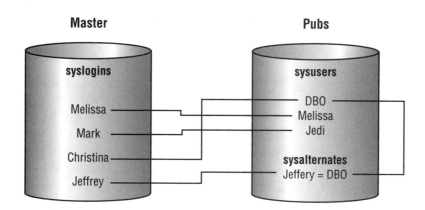

Now let's look at some of the properties of login IDs and usernames and how SQL Server behaves when it encounters them.

The Login ID

The login ID provides server access. There are only two classes of logins: the SA login and everyone else. When SQL Server is installed, by default SA is the owner of every database on the server. The SA user bypasses all security checks, so that user has full control over everything that goes on at that server. Even if another login is later given ownership of a database, or another log creates a database, SA will still have an implied alias as the owner and can still exercise full control.

Every login other than SA must be granted specific rights to do anything on the server. These rights must be granted by SA or the owner of a database.

The User

A username is local to each database. There are two classes of users in a SQL Server database, the database owner (DBO) and regular users. The DBO controls all of the activities and rights in the database. As stated earlier, the SA is often the DBO for many databases.

It is also quite common to have different people acting as DBO for different databases on the same server. This is why DBO must be a database-level distinction, not a server-level distinction. A DBO in one database may have no rights whatsoever in another database on the same server.

You may also have more than one user in a database who needs to act as DBO. This situation can be solved through the use of an alias. Although there is only one login in each database mapped to the user-name DBO, there can be many others who have no usernames of their own and actually access the database aliased as DBO. In this fashion, all objects and activities that take place in the database are through the DBO. This can be a real advantage during the development phase of a particular database. Once you put the database into production, however, you probably will want to restrict the ability of others to act with the power of the DBO.

Exam Essentials

An understanding of the difference between login IDs and usernames and how they interact is essential to passing the exam.

Know the difference between a login ID and a username. Login IDs give you access to SQL Server, but not to any databases within SQL Server. A username is simply a login ID that has been mapped into a particular database. Usernames are stored in the sysusers and sysalternates tables in each database, while login IDs are stored in the syslogins table in the Master database.

Remember that you can have at most one login ID mapped into any single database. If you already have a username in a database, then you cannot also be aliased as someone else in the database. To do something like this, you must drop your username from the database and then remap the login ID as an alias to someone already in the database.

Key Terms and Concepts

Alias: This is the name and mapping that is stored in the *sysalternates* table in a user database.

Login ID: This is the ID you use to gain access to SQL Server. It can be created by hand for use with standard security, or it can be mapped in through the SQL Security utility when using integrated security.

sysalternates: This is a table in every user database that stores login IDs that are not mapped to their own username, but to a user already in the database.

syslogins: This is a table in the Master database where SQL Server login IDs are stored.

sysusers: This is a table in every user database that stores usernames that have been mapped from the syslogins table.

Username: This is the name and mapping that is stored in the sysusers table.

Sample Questions

1. Which of the following is true of login IDs?

A. Login IDs give you access to all databases.

B. Login IDs give you access to databases where your login ID exists.

C. Login IDs give you access to the databases where you login ID exists, as well as the master database.

D. Login IDs don't give you database access, just SQL Server access.

Answer: D is correct. To gain access to a particular database, you must have a login ID mapped to a username or an alias in that database.

2. A login ID can be mapped as many times as necessary into a database.

   A. True.

   B. False. You can have two mappings: one for the username and one for the alias.

   C. False. You can have one mapping.

   D. False. You can have as many as 256 mappings in a single database.

   Answer: Answer C is correct. Your login ID can be mapped once into a single database.

Create a login ID.

As you have seen already, there are two ways to do most things in SQL Server. The exam focuses primarily on how to do things using T-SQL commands and stored procedures. In this section, you will review how to use the *sp_addlogin* stored procedure to create a login ID for SQL Server. You should know how and when to apply the sp_addlogin stored procedure. This exam topic could easily be called "Managing Login IDs" because you will need to know how to drop login IDs, change their passwords, change their default database, and change their default language.

Critical Information

If you are using standard security, then you can create login IDs using the Enterprise Manager or the *sp_addlogin* stored procedure. With the Enterprise Manager, you simply go to the Logins folder and right-click. From the context menu, choose Add Login. Fill in the information in the form, and click the Add button. To add login IDs by hand, you must use the sp_addlogin stored procedure.

Many attributes of existing logins can be modified after the login is created. In fact, the only attribute that can't be modified later is the login name. The attributes that you are allowed to change are:

- Password

- Default database

- Default language

Unlike the Enterprise Manager dialog where you can do all of your modifications in one window, there is a different stored procedure for every attribute of the login that you want to change. These stored procedures are:

- sp_password

- sp_defaultdb

- sp_defaultlanguage

When you no longer want a certain individual to access your SQL Server, you need to drop that person from the Logins list. Unlike Windows NT, SQL Server has no mechanism to simply disable a login. The login must be deleted completely if the individual is to be prohibited from the server.

The simplest way to drop a login from the Enterprise Manager is to select the login from the Logins list in the Server Manager window and press your delete key. You will then be asked to confirm the deletion. If you respond in the affirmative, the login will be removed from the syslogins table. You may be presented with several dialog boxes asking you if you want to drop usernames associated with this particular login ID. This is done because you must first remove the mapping the login ID has in any databases before you can drop the login ID. As with all other factors regarding logins, only the SA has the authority to drop logins from the server.

TIP You will not be allowed to drop a login that owns a database or any objects inside a database.

Necessary Procedures

Understanding how the following procedures interrelate and operate on SQL Server is critical to passing the exam.

Adding New Logins

To add a new login ID, you can run the sp_addlogin stored procedure. This procedure has the following syntax:

```
EXEC sp_addlogin login_id [, password [,defdb
[,deflanguage]]]
```

login_id: The login name that you want to add to the server. This is the only required parameter.

passwd: The password that you want to assign to the login. If this parameter is not provided, the password will be null.

defdb: The default database of the login. The default database is the database that a login will be using immediately after authentication to the server. This should be the most common database for the login. If not provided, this value defaults to the master database.

deflanguage: You may have noticed this option in the earlier dialog. This allows a login to be associated with a specific language if more than one language is known to the server. If not provided, this value defaults to the default language of the server. Most servers have only one language installed.

As you can see, you can add a login ID, assign it a password, a default database, and a default language. You should also note that because this is a system-wide account, only the SA has permission to create it.

You should be comfortable using the sp_addlogin stored procedure to add login IDs to your SQL Server. You can follow these steps to add new logins to SQL Server:

1. Start the ISQL/W utility.

2. Add the following users: Melissa, Mark, Christina, and Jeffrey with passwords that are the same as their names, but in all lower-case letters.

```
EXEC sp_addlogin Melissa, melissa
EXEC sp_addlogin Mark, mark
EXEC sp_addlogin Christina, christina
EXEC sp_addlogin Jeffrey, jeffrey
```

3. To verify their existence, you could run the following select statement:

```
Use Master
GO
SELECT * from syslogins
GO
```

or

From the Enterprise Manager, right-click the logins folder and choose refresh.

Modifying Login IDs

When you want to modify a login ID, you can change the password, the default database, or the default language. You should be familiar with all three of the stored procedures necessary to accomplish these changes.

Modifying a Password

To change the password associated with a login, use the sp_password stored procedure. The syntax of this procedure looks like this:

```
sp_password old, new [, login_id]
```

This stored procedure requires the user to enter the old password for verification before the new password is entered. The password change will always affect the currently logged-in user. The only exception is the SA user who can use the *login_id* optional parameter to change a password for another user.

TIP Any login can change its own password, but only the SA can change the password of another login account.

Now that you have successfully added some login IDs, you should be able to modify their passwords. The next exercise will walk you through the process of using stored procedures to modify passwords:

1. Open the Enterprise Manger Query Tool or ISQL/W.

2. Change the password for the Jeffrey user by executing the following statements:

```
USE master
EXEC sp_password jeffrey, 'jeff', 'Jeffrey'
go
```

Changing a Default Database
To change the default database associated with a login, use the stored procedure sp_defaultdb. The syntax looks like this:

```
sp_defaultdb login_id, defdb
```

Changing a Default Language
Changing the default language will be an issue only if the server knows multiple languages. Installing alternate languages on the server makes available all system messages and dialog boxes in that language. They do not affect character set and sort order. This option can be used if there are multiple languages installed on the server and a user wants to see system messages and dialog boxes in a language other than the system default. In most cases, there will be only one language installed on the server and that language is the default. If desired, the default language for a user can be changed using the stored procedure sp_defaultlanguage. The syntax for this procedure is:

```
sp_defaultlanguage login_id [, language]
```

Dropping a Login

Dropping a login from the server is accomplished through the sp_ droplogin stored procedure. The syntax is as follows:

```
sp_droplogin login_id
```

This action will remove the login from the syslogins system table. If the login has the username DBO in any database or it owns an object in any database, this procedure will fail. You must first drop any object that the username owns and then drop the user from the individual database. You will then be able to drop the user.

To drop login IDs from SQL Server, several things must be true:

- You must be the SA.

- The Login ID cannot have a username is any database that owns objects. If the username owns objects, the objects must first be dropped.

Follow these steps to delete a login ID of Elmo. (Elmo does not currently exist in your Pubs database.)

1. Start the Query Tool in Enterprise Manger or ISQL/W.

2. Run the following query to drop the Elmo login ID.

```
USE master
EXEC sp_droplogin Elmo
go
```

3. Verify that the login was dropped by executing the following query.

```
USE master
SELECT name FROM syslogins
go
```

Exam Essentials

Properly managing your login IDs is essential to administering your database. In addition, the subject makes for some excellent test questions.

Know how to use the sp_addlogin stored procedure to create a new login ID in SQL Server. Remember that the sp_addlogin stored procedure has the following parameters: login ID, password, default database, and default language. The only parameter that is required is the login ID.

Remember that only the SA can manage login IDs. Because login IDs give access to SQL Server in general, only the SA has permissions to create, modify, and delete login IDs.

Know what is required to drop a login's ID. Remember that a login ID cannot be dropped if its mapped usernames own objects in any database. You must first drop the objects.

Key Terms and Concepts

sp_addlogin: This stored procedure is used from ISQL and allows you to create a new SQL Server login. The new login ID and password will be stored in the syslogins table in the Master database.

sp_changepassword: You can use this procedure to change a password for a login ID.

sp_defaultdb: This procedure can be used to change the login ID's default database.

sp_defaultlanguage: This procedure is used to change a login ID's default language.

sp_droplogin: This procedure will drop a login ID from SQL Server.

Sample Questions

1. Which of the following statements will correctly add the user 'Frogger' to your SQL Server and give him a password of 'croak' and a default database of Master?

   A. sp_adduser 'Frogger', 'croak'

   B. sp_adduser Frogger, croak

   C. sp_addlogin 'Frogger', 'Croak'

   D. sp_addlogin Frogger, croak

Answer: D is correct. The parameter list is login ID, password, default database, and default language. If no database is selected as the default database, the user will use Master as the default database. Although Answer C looks correct, it is not. In most databases, your passwords are case-sensitive. The question explicitly asks for a lowercase password. Answer C uses an uppercase first letter.

2. Which of the following statements will correctly change the Frogger password from 'croak' to 'Leap'? (Assume that you are the SA.)

   A. sp_changepassword 'Frogger', 'croak', 'leap'

   B. sp_changepwd Frogger, croak, leap

   C. sp_changepw 'Croak', 'Leap', Frogger

   D. sp_changepassword croak, Leap, Frogger

Answer: D is correct. The parameter list is old password, new password, login ID, and the procedure name is sp_changepassword.

Add a database user.

Adding a database user is the process of mapping a valid login ID into the sysusers or sysalternates tables in each database that you want these login IDs to access. This topic examines how to create and manage database users.

Critical Information

The user is the basic component in database security. A login account simply allows or denies access to the server itself; a username is the login's passport into a database. Without the username, the login would have no entry into the database and no security context for the objects inside the database.

You need to be familiar with the process of adding, managing, and deleting users from a database. As with everything else in SQL Server, you can use the Enterprise Manager or T-SQL to work with users. The test focuses on your understanding of the stored procedures necessary to manipulate database users.

Creating a User

Creating a user adds an entry into the sysusers system table for a login ID. This allows that login to access the resources in the database. Sysusers is held locally in every table and provides some critical information about how the user is allowed to interact with database resources. The sysusers table looks something similar to this:

suid	uid	gid	name	environ
-16386	16386	16386	Melissa	
16385	16385	16385	Mark	
-2	0	0	public	(null)
1	1	0	dbo	(null)

As you look at the structure of the sysusers table, notice the three ID values. Each of them specifies specific attributes of the user.

suid: The value is the server user ID or the numerical ID associated with the login. It is this value that "maps" a login to a username in the database.

uid: The user ID value is the numerical value representing this user elsewhere in the database. When permissions are set, they refer to the uid value.

gid: The group ID value is actually the uid of the group to which this member belongs. Notice that for the groups themselves, the gid and the uid are the same value.

The name is for your convenience so that you have a human-readable value to refer to the uid that is used internally by the system. The environ column is reserved by the system and is not currently being used.

When you create a user, all of this information is written to a record in the sysusers table. You simply provide a username and the login to which you want this user to map. If desired, a group may also be indicated on user creation. The uid will automatically be inserted by the system. You can add users to the database using either the Enterprise Manager or Transact-SQL. You will need to know the Transact-SQL for the exam.

Dropping Users

Once a login no longer needs to access the resources for a particular database, you will want to drop the username from the database. Users can be dropped only if they own no objects inside of the database. If a user owns an object inside the database, the object must be dropped before the user can be dropped. Just as in all previous cases, users can be dropped with either the Enterprise Manager or Transact-SQL.

There are a number of ways to drop users from a database with the Enterprise Manager. The easiest method is simply to select the username in the Groups/Users folder of the database in the Server Manager window and press the Delete key on the keyboard. You will be asked to confirm this deletion, after which the user will be permanently deleted from the database. As discussed earlier, you must know the stored procedures and their parameters for the exam.

Only one person at a time can be mapped into a database as the DBO. Others may be aliased as the DBO, but only one person is actually mapped. You should know how to transfer database ownership to another user.

Transfer of Database Ownership

The ownership of a database may need to be transferred from one login to another. A typical example is the SA login. Only the SA has permission to create databases. The SA login can transfer this permission to another user, but it is strongly recommended that this not be done. Instead, the SA can create the needed databases and subsequently transfer the ownership of these databases to the new DBO user.

As you will remember, the username for the SA login is DBO in every database that the SA creates. When transferring ownership of a database to another user, SA literally assigns the username of DBO in that database to another login. The SA login will retain an implied alias as DBO in that database, so SA does not have to actually give up any control over the database.

WARNING   A login can only have one username or one alias in a database. If you want to transfer ownership of a database to a login who already has a username or an alias in that database, the username or the alias must first be dropped.

Unlike most of the other tasks for which a DBA is responsible, changing ownership of a database can be accomplished only through Transact-SQL. There is no equivalent functionality in the Enterprise Manager.

Aliases

You may want a group of logins to share functional responsibility in a database. For these cases, you have the option of using aliases. An aliased user has exactly the same rights and authorities as the user whose username is used as the alias.

As an example, you may have a group of users you want to act as DBO users. They each need to have the authority to create and drop objects, backup and restore databases, etc. While some of the permissions that fall to the DBO user can be readily transferred, others are required to stay with the DBO, such as the permission to restore databases and transaction logs. No matter how much the DBO may desire to do so, this permission cannot be transferred to other users. There are additional problems with the DBO giving extensive permissions to users in a database.

The advantage of using an alias in this situation is that no permissions actually need to be transferred. When a login which is aliased as DBO accesses the database, the database treats the user as if they are the actual DBO user. There are no limits placed on the functional ability of that user. In addition, any actions that the user takes will be treated as if they were performed by the DBO. If the aliased user creates a table in the database, the owner of the table will be DBO.

Aliases, like usernames, are local to the database. They are stored in the sysalternates system table. This system table is checked when a login attempts to access a database and an entry is not found for that login in the sysusers system table.

TIP Aliases must always refer to a username that already exists in the database. If you have a group of logins that you want to be aliased to a user account, you must create the user account first. One of the logins will be referenced as the actual user, while the remainder can be aliased to that username.

Creating an alias is simply the process of mapping a login to an already existing user account. This allows the login to access the database as the user to which the alias refers. This process can be done through the Enterprise Manger with Transact-SQL code.

Necessary Procedures

You should be able to recognize and use the following stored procedures to create database users, drop users, change database ownership, and add aliased accounts.

Using Transact-SQL to Create Users

Users are added to databases with the stored procedure sp_adduser. This stored procedure uses the following syntax:

```
sp_adduser login_id [, username [, grpname]]
```

Of the three parameters accepted by the procedure, only the login_id is required. These parameters are used as follows:

login_id: The login ID parameter is required and indicates the login ID being mapped to this user.

username: The username parameter specifies the name with which you will associate the mapped login in this database. This parameter is optional and if omitted will default to the same value provided for the login parameter.

grpname: If desired, the user can be immediately assigned to a group using the grpname parameter. This parameter is optional and if omitted the user will remain a member of the Public group but not associated with any user-defined group.

TIP   Be sure to add logins before attempting to add users with sp_adduser. The procedure will not allow you to add a login and a user at the same time.

Use this stored procedure to add users to a database in the "Necessary Procedures" section. Follow these steps to map your login IDs into the Pubs database.

1. Open an ISQL/W window.

2. Run the following code to map our login IDs into the Pubs database.

```
USE pubs
EXEC sp_adduser Melissa
EXEC sp_adduser Mark, Jedi
GO
```

3. In this example, you mapped Melissa in as `Melissa` and you mapped the Mark login ID in as `Jedi`. In your database, his username is Jedi even though his SQL Server login ID is Mark.

4. To verify these two new users, you can run the sp_helpuser stored procedure. This procedure will give a list of users in the current database.

```
USE pubs
EXEC sp_helpuser
GO
```

5. Close the ISQL/W utility.

Using Transact-SQL to Drop Users

Users are dropped from a database using the sp_dropuser stored procedure. The syntax of this procedure is:

```
sp_dropuser username
```

When dropping a user from a database, make sure the correct database is being used. You might accidentally drop a user with the same name from a database other than the one with which you are working. As an example, if the DBA of our sample database wanted to drop the Mark user from the database, the following statements would be executed:

```
USE pubs
EXEC sp_dropuser Mark
go
```

To drop a user from the database, follow these steps:

1. Open up the ISQL/W utility.

2. Run the sp_helpuser stored procedure on the Pubs database to ensure that the Login ID Mark which is mapped in as Jedi exists here.

   ```
   USE pubs
   EXEC sp_helpuser
   GO
   ```

3. Now drop user Jedi.

   ```
   USE pubs
   EXEC sp_dropuser Jedi
   GO
   ```

4. Jedi should now be dropped from the Pubs database. Rerun Step 2 to ensure that this is the case.

5. Close the ISQL/W utility.

Transferring Database Ownership

Transferring ownership of a database is accomplished with the stored procedure sp_changedbowner. The syntax of this procedure looks like this:

```
sp_changedbowner login_id [, true]
```

You must be using the database that you are transferring before executing the stored procedure. The login_id parameter represents the login name that will receive ownership of the database. An optional flag is provided to allow aliases and their permissions to be transferred to the new owner. If the "true" flag is used, all logins currently aliased as DBO will retain their aliases and permissions in the database after the transfer in ownership. If this flag is not used, all aliases to DBO in the database will be dropped after the change in ownership.

The following steps explain how to transfer ownership of the Pubs database from the SA to Mark. You can do this because Mark no longer has a username in the Pubs database.

1. Open the Query Tool or ISQL/W.

2. Verify current ownership of the database by entering and executing the following statements. The results of this query should show the login ID as the DBO user in the database.

   ```
   USE pubs
   EXEC sp_helpuser dbo
   go
   ```

3. Assign ownership of this database to the Mark login. Now transfer ownership of the database to Mark by executing the following statements:

   ```
   USE pubs
   EXEC sp_changedbowner Mark, true
   go
   ```

4. Verify that the ownership has been transferred by executing the statements in Step 2 again. This time you should see that the Mark login has been associated with the DBO username.

5. Close the Query Tool or ISQL/W.

Adding an Alias to a Database

The sp_addalias stored procedure is used to add aliases into a database. The syntax for this procedure uses the login name and the aliased username as follows:

```
sp_addalias login_id, username
```

If you were to add an alias as DBO for the Mark login in the Pubs database as in the earlier examples, the statements would look like this:

```
USE pubs
EXEC sp_addalias Mark, dbo
go
```

WARNING   When adding aliases using Transact-SQL, remember that a login can have either a username or an alias, but not both. If the login that you want to map with an alias already has a username in the database, you must drop the username for that login before the alias can be created.

As a final step in this set of procedures, alias some other login IDs. Alias Jeffrey as the DBO in the Pubs database, and also alias Christina as Melissa in the Pubs database.

1. Open the Query Tool or ISQL/W.

2. Run the following query to alias our two users:

```
USE pubs
EXEC sp_addalias Jeffrey, dbo
EXEC sp_addalias Christina, Melissa
GO
```

3. Verify that this procedure worked correctly by running the following stored procedure:

```
USE pubs
EXEC sp_helpuser
GO
```

4. When you are finished, close the ISQL/W utility.

Exam Essentials

Stored procedures of all types (especially security) are stressed on the exam.

Remember the stored procedures and what they do.   The stored procedures that you looked at in this section are: sp_adduser, sp_changedbowner, sp_addalias, and sp_dropuser. Remember that the sp_adduser procedure will allow you to specify a login_id, a user_name (which may be different from the login_id, although it is not recommended), and a groupname.

Key Terms and Concepts

Aliasing: You can use aliasing in your databases to allow a particular login ID access to your database in the context of another individual in the database. For example, developers are often aliased as the DBO of the database. In this manner, all objects created in the database are owned and controlled by a single username: the DBO.

Database Users: Database users are different than SQL Server login IDs. A login ID will give access to SQL Server, but does not give you permissions in any database. You must have a mapped login ID to a database username in order to gain access to that particular database.

Sample Questions

1. Which system table holds information about user aliases?

A. sysusers

B. syslogins

C. sysprotects

D. sysalternates

Answer: D is correct. Sysusers stores mapped login IDs in each database. Syslogins is in the Master database and stores login IDs. Sysprotects stores permissions for users in a database.

2. There can be only one user acting as the database owner in a database. (Select the best answer.)

   A. True. There is only one DBO is any database.

   B. True. The SA is always the DBO is a database.

   C. False. The SA can be the DBO as well as one other person.

   D. False. You can alias users in a database as the DBO.

   Answer: D is correct. You can have only one database owner, but you can alias as many users as you like to the DBO. The SA is always a DBO in every database.

3. Which stored procedure is used to change ownership of a database to another user?

   A. sp_defaultdb

   B. sp_helpdb

   C. sp_changedbowner

   D. sp_addalias

   Answer: C is correct. Sp_defaultdb is used to change a login ID's default database. Sp_helpdb is used to gather information about databases. Sp_addalias is used to alias a login_id to a user_name that already exists in a database.

4. An SA user attempts to transfer ownership of a database to another login, and this action returns an error. What might be the problem?

   A. The login is accessing the database under a standard connection.

   B. The login has an entry in the sysalternates system table in that database.

   C. The SA does not have the authority to transfer ownership, only the DBO has this authority.

D. The database is corrupt and must be repaired before the transfer of ownership can take place.

Answer: B is correct. Because the login ID has already been mapped to that database once, it cannot be mapped a second time. In order to solve this problem, use the sp_dropalias procedure to remove the mapping and then rerun the sp_changedbowner procedure again.

5. After ownership of a database was transferred from SA to another user, all users who used to be able to access the database under DBO aliases report that they can no longer access the database at all. What went wrong?

   A. The database ownership was transferred with the Enterprise Manager. This is a known bug in the Enterprise Manager.

   B. When the sp_changedbowner stored procedure was called, the true flag was not included.

   C. Nothing went wrong. It is impossible to retain aliases to DBO during ownership transfer.

   D. The users who were formerly aliased as DBO already had usernames in the database. Aliases cannot be maintained unless these usernames are dropped.

Answer: B is correct. If you want users who are aliased as the DBO to continue being aliased as the DBO during a transfer of database ownership, then you must specify the TRUE option as shown here:

```
EXEC sp_changedbowner login_id, TRUE
```

Add and drop users for a group.

Placing users in groups can ease your task as an administrator. Knowing how to create groups and modify group membership is important to understand for the exam.

Critical Information

A group is nothing more than a security context inside of which you place your users. When planning database access, you probably will want to include groups in your strategy. When you assign permissions to a group, every member of that group will have the permissions that you specify unless you override group permissions at the user level. Using groups can make the process of managing permissions much easier.

By adding groups, permissions are assigned at the group level rather than at the user level. The difference revolves around the fact that SQL Server only allows a user to be a member of one group other than the Public group. A user is always a member of the Public group.

Creating Groups and Dropping Groups

Because groups are database specific, you must first select the appropriate database, and then create your groups. Anyone with DBO permissions in a database can create and modify groups. Use the *sp_addgroup* stored procedure to add a new group to a database.

The only modifications that can be made to a group are its membership and the permissions that have been assigned to the group. If you want to change a group name, you must drop and re-create the group. To drop a group, use the *sp_dropgroup* stored procedure.

Group Membership Modification

As your users' jobs or data-access needs change, you may find it necessary to change the group association. This can be done quite easily by using either the Enterprise Manager or Transact-SQL. When considering a user's movement between groups, be sure to consider the fact that a user is always a member of the Public group, no matter which user-defined group may hold that user as a member.

Necessary Procedures

You will need to understand how to add groups, add users to a group, remove users from a group, and drop groups for the exam. All of these activities can be accomplished through the Enterprise Manager or through stored procedures. The exam focuses on using the stored procedures to accomplish these tasks.

Adding Groups

Create groups with the sp_addgroup stored procedure. Before executing the stored procedure, you must use the appropriate database first, or else you will be adding the group to the wrong database. The syntax is:

```
sp_addgroup grpname
```

Follow these procedures to create a new group called Admins and a group called Grunts in the Pubs database.

1. Open the ISQL/W utility.

2. Run the following code to create the Admins and Grunts groups in the Pubs database.

```
USE pubs
GO
EXEC sp_addgroup Admins
EXEC sp_addgroup Grunts
GO
```

Modifying Groups and Group Membership

You can add users to a group using the sp_adduser stored procedure by specifying an optional group name, or you can change a user's current group to another group using the sp_changegroup stored procedure. The following syntax is used to change a user's group.

```
sp_changegroup grpname, username
```

In this procedure, the grpname parameter represents the group to which you want to assign membership for that user. If the Public group is referenced in this parameter, any group membership other than Public is revoked from that user.

TIP   Before you can drop a group using *sp_dropgroup*, the group must have no members. To remove members from a group, execute the *sp_changegroup* procedure for all users in the group, transferring their memberships to another group or to the Public group. After this is done, the group can be freely dropped.

Groups are dropped with the stored procedure sp_dropgroup. The syntax for this stored procedure is:

```
sp_dropgroup grpname
```

Unlike using the Enterprise Manager, groups cannot be dropped with Transact-SQL unless the group is empty. If the group has members, the stored procedure will fail. To remove members from a group, you can drop the user or transfer the user to another group or to Public. To accomplish this, you can run either the *sp_dropuser* command or the *sp_changegroup* command.

In the following steps, you will drop your aliased users Christina and Jeffrey. You will then use the sp_adduser stored procedure to add them to a particular group. You will then use the sp_changegroup stored procedure to change a user's group from one to another. Finally, you will drop users, and then drop the group.

1. First drop the aliased users Christina and Jeffrey, and then re-create these users in the Pubs database. Notice that part of the sp_ adduser statement allows you to specify a group as well. Place both

Christina and Jeffrey in the Grunts group. Then change Melissa's group from nothing/Public to Admins/Public.

```
USE pubs
EXEC sp_dropalias Christina
EXEC sp_dropalias Jeffrey
GO
EXEC sp_adduser Jeffrey, Jeffrey, Grunts
EXEC sp_adduser Christina, Christina, Grunts
GO
EXEC sp_changegroup Admins, Melissa
GO
```

2. You can verify that the groups have been set up properly and that the users exist in them by running the sp_helpgroup stored procedure or the sp_helpuser stored procedures.

```
USE pubs
EXEC sp_helpgroup Admins
GO
EXEC sp_helpuser Melissa
GO
```

3. To remove users from a group, you can either drop them from the database or change their group. In this example, move Melissa from the Admins to the Public group and drop Jeffrey from this database.

```
USE pubs
sp_changegroup 'public', Melissa
EXEC sp_dropuser Jeffrey
GO
```

4. Verify that the users have changed groups appropriately.

5. Now remove the Admins group from the Pubs database. Run the following code:

```
USE pubs
EXEC sp_dropgroup Admins
GO
```

6. Again, run the sp_helpgroup stored procedure to view the groups and the users that belong in them.

Exam Essentials

Again we see that security is stressed on the exam. Make sure you know these different stored procedures and when to use them.

Know the stored procedures for dealing with groups. This includes the following stored procedures: sp_addgroup, sp_dropgroup, and sp_changegroup.

Know how to modify a user's group affiliation. This gets kind of tricky. Remember that a user's group can be modified by using the following stored procedures: sp_adduser (remember there was a group parameter here), sp_changegroup, and sp_dropuser (you are removing the user from the database and, therefore, that user's group affiliation).

Key Terms and Concepts

sp_addgroup: This will add a new group to the database.

sp_changegroup: This will change a user's membership from one group to the next.

sp_dropgroup: This will drop a group from the database.

Group membership: A user in a database is always a member of the Public group. A user can be a member of one group in addition to Public.

Sample Questions

1. The SA is attempting to drop a group from a database using sp_dropgroup. This statement fails on execution. What might be the problem?

A. One of the users in the group owns an object in the database. The group and its users can't be deleted with sp_dropgroup if any user owns any objects.

B. The SA does not have authority to drop groups from a database. Only the DBO has that authority.

C. The group is empty, and deleting it would have no effect.

D. The group is not empty, and you cannot drop a group with members.

Answer: D is correct. When you issue the sp_dropgroup stored procedure, there must be no members in the group being dropped. You can remove members from a group using the sp_changegroup command or the sp_dropuser command.

2. A user can be a member of how many groups including Public?

A. 1

B. 2

C. 3

D. 4

Answer: B is correct. A user is always a member of the Public group and, at most, one additional group per database.

3. Which of the following statements will drop the Grover user from the Monsters group?

A. sp_dropgroup Monsters, Grover

B. sp_helpgroup Grover, Monsters

C. sp_transfergroup null, Grover

D. sp_changegroup 'public', Grover

Answer: D is correct. You can use the sp_changegroup or the sp_dropuser statements to remove a user from a group. Dropping a user will remove that user from the database.

CHAPTER

6

Managing Permissions

Microsoft Exam Objectives Covered in This Chapter:

▶ **Grant and revoke permissions.** *(pages 191 – 200)*

▶ **Predict the outcome of a broken ownership chain.** *(pages 201 – 206)*

▶ **Identify system administrator functionality.** *(pages 207 – 209)*

▶ **Implement various methods of securing access to data.** *(pages 209 – 222)*

The objectives for this portion of the exam cover your ability to implement security within a database. As you know, there are three levels, or stages, of authentication. At the top level, or server stage, you must have a valid login ID to get into the SQL Server system. The next level, the database stage, requires that you have a username in your database. However, even though you have a username in a database, you still cannot do things like access data or create objects. For these actions, you must have permissions for that database and its objects, which comprise the third level of security at the database object level.

Each database has its own independent permissions. To prepare for the test, you need to explore the two different types of user permissions: statement and object. You should also review the database security hierarchy, which delineates who has what permissions and who can grant or revoke those permissions to others.

When you grant permissions to others, you create chains of ownership. These ownership chains can become complex and tricky. You must learn how to predict the permissions needed by users at different locations within the ownership chains.

Permissions can be granted to database users and database groups. The exam tests your knowledge of how these permissions are enforced.

Grant and revoke permissions.

This exam objective tests your understanding of the permissions structure and the granting and revoking of permissions. This topic is fairly broad and covers a lot of territory. For the exam, you must understand the types of permissions and how they are applied.

Critical Information

To create objects and access data, you must have *permissions*. There are two main types of permissions: statement permissions and object permissions. With statement permissions, you can create database objects, such as tables and views. With object permissions, you can view and modify data in those database objects.

Statement Permissions

Statement permissions allow you to use certain statements in a database. These permissions are generally related to the creation of database objects. Table 6.1 lists the statement permissions and who can grant them to others.

TABLE 6.1: Statement Permissions

Statement	Can Be Granted By
Create Database	Only the SA
Create Default	SA or DBO
Create Procedure	SA or DBO
Create Rule	SA or DBO
Create Table	SA or DBO

T A B L E 6.1:   Statement Permissions *(continued)*

Statement	Can Be Granted By
Create View	SA or DBO
Dump Database	SA or DBO
Dump Transaction	SA or DBO

When you use a Create statement to create an object, you become the DBOO (Database Object Owner) and then can grant or revoke all *object* permissions on that object.

NOTE   Only the SA or someone with SA privileges has the ability to use the GRANT ALL statement. The only recipient of a GRANT ALL is a DBO. This is because only the SA can grant the CREATE DATABASE statement permission and only to a DBO.

Object Permissions

Object permissions generally allow users to manipulate data that a database object controls. Object permissions are used to manipulate data through the database objects. For example, to view the data in a table, you must first have Select permission on that table. If you want to run a stored procedure, you must first have Execute permission on that stored procedure.

Object permissions can be granted by the SA or the DBOO. Table 6.2 lists the object permissions and what objects they affect.

T A B L E 6.2:   Object Permissions

Permission	Performs	Objects Affected
Delete	Deletes data from object	Table, View

TABLE 6.2: Object Permissions *(continued)*

Permission	Performs	Objects Affected
Drop *<object>*	Removes an object	Default, Table, Procedure, Rule, View
Execute	Runs a stored procedure	Stored Procedure
Insert	Adds new data to object	Table, View
References	Creates a foreign key reference	Table, Column
Select	Views data in object	Table, View, Column
Update	Modifies data in object	Table, View, Column

Tables have additional object permissions (like indexes and triggers) attached to them. Table permissions are listed in Table 6.3.

TABLE 6.3: Implied Table Permissions

Permission	Performs
Alter Table	Allows you to add columns to a table
Create Index	Allows you to create an index
Create Trigger	Allows you to create a trigger
Drop Index	Deletes an index
Drop Table	Deletes a table
Drop Trigger	Deletes a trigger
Truncate Table	Deletes all information in a table, but keeps the table schema intact
Update Statistics	Updates the statistical information stored in the indexes on a table

---

TIP   Although you can grant permissions on columns, it is not rec-ommended because any Transact-SQL statement that touches that table must check permissions on each column. Rather than grant per-missions on columns, you should create a view on the required columns and then assign permissions to that view. This way, permis-sions are checked only once on the entire view rather than on each column within the view.

Necessary Procedures

You should be able to read and understand what the GRANT and REVOKE statements are trying to accomplish.

Granting and Revoking Statement Permissions

You can grant and revoke permissions using the Transact-SQL commands GRANT and REVOKE. Here is the syntax used for statement permissions:

```
GRANT {ALL | statements }
TO {PUBLIC | users }

REVOKE {ALL | statements }
TO {PUBLIC | users }
```

The *statements* parameters that you can specify are the ones listed in Table 6.1. The *users* parameter can be users (separate usernames with commas) and/or groups. For example, to grant the Create View permission to Luanne and Mark, you could run the following query as either the SA or the DBO:

```
USE pubs
GRANT CREATE VIEW
TO Luanne, Mark
```

You should get the following response:

```
This command did not return data, and it did not return
any rows
```

NOTE You cannot grant permissions to both the group Public and individual users in the same Grant statement.

Granting and Revoking Object Permissions

As with statement permissions, you can use the Transact-SQL GRANT and REVOKE statements to grant and revoke object permissions. Here is the syntax for object permissions:

```
GRANT {permissions}
ON {object}
TO {users}
[WITH GRANT OPTION]

REVOKE [GRANT OPTION FOR]{permissions}
ON {object}
FROM {users}[CASCADE]
```

For example, the following statements grant permissions on the Authors table to Melissa:

```
GRANT SELECT, INSERT, DELETE
ON authors
TO Melissa
```

The GRANT and REVOKE statements have two additional options when they are used for object permissions: WITH GRANT OPTION and CASCADE.

When a database object owner grants permission on an object to another user with the WITH GRANT OPTION, the other user can then grant those same permissions to others. For example, if the DBO granted Melissa Select and Insert permissions on the Authors table with the WITH GRANT OPTION, Melissa could then grant Select and Insert permissions to Anthony, like this:

```
GRANT SELECT, INSERT
ON authors
TO Anthony
```

If Melissa was not given the WITH GRANT OPTION permissions, she could not pass on the permissions to others.

As you can see, the use of WITH GRANT OPTION can potentially cause problems because the DBO begins to lose control over who has access to the object that he or she owns. This is where the CASCADE option comes into play. If the DBO simply revoked permissions on the Authors table from Melissa, like this:

```
REVOKE SELECT, INSERT
ON authors
FROM Melissa
```

then Anthony would still have all the permissions that Melissa granted him. The DBO may or may not know about what permissions Anthony has. To revoke permissions from Melissa (as well as from anyone Melissa granted permissions to), you can use the CASCADE option, like this:

```
REVOKE SELECT, INSERT
ON authors
FROM Melissa
CASCADE
```

You can use the following steps to check current permissions, grant and revoke permissions, and test these permissions:

1. Start SQL Enterprise Manager and drill down to the Pubs database.

2. Right-click on the Pubs database, and choose Edit from the context menu.

3. Click on the Permissions tab to view the current permissions.

4. If Melissa does not have the Create View permission, give it to her now. (Click on her Create View checkbox to place a green checkmark there.) Then click OK to close the Edit Database dialog box.

5. Start ISQL/W and enter and execute the following query:

```
USE pubs
GO
REVOKE ALL
FROM Melissa
```

You should get the following results:

```
This command did not return data, and it did not return
any rows
```

6. Close the ISQL/W window.

7. Return to the Permissions tab in SQL Enterprise Manager's Edit Database dialog box to view the permissions that Melissa now has. The checkmark should be gone from the Create View box.

8. If it is not, close this window and Refresh the databases and then repeat Step 7. Melissa has had all statement permissions revoked.

9. Now, test to see if Melissa can select any information from the Employees table. Open the ISQL/W utility by running: Start ➢ Program Files ➢ Microsoft SQL Server 6.5 ➢ ISQL/W. When you are prompted for your login credentials, enter the following: Login ID: **Melissa**, Password: **melissa**. Use a nontrusted connection. You are now logged in to the database as Melissa.

10. Now run the following script to test whether or not Melissa can select anything from the employees table.

```
USE pubs
GO
SELECT * FROM employees
GO
```

11. You should not be able to select anything. Now let's grant Melissa SELECT and INSERT permissions. Start another ISQL/W window and log in as SA, with no password and with a trusted connection. Run the following script.

```
USE pubs
GO
GRANT SELECT, INSERT
ON employees
TO Melissa
GO
```

12. Once this has run successfully, try to rerun your SELECT statement as shown in Step 10. You should be able to access the data now.

13. Close the ISQL/W utilities when you are finished.

Exam Essentials

This objective is stressed on the exam. You must be able to effectively read and understand what a particular grant or revoke statement does.

Know the difference between statement and object permissions. Statement permissions cannot be granted to others. They are available only to the object owner. Object permissions can be granted to others. These include permissions like SELECT, INSERT, and DELETE.

Understand how the WITH GRANT OPTION and CASCADE options work. When you grant permissions to others with the WITH GRANT OPTION, they can grant those same permission to others. The REVOKE .. CASCADE command will revoke any permissions that you gave to someone and any permissions that person gave to others on your object.

Key Terms and Concepts

GRANT .. WITH GRANT OPTION: Allows a DBOO to grant permissions on an object to another. In addition to giving permissions on the object to that user, the WITH GRANT OPTION allows the new user the ability to grant those same permissions to someone else.

REVOKE .. CASCADE: Allows the DBOO who has given permissions to another user with the WITH GRANT OPTION to revoke that user's permissions and to also revoke any permissions on the DBOO's object that the user might have granted to someone else.

Sample Questions

1. Which of the following is true about permissions?

   A. Statement permissions can be granted to others.

   B. Statement permissions cannot be granted to others.

   C. Object permissions can be granted to others.

   D. Object permissions cannot be granted to others.

   Answer: B and C are correct. You cannot grant statement permission to others, but you can grant object permissions to other users in the database.

2. Which of the following is true about column-level permissions?

   A. You should grant column-level permission to users in order to keep your database more secure.

   B. You should grant column-level permission to users instead of creating views because this is more efficient.

   C. You should create a view on desired columns, and then give permissions on the view because this is more efficient than column-level permissions.

   D. You cannot create column-level permissions.

   Answer: C is correct. Granting permission on a view is much more efficient than granting permissions on columns. Permissions will be checked only on the view, and only when the view is used, rather than every column, every time a column is referenced.

3. If you grant a permission with the WITH GRANT OPTION option, which of the following is true?

   A. The grantee will be able to pass those permissions on to other users.

   B. The grantee will be able to pass all permissions on that object to other users.

   C. The grantee will not be able to pass those permissions to other users.

   D. The grantee can pass those permissions only to the DBOO.

   Answer: A is correct. This can be a dangerous thing to do because the DBOO can quickly lose control over his/her object.

4. If you want to revoke permissions from grantees and anyone else who may have been granted permissions by your grantees, you can use the REVOKE statement with the CASCADE option.

   A. True. This is how the REVOKE with CASCADE works.

   B. False. The REVOKE with CASCADE revokes all permission on the individual grantee.

   C. True. The grantee will also lose any other permissions on other database objects.

   D. False. The grantee and anyone the grantee gave permissions to will lose any other permissions that they have on other database objects.

   Answer: A is correct. To REVOKE permissions that a grantee might have passed along to others on your object, REVOKE those permissions with the CASCADE option.

Predict the outcome of a broken ownership chain.

Ownership chains are a fact of life in SQL Server. There are ways to avoid them, but understanding how they are created and where permissions will be checked is a necessary skill for any administrator. This exam objective is designed to test your ability to find breaks in an ownership chain and how those breaks will affect a user trying to use an object.

Critical Information

To understand ownership chains, look at a few examples of how they are created and how permissions are checked against them.

For example, if Melissa owns a table and she creates a view based on her table, she has created an ownership chain. This ownership chain has only one object owner. Figure 6.1 illustrates what has just happened.

FIGURE 6.1: An unbroken ownership chain

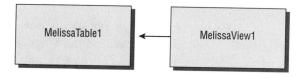

Melissa could grant Select permissions to Mark on her view. When Mark attempts to select from MelissaView1, permissions would be checked on MelissaView1 as shown in Figure 6.2. Permissions are checked only where a break in ownership takes place. Because Mark is trying to look at an object that he doesn't own, permissions will be checked on the View. The view is based on a table that Melissa owns. Because the view and the underlying object (Melissa's table) are both owned by the same person, permissions will not be checked again.

FIGURE 6.2: Permissions are checked only once in an unbroken ownership chain.

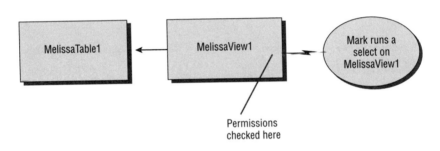

Permissions checked here

If Mark created a view based on Melissa's view, this now becomes a *broken* ownership chain because different users *own objects* within the permission chain. If Mark granted permissions to Luanne on his view, permissions would be checked on MarkView1 for Luanne and on MelissaView1 for Luanne, as illustrated in Figure 6.3.

If Luanne has Select permissions on both MarkView1 and Melissa-View1, then she could select successfully from MarkView1. If anywhere in the permission chain, Luanne does not have permission where permissions are checked, then she would not be able to select from MarkView1. Permissions are checked *every* time ownership changes. This doesn't seem too bad at first glance, but take a look at Figure 6.4 to see what could happen if you let your database developers create dependent objects as needed.

FIGURE 6.3: Permissions are checked every time ownership changes in a broken ownership chain.

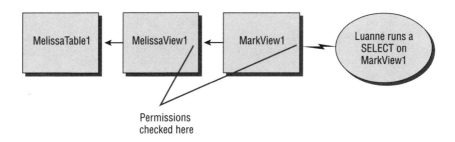

FIGURE 6.4: A complex, broken ownership chain

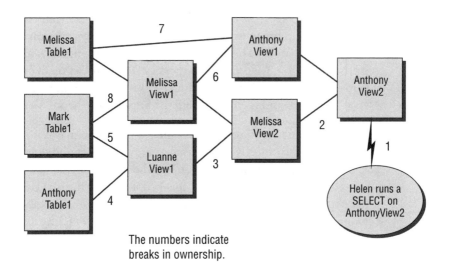

Figure 6.4 illustrates a complex, broken ownership chain. Determining where permissions would be checked for user Helen can be

confusing. Each break in ownership must have a permission check, as listed here:

- AnthonyView2
- MelissaView2
- LuanneView1
- AnthonyTable1
- MarkTable1
- MelissaView1
- MelissaTable1

One of the best ways to avoid this problem is to alias your database developers as DBO. In this manner, the DBO is the owner of all objects that are created by the aliased developers. This means that you do not have a break in the ownership chain, and permissions will be checked only once. This is not to say that you should alias all of your users as DBO. Alias the developers as DBO, and let them create the objects as needed. Once the database is in production, add your users and groups and then give them the appropriate permissions.

There is one more detail to cover for the exam, although it is not formally listed in the objectives. If a user creates an object and does not give the DBO permissions on that object, the DBO cannot touch that object. There is a workaround for this problem. It is the SETUSER statement. The SETUSER statement allows the DBO to assume the persona of the user in question. In this way, the DBO (acting as the user) can then grant permissions on the objects owned by the user to the DBO.

Exam Essentials

Ownership chains are stressed on the exam. You must understand how ownership chains affect permissions and how ownership chains can be avoided. These questions are much less difficult to deal with when you use scratch paper and build figures similar to those presented here. In this manner, it should be simple to follow the ownership chains.

Understand how ownership chains are created. Ownership chains are created when you have objects that depend upon each other and those objects have different owners.

Understand where in the ownership chain permissions will be checked. Permissions will be checked at each break in ownership.

Understand how to avoid broken ownership chains. To avoid broken ownership chains, only allow one user (or several users aliased as that one user) the ability to create objects in the database. If you alias developers as DBO, the DBO still owns the objects if a developer ever leaves.

Remember what the SETUSER statement does. The SETUSER statement allows a DBO to impersonate a user in his or her database. This can be useful if the user has created objects, but has not given the DBO permissions on those objects.

Key Terms and Concepts

Ownership chain: An ownership chain is created when an object owner creates new objects based on the original object.

SETUSER statement: The SETUSER statement is used by a DBO to temporarily take on the persona of a user in his or her database. This allows the DBO to always retain control over objects created by users in their database.

Sample Questions

1. If a user in a database has created an object, and has not given permissions on that object to the DBO, the DBO can still access the object due to which of the following?

    A. The SETUSER statement allows the DBO to impersonate a user, thereby giving him access.

    B. The DBO Use Only database option allows the DBO to access all objects in a database.

    C. The DBO cannot access an object that it doesn't own.

    D. Nothing needs to be done. The DBO can always access all objects in his or her database without any further work.

Answer: A is correct. This is one of the intended uses of the SetUser statement.

2. If James creates a table, and then James creates a view on his table and gives Laura permission on his view, which of the following is true?

    A. Laura can select from the view and permissions will be checked only once on the view itself.

    B. Laura can select from the view and permissions will be checked on the view and on the table on which the view is based.

    C. Laura cannot select from the view because she doesn't have permissions on the underlying table.

    D. Laura can select from the view, and permissions will not be checked.

Answer: A is correct. There is only one owner of all objects in this chain.

3. James creates a table, and then James creates a view on his table and gives Laura permission on his view. Laura creates a view based on James' view, and then gives Amanda permissions on her view. Where will permissions be checked? (Choose all that apply.)

    A. On Laura's view

    B. On James' view

    C. On James' table

    D. Permissions will not be checked.

Answer: A and B are correct. Permission will be checked at every break in ownership.

Identify system administrator functionality.

This exam objective reflects your knowledge of what the SA can and can't do. It may sound a little overwhelming at first, but there is a simple solution. The SA has no restrictions on what it can do in a database. Your job for the exam is to know what permissions are the exclusive rights of the SA.

Critical Information

There are no restrictions on what the SA can do in SQL Server. The SA is automatically granted all permissions, and can grant most of those permissions to others.

In addition to the permissions listed in Tables 6.1 and 6.2, the SA has some permissions that cannot be granted to others. Table 6.4 lists these permissions.

T A B L E 6.4: Permissions Reserved for the SA

Permissions	Tasks
Add/Drop *extended stored procedures*	Add or drop extended stored procedures
Disk {Init, Mirror, Refit, Reinit, Remirror, Unmirror}	Device-related tasks
Kill	Stop a process (but not a system process; you cannot kill a system process)
Reconfigure	Reconfigure SQL Server

T A B L E   6.4:   Permissions Reserved for the SA *(continued)*

Permissions	Tasks
Shutdown	Shut down SQL Server
DBCC <statements>	Database consistency checker statements. (Some of these *can* be granted to DBOs.)

When something affects SQL Server as a whole, or something is done outside the boundaries of SQL Server, then it is an SA permission only and cannot be granted to others. For example, only the SA can create new devices. These devices are preallocated hard disk space. These files on hard disk are outside the realm of SQL Server. Only the SA can reconfigure SQL server, etc.

Exam Essentials

Certain permissions are available only to the SA and cannot be granted to others. This topic will appear on the exam.

Know what permissions the SA has that cannot be granted to others.   Knowledge of the SA abilities is not strenuously tested on the exam. You should, however, be familiar with what is the sole province of the SA. In other words, you should know what permissions the SA has that cannot be granted to others. This includes the KILL statement, most DBCC commands, and any SQL Server configuration changes.

Key Terms and Concepts

DBCC: DBCC stands for Database Consistency Checker. It is a set of statements that are geared toward reporting inaccuracies in your database. In general, these statements only report problems, they do not fix them. To fix most problems, you should use stored procedures and Transact-SQL.

Kill: The KILL statement is an SA-only statement. It allows the SA to kill active processes. You cannot kill a system process.

Sample Questions

1. Which of the following are permissions restricted for SA use only?

    A. KILL statement

    B. CREATE DATABASE statement

    C. DISK INIT statement

    D. DUMP DATABASE

Answer: A and C are correct. The CREATE DATABASE permission can be granted to a DBO. The DUMP DATABASE statement is a DBO permission by default. The KILL statement allows the SA to kill a currently running process. DISK INIT is used to allocate disk space for database storage.

Implement various methods of securing access to data.

This exam objective is a sort of catch-all for everything that is not covered elsewhere in this chapter. You need to know the difference between standard security and integrated security, and how it affects login IDs. You can revisit users and groups and review how permissions are enforced through permission precedence. You can finish up with a look at how permissions are handled in regards to views.

Critical Information

To this point, you have reviewed how SQL Server authenticates users to the server independently of the Windows NT environment. This approach is called *standard security*. When a user logs in to a Windows NT server, he or she is still required to authenticate to the SQL Server service to access SQL Server resources. This requires two logins. If desired, another security approach can be used called *integrated security*. Integrated security is also sometimes called *trusted security* because SQL Server trusts the authentication of Windows NT, thereby eliminating the need for multiple logins. The connections that are made to SQL Server by using Windows NT account information for authentication are called *trusted connections*.

SQL Server uses three security models: standard, integrated, and mixed. To prepare for the exam, you need to explore the rationale and mechanics for using these models.

NOTE   The security models discussed in this section relate only to server access. Only the behavior of the first gatekeeper, the SQL Server, can be modified using alternate security models.

Standard Security

When SQL Server is installed, it is initially configured for standard security. In the standard security model, the SQL Server is responsible for authenticating all users to the server without any assistance from the operating system. The fact that a user is able to authenticate to the NT Server is irrelevant from the perspective of SQL Server. Upon attempting access to SQL Server, you will be forced to provide a SQL Server login ID and password to get by the first gatekeeper. Everything discussed in this chapter to this point with regard to login accounts has assumed a standard security implementation.

You can verify the current security model by checking the Security Options dialog in the Enterprise Manager. This can be done by following these steps.

1. From the Enterprise Manager menu, select Server ➢ SQL Server ➢ Configure.

2. In the Server Configuration/Options dialog, click the Security Options tab.

3. You will see three option buttons (one for each of the three security models) in the Login Security Mode frame. Verify that the Standard option button is selected.

4. Choose the OK button to close the dialog.

5. If you changed security modes, you must stop and restart SQL Server.

WARNING   The security mode option is not dynamic. If you ever make any changes to the security mode, you will need to stop and restart your server for the changes to take effect.

You can test standard security by attempting to log in under a login name that has not been added to the server. You will have a chance to do this in the "Necessary Procedures" section.

By only providing a valid login ID and password, you were able to connect to the SQL Server. This is the case no matter what your NT Server login may be. You could be logged in to Windows NT as Administrator and you still would be unable to connect to the SQL Server without providing a valid SQL Server login ID and password.

The steps for implementing a standard security model mirror are:

1. Create login IDs for every server user you want to have access to the SQL Server.

2. Create usernames for these login IDs in the database to which access is desired.

Trusted Connections with Standard Security

Although integrated security will not support standard connections, standard security will support trusted connections if a trusted connection is requested from the client. It is actually very common for system processes and some ODBC applications to request trusted connections even when the security model is set to standard. Follow these steps to test a trusted connection:

1. Verify that you are logged in to Windows NT as Administrator. If this is not the case, log out of Windows NT and log back in as Administrator.

2. Open ISQL/W and set the security option buttons in the Connection dialog to Integrated Security.

3. Click the Connect button. You should be authenticated to SQL Server. If you look in the title bar of the Query window, you should see that you are logged in to SQL Server as SA.

4. Close ISQL/W.

You were logged in to SQL Server with a trusted connection even though the security mode was set to standard security. This is why you were not required to enter any authentication information. You connected to the SQL Server as SA because you were logged in to Windows NT as Administrator. NT Administrators have default mappings to SA for trusted connections.

Integrated Security

When using the integrated security model, the SQL Server will trust the NT Server authentication as valid and either connect or deny connection to the SQL Server based on the Windows NT identity of the user.

When running a strict integrated security model, only trusted connections are allowed. Trusted connections can be made to a SQL Server from the following clients:

- Windows NT Servers or Workstations
- Windows for Workgroups clients

- Windows 95 clients

- Microsoft LAN Manager clients running Microsoft Windows or MS DOS

- Windows 3.1 clients on Novell® Netware®

WARNING Trusted connections are allowed only on named pipes or multi-protocol sessions. No other SQL Server Net-Libraries support integrated security. Consider this fact when planning your client access and installing Net-Library components.

When a SQL Server receives a server authentication request while running under integrated security, one of three possible connections can be made. The type of connection depends on the identity of the NT user. The types of connections that can be made are:

Standard user: If the SQL Server has a valid mapping of the NT user account to a SQL Server login account, then that user is authenticated under the mapped ID. The mapping is done with a utility called the *Security Manager*.

SA user: If no valid mapping exists to a SQL Server user, the NT login is checked to see if it has NT Administrator authority or has been mapped to SQL Server SA authority. If this is the case, the NT user will be authenticated as SA. This mapping is also done with the Security Manager.

Guest: If you want to, you can add a guest login to the server to allow authentication for individuals who do not meet either of the previous criteria. The name of this login account can be specified in the Security Options Tab of the Server Configuration dialog.

NOTE Integrated security provides access to the server only. If you want the users that access the server using integrated security to have access to database resources, usernames in each database must still be added. The login ID you will use for username mapping will be the same as the Windows NT login IDs.

Implementing integrated security requires you to change the security mode of your SQL Server and add some mappings from the Windows NT groups and users to SQL Server groups and users. The process can be executed in the following steps.

1. **Organize your Windows NT accounts:** It is much easier to map Windows NT groups to SQL Server accounts than to deal with individual NT user accounts. You might consider creating two groups: one for NT users who will receive SA authority and another for NT users who will access the SQL Server as standard users.

2. **Map NT groups and users to SQL Server:** Using the Security Manager utility, Windows NT groups and users can be given mappings to SQL Server. When you map a user who will connect to SQL Server with standard user authority, this process will actually create the SQL Server login ID in the server for you.

3. **Reset the SQL Server security mode:** In the Security Options dialog, change the option selection from standard to integrated security. This will disallow any nontrusted connections.

4. **Stop and restart SQL Server:** Because the change in security mode is not dynamic, the SQL Server must be restarted for the process to complete.

You will have a chance to try this in the "Necessary Procedures" section. An interesting way to test your Integrated security is to log in to the ISQL/W utility. Try providing a false ID and password. You will be logged in with your mapped NT ID. The login dialog box ignores your ID and password.

There are many benefits to using Windows NT integrated security. The first, of course, is that you are not required to authenticate to the SQL Server when you want to make a connection. This can eliminate much duplicated effort and frustration on the part of your users.

Another advantage is that SQL Server security can be managed from the operating system level. This means that you may not need two administrators, the network Admin and the DBA, both managing security. The DBA may be freed for other tasks.

Although there are advantages, there are also disadvantages and barriers to using integrated security. The single most prohibitive barrier is that integrated security is allowed only on named pipes and multi-protocol connections. If you are using any other Net-Libraries, you will not be able to support integrated security.

Another disadvantage is that unless the DBA also has full Admin authority on the network, integrated security takes the ability to properly secure database access and turns this over to the network administrator. Although this may not be problematic in most companies, it is something that you must consider.

Mixed Security

Some clients cannot make a trusted connection to a SQL Server. A Macintosh client, for example, while able to connect to a Windows NT server, is not able to establish a trusted connection to SQL Server. Other clients may be using Net-Libraries other than named pipes and multi-protocol. For these situations, and any other where a trusted connection is not desired, mixed security is supported.

Mixed security is the perfect solution when trusted connections are preferred, but standard connections must be supported. Standard security, while it still supports trusted connections, has preference for standard connections. Trusted connections must be requested specifically. Integrated security does not support standard connections in any form. Mixed security provides the best of both worlds.

When a SQL Server is running in mixed-security mode, a client requesting a connection will first be attempted as a trusted connection. If it is possible for a trusted connection to be made, then a trusted connection will be granted. If a trusted connection cannot be made, the server reverts back to standard security, checking the syslogins system table for a login ID for that user. If the user can be authenticated at this level, a standard connection will be granted. If not, the connection will be denied.

Implementing mixed security is done by implementing both integrated and standard security on the same system and setting the security mode of the server to mixed. Mappings are created for users accessing the server through trusted connections, and logins are added to the SQL Server for those making standard connections.

Permission Precedence

The permission precedence in SQL Server 6.5 tells us in what order permissions are enforced in SQL Server. Unfortunately for those of you who are Windows NT gurus, SQL Server handles group and user permissions differently than Windows NT does. The best way to describe the permission precedence in SQL Server is to go through several scenarios. But first, here is the skinny on how permissions are enforced:

1. User permissions take precedence over group permissions.

2. Group permissions take precedence over Public group permissions.

3. Public group permissions don't take precedence over anything.

Here are some scenarios to consider. Assume that Rosa is a user who is a member of the Sales group as well as the Public group. (Remember that you are *always* a member of the Public group.)

> **Scenario 1:** The SA revokes object permissions from Rosa. The SA then grants object permissions to the Sales group. Will Rosa still have access? No, because the more specific user-level permissions take precedence.

> **Scenario 2:** The SA grants object permissions to the Sales group. The SA then revokes object permissions from the Public group. Will Rosa still have access? Yes, because the more specific group-level permissions override the Public permissions. Because Rosa was neither denied nor granted permission at the user level, the group permissions are checked.

> **Scenario 3:** The SA grants object permissions to the Public group. The SA then revokes object permissions from the Sales group. Will Rosa have access? No, because the more specific group-level permissions take precedence over the Public permissions.

Permissions on Views

Permissions on views are a special case because permissions on dependent-view objects are checked when the view is run, not when it is created. A database user could create a view based on a table to which he or she does not have access. He or she could then grant permissions on his or her view to another user. If that other user has permissions on the dependent objects, then he or she will be able to run the view, even though the user who created the view is unable to use it.

As stated earlier, this section was a little choppy because it was a catch-all for what was not covered by specific topics. Take a look at the "Necessary Procedures" section to examine how to set up and test various connections.

Necessary Procedures

The following procedures are designed to highlight the differences between standard and integrated security. Understanding these differences will help you to better understand several questions and answers on the exam.

Testing Standard Security

To test your standard security, follow these procedures:

1. Open the ISQL/W application and ensure that the Login Information options in the Connect dialog are set for standard security.

2. Enter the login ID of **Melissa** and a password of **melissa**.

3. Click Connect. Melissa has just authenticated to the server. Notice that the title bar of the query window shows that you have authenticated as the Melissa login.

4. From the ISQL/W menu, choose File ➤ Disconnect to drop the connection.

5. Attempt another login by selecting File ≻ Connect from the ISQL/W menu.

6. Enter a login ID of **Grover**. Leave the password null. Click Connect.

7. The login attempt will fail. Click the OK button on the failure message box and click Cancel on the Connection dialog.

8. Close ISQL/W by selecting File ≻ Exit from the menu.

Implementing Integrated Security

You will be tested on your ability to implement integrated security. This takes several steps, but it is worth understanding, not only for the exam, but for the real world as well.

1. Create two new NT Groups using the User Manager for Domains. Call these groups SQLUsers and SQLAdmins.

2. Create two new NT user accounts using the User Manager for domains. The account names will be **Grover** and **Oscar**. Leave the passwords null. Clear the "User Must Change Password at Next Logon" checkbox. Select the checkboxes for "Password Never Expires." These options are for ease of demonstration. Your own password options may be different.

3. Assign Grover to the SQLAdmins group and Oscar to the SQLUsers group.

4. Open the Security Manager by using the Windows NT Start menu and selecting Start ≻ Programs ≻ Microsoft SQL Server 6.5 ≻ SQL Security Manager. (For a more comprehensive discussion on the SQL Security Manager, see *MSCE: SQL Server 6.5 Administration Study Guide* by Sybex.)

5. Enter your server name, and log in as SA.

6. From the menu, select View ≻ SA Privilege.

7. You should see that the Administrators Group has been granted SA authority. From the menu, select Security ≻ Grant New.

8. Select SQLAdmins from the list of groups, and click Grant. Click OK on the message acknowledging the action, and click Done to

close the list. You have just granted SA authority to the SQL-Admins group.

9. From the menu, select View ➤ User Privilege. No NT users or groups currently have user privileges.

10. From the menu, select Security ➤ Grant New.

11. Select SQLUsers from the list. Notice that a checkbox is selected adding login IDs for the members of the group. Leave this option selected. The second checkbox gives you the option of adding user-names in a database for members of this group. Leave this option cleared.

12. Click Grant. You will now see a report indicating how many login IDs were added. This action should report two, one for Oscar and one for Administrator (also a member of the SQLUsers Group). Click Done on this report and Done on the Security dialog.

13. Close the Security Manager by selecting File ➤ Exit from the menu.

14. To complete the process, open the Enterprise Manager, access the Server Configuration dialog, and click the Security Options tab. Set the security mode to Windows NT Integrated and click OK.

15. Stop and restart the server for the new security mode to take effect.

NOTE At this point you will no longer need to enter any authentication information to connect to your SQL Server.

Testing the Security Mode

WARNING When using integrated security, you may discover that your Windows NT login names use characters that are not valid in SQL Server. Characters such as the domain separator, the hyphen, ampersand, etc. can be mapped to valid SQL Server characters in the Security Options tab of the Server Configuration dialog. Learn these default mappings for the exam!

---

1. Verify that you are logged in to Windows NT as Administrator. If this is not the case, log out and log back in to NT as Administrator.

2. Open ISQL/W. Verify that the Login Information option is set to standard security.

3. Without entering a login ID or password, click the Connect button. You should be connected to SQL Server as SA. Normally, this action would fail, but because you are using integrated security, you are required to use a trusted connection.

4. Close ISQL/W. Log off Windows NT and log back in as Oscar. Remember that the Oscar Windows NT user was mapped to User authority in SQL Server.

5. Open ISQL/W. Verify that standard security is selected, and enter SA as a login ID. Enter the SA password if one exists. Click the Connect button.

6. You will be connected to SQL Server as Oscar. Because you have enabled integrated security, you are given a trusted connection no matter what type of connection is actually requested.

7. Close ISQL/W and Log off Windows NT as Oscar. Log back in to Windows NT as Administrator.

Exam Essentials

Knowledge of the difference between integrated and standard security is covered on the exam. Remember that when you are using integrated security, you will always use a trusted connection to SQL Server. Under standard security, you may be using a trusted or a nontrusted connection.

Know the difference between a trusted and a nontrusted connection. Trusted connections are used with integrated security. A trusted connection may be requested through standard security, but the default in standard security is to use a nontrusted connection.

Remember that permissions on views are checked when the view is used, not when the view is created.   Remember that users can create a view on objects on which they do not have permissions. This is because the permissions on the view are not checked until the view is run.

Key Terms and Concepts

Nontrusted connections: These connections occur when you use standard security. With this type of connection, all users are authenticated by SQL Server independently of Windows NT.

Trusted connection: A trusted connection occurs when Windows NT does authentication for SQL Server. For this to work, your must have valid NT user accounts mapped into SQL Server. You can accomplish this using the SQL Security Manager.

Sample Questions

1. When are permissions on a view checked?

    A. When the view is created

    B. When the view is run

    C. Never

    D. Views do not have permissions

Answer: B is correct. Permissions on a view are not checked until the view is run. In this way, it is possible for users to create a view on objects on which they do not have permissions.

2. Trusted connections can be used with which type of security?

    A. Integrated

    B. Standard

    C. Mixed

    D. None of the above

Answer: A, B, and C are correct. Trusted connections are normally used with integrated security. It is possible to request a trusted connection with standard security. Mixed security uses both trusted and nontrusted connections.

3. Of the following, which user has the most permissions in a database?

   A. User who has been granted all permissions

   B. A database object owner

   C. The DBO

   D. They are all equal

   Answer: C is correct. A user who has been granted all permissions has really only been granted all object permissions. He or she does not have any statement permissions. Database object owners have all permissions on the objects they create; however, they have no control over any other aspect of the database. The DBO has total control within its database.

4. You have a Novell Server which is being used to validate users in the west wing of your office. You also have an NT Server which validates users in the east wing of your office. The NT Server is also running your SQL Server 6.5 database. What type of security will be the best choice to support both your Novell and NT Server logins?

   A. Standard

   B. Mixed

   C. Integrated

   D. You cannot support both Novell and NT Users at the same time.

   Answer: B is correct. Mixed security is your best choice. This will allow users connected to your Windows NT Server to use integrated security and users from the Novell Server to use the standard side of mixed security. You could use standard security for all users, but you would lose the benefits of integrated security.

CHAPTER

7

Server Alert Processing
and Task Scheduling

Microsoft Exam Objectives Covered in This Chapter:

▶ **Identify the role of the MSDB database.** *(pages 224 – 226)*

▶ **Identify the role of SQL Executive service.** *(pages 227 – 228)*

▶ **Identify conceptual relationships among the Scheduler service, the MSDB database, and the Windows NT event log.** *(pages 229 – 231)*

▶ **Set up alerts.** *(pages 232 – 236)*

▶ **Schedule tasks.** *(pages 236 – 241)*

The objectives for this portion of the exam cover your understanding of the concepts involved with the proactive administration of SQL Server. This includes the relationships between the SQL Executive service and the MSDB database. You must also know how to set up alerts and schedule tasks.

▶ Identify the role of the MSDB database.

This topic identifies what the MSDB database is used for in the SQL Server environment. Starting with SQL Server 6.0, Microsoft added the ability to schedule tasks to operate at pre-defined intervals. SQL Server also allows operators to be defined, who can be e-mailed or paged on either successful or failed attempts at doing the task. SQL Server can also have alerts defined, which tell SQL Server what to watch for, what task to do if a particular event occurs, and who to notify if and when the event occurs.

Critical Information

The database that holds all of the tasks, alerts, and operators is the MSDB database, which is installed by default, although there are no tasks, alerts, or operators defined by default.

The MSDB database is a system database that is created automatically when SQL Server 6.0 or higher is installed. The MSDB database contains tasks, alerts, and operators. The MSDB data portion of the database is contained on the msdb_data.dat device, and the msdb_log.dat device contains the log.

There are five system tables in the MSDB database (besides those that are contained in every database). The tables are:

Systasks: This table is the one that tracks the tasks that have been created. SQL Executive looks in this table for not only the task and what it entails, but also the schedule for the task. Doing a query on the systasks table shows similar information to that of the Manage Tasks menu of Enterprise Manager.

Sysalerts: This table holds all of the alerts that have been defined for the system. The individual columns list the NT events that SQL Executive looks for, and what task to perform if the event is found.

Sysoperators: This table holds all of the information about various operators, including how they have been defined to SQL Server. E-mail addresses and paging numbers can be defined for each operator, and their hours of responsibility can also be defined. A failsafe, or operator of last resort, can also be defined in case there are no available operators.

Sysnotifications: This table relates alerts to the operators who will be notified if the alert is triggered.

Syshistory: This table holds the history of attempted tasks, retaining information about the success or failure of the task, how long the task took, and when the task operated. This table can be accessed inside the Manage Tasks screen by choosing the History icon.

Exam Essentials

The MSDB database is a key ingredient in the proactive administration of SQL Server. You should be familiar with its uses and its tables.

Know the uses for the MSDB database. Remember that the MSDB database is used by the SQL Executive service to store information about tasks, alerts, events, and replication tasks. This information is stored in five main tables: systasks, sysalerts, sysoperators, sysnotifications, and syshistory.

Key Terms and Concepts

MSDB history: The MSDB history is used to track all tasks, alerts, events, and replication tasks that have taken place. You should periodically clear out the history to keep the size of your MSDB database manageable.

Operator: An operator is an e-mail address where e-mail messages can be automatically sent when a task or alert has been configured to do so.

Sample Questions

1. Which of the following is true of the MSDB database?

   A. The MSDB database is used to store replication tasks.

   B. The MSDB database is used to store scheduled events.

   C. The MSDB database is used to store alerts.

   D. The MSDB database is used to store all of the other database information in SQL Server.

   Answer: A, B, and C are correct. The MSDB database is used by the SQL Executive service to store information about tasks, events, alerts, and replication information.

Identify the role of the SQL Executive service.

This topic identifies what role the SQL Executive service plays in the SQL Server environment. The SQL Executive service is essentially a group of four utilities that allow for proactive administration of your SQL Servers.

Critical Information

The SQL Executive service is in charge of finding and carrying out tasks and alerts, and notifying operators about the success and/or failure of those tasks and alerts. This allows for the proactive administration of your SQL Server. In the past, you had to wait for problems to occur and then take corrective action. The ability to set alerts to fire off when a particular set of conditions are met and then take action has greatly improved the reliability of the SQL Server database.

For example, you could schedule a task to fire off every two hours that will check the space used in a transaction log. When the log reaches 80% full, that task can fire an alert that the log is 80% full. That alert can then send an e-mail message to an operator that the log is 80% full. The alert can then take further action by running its own transaction log backup task. More e-mail can then be sent when the backup task works, or fails.

Exam Essentials

The SQL Executive service plays a major role in the administration of your SQL Server. Understanding how this service is integrated with the rest of SQL Server is essential for administration as well as for the exam.

Know why the SQL Executive service is used. Remember that the SQL Executive service is a suite of utilities that allows you to pro-actively work with your database administration. These utilities administer scheduling tasks, firing alerts, looking for events, and running replication.

Key Terms and Concepts

Alerts and the NT Event log: SQL Server will not fire an alert unless it finds information in the Windows NT Event log. If an event in SQL Server is not sent to the NT Event log, then an alert will not be fired.

SQLExecutive: This is the name of the SQL Executive service that runs on Windows NT. The service uses the MSDB database to run tasks, alerts, events, and replication.

Sample Questions

1. Which of the following is true about the SQL Executive service?

   A. The SQL Executive service is used to run tasks.

   B. The SQL Executive service is used to generate alerts.

   C. The SQL Executive service is used to run replication.

   D. The SQL Executive service is used to run SQLMail.

   Answer: A, B, and C are correct. Although you can send mail from SQL Server, it is not the sole province of the SQL Executive service. The mail service is supported by MAPI.

Identify conceptual relationships among the Scheduler service, the MSDB database, and the Windows NT event log.

This topic focuses on how the scheduler, the MSDB database, and the Windows NT event log feed off of each other. The SQL Executive service is the overall controlling service for tasks, alerts, operators, and events. There are separate engines for tasks, alerts, and events, but the SQL Executive is the controlling service for these engines and uses the Windows NT event log to coordinate certain services.

Critical Information

The best way to look at these relationships is to work through an example. Look at what happens to a common error before and after SQL Executive has been configured.

Suppose the Pubs database log fills up and generates an 1105 error (the standard error code that a full log will generate). This error will be written to the SQL Server error log, and in most cases, the error will also be written to the Windows NT Application log as shown in Figure 6.1. SQL Server's own internal error generator will create the 1105 error; however, without SQL Executive to watch for and do something when the error occurs, the problem will have to be fixed by hand. Because the log is full, users will not be able to use the database.

Now if you create an alert and a task, the alert engine will look for the 1105 error in the NT event log. When it finds it, a backup task will be triggered that will truncate (clean out) the log.

F I G U R E 7.1: Flowchart of standard SQL error messages

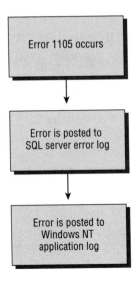

When SQL Server generates an 1105 error, the alert engine finds it and acts on it by triggering the task. The database log is truncated, and users can resume using the database normally. If the backup failed to work, another error would be generated. At that point the operator could be e-mailed and/or paged in order to fix the problem by hand.

The real key here is that the alerts engine scans the NT Application log for SQL Server errors. If a SQL Server error or event is not sent to the NT Application log, then the alerts engine will never see it.

Exam Essentials

Windows NT and the SQL Executive services allow you to create proactive tasks and alerts in SQL Server. This concept is important for the exam.

Remember the relationship between the SQL Executive service and the NT Application log. If an event is not sent to the NT Application log, the alerts manager cannot act upon it.

Key Terms and Concepts

Alerts manager: A part of the SQL Executive utility. The alerts manager scans the NT Application log looking for SQL Server events and errors.

NT Application log: A part of the NT Event log. The NT Event log tracks all manner of events and errors in Windows NT. SQL Server has the ability to send events and errors to the NT Application log.

Sample Questions

1. Which of the following must be true for the alerts manager to work?

   A. Errors and events must be sent to the NT Application log.

   B. The SQL Executive service must be configured for auto-start.

   C. The SQL Executive service must be configured to read the NT Application log.

   D. Nothing needs to be done. Alerts fire automatically when there are problems with SQL Server.

   Answer: A is correct. As long as the SQL Executive service is running (by auto-starting, or started by hand), it will look in the NT Application log for events and errors. No configuration is needed for the SQL Executive to read the NT Application log.

Set up alerts.

$\mathbf{A}$t first glance, this exam objective appears to look at the process by which you set up an alert. This is true to a degree. In addition to understanding the process, you need to know the different options available to you when you set up alerts. This includes the alert itself, a task to perform, and activation.

Critical Information

By defining an alert, you are telling SQL Server which error codes to look for in the NT Event logs, and what action to take if an event is found.

Creating an Alert

Creating alerts is somewhat intuitive. There are three or four basic steps:

1. Define the error. Alerts can be based on a generic error message number, an error severity, or an error happening in a specific database.

2. (Optional) Define the database in which the error must occur. An alert can filter error messages based on the database in which the error occurs. For instance, an alert can be created that watches the Pubs database in case it fills up. This alert would operate only on the Pubs database. If any other database filled up, the alert wouldn't do anything.

3. Define the task to perform. Alerts are usually created to perform a task when the alert condition is met. A task can be defined that will occur when the alert is triggered. Tasks can either do T-SQL commands, or they can run command prompt programs.

4. (Optional) Define who will be notified, and how. Operators can be defined so that they are e-mailed and/or paged when an alert is triggered. Operators are covered in more detail later.

Cascading Alerts

If you have more than one SQL Server, you can define a central server that will receive events from others servers for which you have not defined alerts. This is called an Unhandled Event Forwarding Server.

NOTE   The server that is designated as the Unhandled Event Forwarding Event Server must exist or be created in Enterprise Manager.

Operators

SQL Server is MAPI compliant, which means that SQL Server can send and receive e-mail. This gives SQL Server the ability to define operators and their e-mail addresses, so that SQL Server can notify operators upon the success and/or failure of scheduled or triggered tasks and alerts.

Necessary Procedures

You need to be able to create an alert that will watch for the log of the Pubs2 database to become full, and will then dump the transaction log (thereby truncating the log) if and when the alert is triggered.

Alerts

In the following steps, you will create a new alert that will search the NT Application log looking for a particular error. Once that error shows up, your alert will take corrective action.

1. Start Enterprise Manager.

2. Open the Alert menu by choosing Alerts/Operators… from the Server menu or highlighting SQL Executive. Right-click and choose Manage.

3. You should see nine prebuilt alerts. To add a new alert, choose the exclamation point with the highlight.

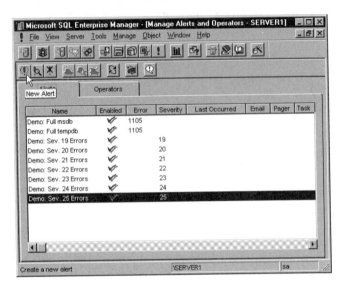

4. Create an alert with the name "Detect Full Pubs2 Transaction Log." Have it look for error 1105 in the Pubs2 database.

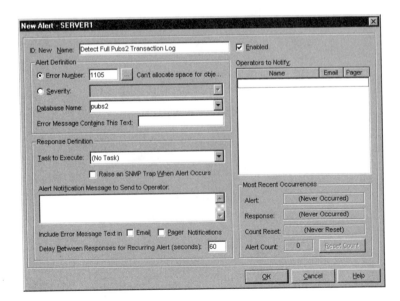

5. Now create a task to occur if and when the alert triggers. Choose New Task. This will open the Task Creation screen.

6. Give the task a name (for example, Dump the Pubs2 log when an alert is triggered), and enter the T-SQL code as:

   ```
   Dump transaction pubs2 to pubs2_tl_backup
   ```

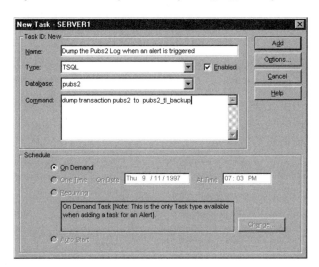

7. Choose Add, and then Close to save the alert.

Exam Essentials

Alerts are very useful in the administration of your SQL Server databases. Alerts will be examined on the test.

Remember what alerts can and can't do.   Alerts need to scan the NT Application log looking for error messages that you have specified. Once an error is found, you can have the alert fire off a task to take care of the error.

Key Terms and Concepts

Operator: This is simply someone to whom you can send e-mail when an alert or event is processing.

Sample Questions

1. Which of the following are options available in the alerts management screens?

   A. Error number to look for

   B. Task to perform

   C. Activate/deactivate the alert

   D. Define an operator to send an e-mail message to

   Answer: A, B, C, and D are correct. You can do all of these things when you are working with alerts.

Schedule tasks.

As with alerts, this exam objective talks not only about scheduling tasks, but also the different options that are available when you schedule a task and the different types of tasks.

Critical Information

SQL Server provides the ability to create tasks that can be run at regular intervals or when an alert is triggered. Different types of tasks can be scheduled.

The Different Types of Tasks

SQL Server supports five different types of tasks:

TSQL tasks: These tasks are written using T-SQL commands. These commands are often used to back up the database, rebuild indexes, and to perform various routine maintenance on databases.

CMDEXEC: These tasks literally open a command prompt and do some sort of batch file or .EXE file. Common tasks are those created by the Maintenance Wizard or by the WWW Connection Wizard.

Distribution: This task deals with replication and when the data is sent out to subscribing sites.

Logreader: This task deals with replication and when to look for changed data.

Sync: This task deals with replication and keeping databases in sync.

Task Scheduling

Tasks can be scheduled in one of three ways:

On demand: This is how tasks that are created for alerts are made. They are executed only if the alert triggers.

One time only: Relatively self-explanatory, this type of task is usually created for a special purpose. It is a one time task that will execute only once on its scheduled date.

Recurring: This type of task happens on a regular basis: daily, weekly, or even monthly.

Creating Tasks

There are various ways to create tasks. The most common ways are:

Manually

Enterprise Manager: Enterprise Manager has the ability to create various tasks, the most common of which is the backup task.

Maintenance Wizard: The Maintenance Wizard that comes with SQL Server 6.5 creates a task in order to do routine maintenance and back up databases.

WWW Connection Wizard: The WWW Connection Wizard, if used to create updates to a Web page that happen on a regular interval, will create a recurring task.

Replication: Will be covered in Chapter 11.

NOTE The Maintenance Wizard creates a command task, not a T-SQL task. The task that is created starts a program called "maintsql.exe" which was expressly written for SQL Server 6.5 maintenance.

Necessary Procedures

Tasks can easily be created manually. The required elements of a task are the type, schedule, and command to be executed.

Manually Creating a Task

To manually create a task, follow these steps.

1. Open the Tasks window of Enterprise Manager by highlighting SQL Executive, right-clicking, and choosing Manage Scheduled Tasks.

   or

   Open the Tasks window by choosing Scheduled Tasks... from the Server menu of Enterprise Manager.

2. Create a new task by choosing the far-left icon (a clock with a checkmark).

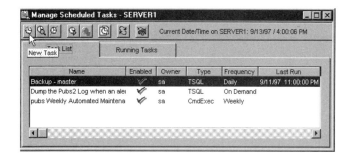

3. Give the task a name (for example, "Back up Pubs2 database every night").

4. Make sure that it is a TSQL task.

5. For the command, enter:

```
Dump Database pubs2 to pubs2_backup with init
```

6. Select the Change button by the scheduling information and change the date and time of the task to every day at 12:30 AM.

7. Choose OK and ADD to save the task.

Task History

One of the best things about tasks is that a history of both the time of execution and whether the task was successful or not is kept. Follow these steps to examine the history of your tasks to see if they were successful.

1. Open the Tasks window of Enterprise Manager.

2. Highlight the task created earlier.

3. Open the history of the task by selecting the icon with a clock and pieces of paper.

4. You should see that your task was successful. Choose OK to close the screen.

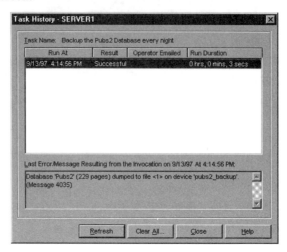

5. Check the maximum size of the History table by choosing the Options icon (the car with the open hood).

6. The defaults are 1,000 possible lines of history with 100 per task. Choose Cancel to leave the screen.

Exam Essentials

Tasks play an important role in both the exam and in the real-life administration of your SQL Server database. Keep these points in mind when studying for the exam.

Remember the different types of tasks that can be created.
There are three main categories of tasks: T-SQL, CMD execution, and replication tasks.

Remember the different scheduling options for tasks.   Tasks can be scheduled to fire on demand, one-time, or on a recurring basis.

Key Terms and Concepts

CMDExec: This is a command execution that can be scheduled to run as opposed to a replication task or a Transact-SQL command.

Sample Questions

1. What kind of tasks can be created?

   A. Alert processing tasks

   B. T-SQL tasks

   C. CMDExec tasks

   D. Replication tasks

   Answer: B, C, and D are correct. There is no such thing as an alert processing task.

CHAPTER

8

Managing Data

Microsoft Exam Objectives Covered in This Chapter:

▶ **Identify the best uses for the dumping command and the loading command in managing data.** *(pages 245 – 247)*

▶ **Identify the best uses for BCP when managing data.** *(pages 247 – 254)*

▶ **Identify the appropriate replication scenario to use.** *(pages 254 – 261)*

▶ **Identify the functionality of dynamic backup.** *(pages 262 – 263)*

▶ **Identify how automatic recovery works.** *(pages 264 – 266)*

▶ **Perform a database dump.** *(pages 266 – 268)*

▶ **Perform a striped backup.** *(pages 269 – 270)*

▶ **Create a dump device.** *(pages 271 – 273)*

▶ **Dump a transaction log.** *(pages 274 – 277)*

▶ **Load a database dump.** *(pages 278 – 281)*

The objectives for this portion of the exam cover your ability to correctly identify which type of data management technique is appropriate in which situations. This includes the backup and restoration of data. You will also need to determine when to use BCP versus the Transfer Manager Interface. An understanding of the backup process itself is also focused on in the objectives.

Identify the best uses for the dumping command and the loading command in managing data.

This exam objective really focuses on knowing when it is appropriate to use backup and restorations for the movement of data. The DUMP and LOAD commands can be very powerful weapons in your data management arsenal.

Critical Information

You can use the DUMP and LOAD commands for backing up and restoring data. You may want to use these commands to get a copy of the data, to move it to another device, to move it to another SQL Server machine, or to upgrade from an earlier version of SQL Server. Keep in mind that when you run a backup or a restoration, you will move all database data and database objects in the database.

You should use the LOAD and DUMP commands in all of the following scenarios:

- Normal day-to-day backups of your databases
- To place data on a backup or standby server
- To re-create a database on a new device
- To upgrade from a SQL Server 4.2x or 6.0 database to 6.5
- To perform a manual synchronization for a replication process

You should *not* use the LOAD and DUMP commands in these situations:

- To upgrade or move a database from one processor architecture to another
- To change the sort order
- To change the character set
- To load or dump individual database objects and permissions

Exam Essentials

Loading and dumping database information is one of the most important tasks that you will perform as an administrator. As for the exam, be sure you know when it is appropriate to use the LOAD and DUMP statements.

Know which situations are appropriate for the use of LOAD and DUMP. You should use the LOAD and DUMP statements for backups and restorations of data, to create a standby server, to upgrade from an earlier version of SQL Server to a newer version of SQL Server on the same processor architecture, and to manually synchronize a replication process.

You should *not* use the LOAD and DUMP commands to upgrade from one processor architecture to another, or if a sort order or character set has been changed. You cannot use the dump and load procedures to move specific database objects like views from one place to another. DUMP and LOAD move all data, objects, and permissions.

Key Terms and Concepts

DUMP: The term used for a backup of your database

LOAD: Loads the data from a backup into a database

Sample Questions

1. Which of the following are good uses for the DUMP and LOAD commands?

    A. To perform day-to-day backups and restorations of your data

    B. To upgrade a database from SQL Server 4.21 on a DEC Alpha to SQL Server 6.5 on a Pentium PC

    C. To upgrade a database from SQL Server 6.0 on a DEC Alpha to SQL Server 6.5 on a DEC Alpha

    D. To create a standby or backup server

Answer: A, C, and D are correct. These are all valid uses for DUMP and LOAD commands. You cannot upgrade data from one processor architecture to another using backup and restore. You should use either the BCP commands or the Transfer Manager Interface.

Identify the best uses for BCP when managing data.

This test objective examines not only when you should use BCP (as opposed to backup and restore or the Transfer Manager Interface), but also what permissions are needed to use BCP and the parameters of the BCP statement.

Critical Information

The BCP.EXE command-line program, which comes with SQL Server, is designed to bring ASCII and native (binary) data into or out of SQL Server. To be properly prepared for the exam, you should review the permissions needed to run a bulk copy, the difference between a fast and slow bulk copy, the BCP parameters, additional BCP rules, and when you might want to use bulk copy.

Permissions

To use BCP, you must have the following permissions:

Copy data out: SELECT permissions on the tables and views with which you want to work

Copy data in: INSERT permissions on any of the tables and views with which you want to work

Although any user with the appropriate permissions can use the BCP utility, the DBO usually has the responsibility.

Fast versus Slow BCP Sessions

There are two ways to conduct an import session with BCP. You can have a fast bulk copy or a slow bulk copy.

- Fast bulk copy occurs when there *are no* indexes on the table being imported to and the Select Into/Bulk Copy database option has been set.

- Slow bulk copy occurs when there *are* indexes on the table and/or the Select Into/Bulk Copy database option has *not* been set.

Fast BCP has the advantage of being considerably faster for importing data because there are no indexes to be updated for each row. Another advantage is that because the import is not logged, there is little chance of the transaction log filling up during the import process.

In some cases, using fast BCP may be the only option. This will depend on the size of the database and the amount of data that needs to be imported. For example, suppose that you have a 50MB database that has a 20MB transaction log, and you want to import 30MB of data; if the import is logged, it will fill the transaction log before it can be completed. Even though the data will all fit into the database, the size of the transaction log limits the amount of data that can be imported before the transaction log needs to be truncated.

The BCP Command

BCP supports command-line keywords and switches to control the way it works. The command line has the following syntax:

```
bcp <database..table> in/out <filename> <filetype>
<field delimiter> <row delimiter> /S<server> /U<user>
/P<password>
```

Table 8.1 lists the BCP keywords and switches. Note that the switches are case-sensitive.

T A B L E 8.1: BCP Switches

Keyword or Switch	Function
in/out	Specifies whether the data is going into the specified database and table or out of it.
/a	Sets the packet size. Valid packet sizes are from 512 bytes to 64KB. This setting may have little effect, or it may help to speed up BCP. It depends on your network topology and equipment.
/b	The number of rows included as a batch. Each batch is sent as a single transaction (if logging is enabled).
/c	Specifies the data is to be read from/stored in ASCII format. The /c switch also implies the /t and /r switches (which are delimiters).
/E	Specifies how Identity datatypes in fields will be handled.
/e <error file>	Creates an error file.
/F	Specifies the first row with which to start. If omitted, BCP will start with the first row encountered.

T A B L E 8.1: BCP Switches *(continued)*

Keyword or Switch	Function
/f <format file>	Specifies a format file to be used.
/I <input file>	Specifies an input file.
/L	Specifies the last row with which to end. If omitted, BCP will end with the last row encountered.
/m	The maximum number of errors allowed before the BCP operation will cancel. The default (if not specified) is 10.
/n	Specifies the data is to be read from/stored in native or binary format. This format works only when you are transferring data between compatible SQL Server machines.
/o <output file>	Specifies an output file.
/r	Specifies the row delimiter. One of the most common delimiters is the end-of-row or carriage return, which is specified by \n.
/t <"delimiter">	Specifies the field delimiter. For example, /t "," specifies a comma-delimited file.

TIP Because you may not want every column to be imported or exported, BCP allows the creation and use of format files. Not only can format files be used to specify which columns to ignore, they can also be used to set up an unattended BCP session. In order to create a format file, do an initial bulk copy without using the /c or the /n switches. You will be prompted through the BCP session, and a format file will be created. To reuse the format file, specify the file after the /f switch.

BCP Rules to Remember

Here are a few other factors that you should memorize about bulk copy:

- Importing data into a table is a dynamic process. Others may be using the table during the bulk copy procedure.

- Exporting data should not be dynamic. When you export data, changes to the data by other users may not be included. For this reason, you should set the database to single-user and then export your data.

- When importing data, datatypes and defaults will always be enforced.

- Rules, triggers, keys, and constraints are always ignored when data is imported.

- BCP imports data only. It will not import other database objects or permissions.

When to Use BCP

BCP is most useful when you are trying to import or export flat files. Many mainframe databases generate text-delimited flat files. Once a flat file has been created, using BCP to import that file into a SQL Server table is a simple process. You can also use BCP to export a table or view to a flat file. That new file can then be imported into another database, spreadsheet, or program.

BCP does not import any database objects or permissions. To import objects and permissions, you should use the Transfer Manager Interface in SQL Enterprise Manager.

Exam Essentials

Although the BCP command has only one test objective listed, it is stressed on the exam. Keep the following points in mind when you take your test.

Know what permissions are required to import data and export data using BCP. Remember that you must have SELECT permissions on the data to which you want to export and INSERT permission on the tables and views from which you want to import.

Remember the difference between a fast bulk copy and a slow bulk copy. A fast bulk copy occurs when there are no indexes on the table being imported to and the select into/bulk copy database option has been set.

Know why each of the BCP parameters are used. On the exam, you may need to decide which parameter of many is used for which option when presented with a BCP command.

Remember the BCP rules. Importing data is dynamic, exporting data is not. Rules, triggers, and keys are always ignored and datatypes and defaults are always enforced when you import data.

Know when it is appropriate to use BCP. BCP imports data only. If you need to import other database objects (like permissions, views, etc.) you must use either the DUMP and LOAD commands, or the Transfer Manager Interface.

Key Terms and Concepts

BCP enforces: BCP enforces defaults and datatypes when it is importing data into a database.

BCP ignores: BCP ignores rules and triggers when it is importing data into a database. You should run queries to verify imported data.

Sample Questions

1. Which tool would you use to import a mainframe data tape to SQL Server?

  A. Replication

B. Backup and restore

C. Transfer Manager Interface

D. BCP

Answer: D is the best choice. Generally, a mainframe will create flat ASCII text files. These files will normally have some type of text delimiter that you can use BCP to import the raw data into a SQL Server table.

2. What rights do you need on a table when using BCP to export records?

   A. SA rights

   B. DBO rights

   C. Insert rights

   D. SELECT/EXECUTE rights

   Answer: D is correct. To export data using BCP, you must have SELECT and/or EXECUTE permissions on the tables, views, or stored procedures that you want to use for export.

3. What rights do you need to import when using BCP?

   A. SA rights

   B. DBO rights

   C. Insert rights

   D. SELECT/EXECUTE rights

   Answer: C is correct. You only need INSERT permissions in order to import data using BCP.

4. BCP ignores which of the following when doing an import? (Select all that apply.)

   A. Rules

   B. Triggers

   C. Datatypes

   D. Defaults

Answer: A and B are correct. BCP always ignores rules and triggers when importing. However, note that defaults and datatypes are always enforced during an import.

5. Which of the following is true when performing a fast BCP?

   A. All inserts are logged to the transaction log.

   B. You must not have any indexes.

   C. Select Into/Bulk Copy must be turned on.

   D. You must be the DBO in the database.

   Answer: Answer B and C are correct. For a fast BCP to succeed, you must not have indexes on your table and the Select Into/Bulk Copy database option must be set.

Identify the appropriate replication scenario to use.

This exam objective focuses on the key features of the different replication scenarios. You must understand the benefits of each scenario and be able to apply that knowledge in a given business situation.

Critical Information

You have several different replication models from which to choose. Each model has benefits that are useful for different business scenarios. To prepare for the exam, you should understand the scenarios and the business situations in which they will be the most useful. This topic is stressed heavily on the exam. Fortunately, understanding the key benefits of each model makes these exam questions very straightforward.

The five different replication models are:

- Central publisher
- Central publisher using a remote distributor
- Publishing subscriber
- Central subscriber
- Multiple publishers of one table

Here are a few definitions that you need to understand:

Publisher: The SQL Server that will publish information to which other SQL Servers can subscribe

Subscriber: The SQL Server that will subscribe to information that has been published

Distribution: The SQL Server that captures the transactions published by the publishing server and then moves those transactions to the subscribing servers

Central Publisher

As shown in Figure 8.1, both the publishing database and the distribution database are on the same SQL Server. This model is useful in the following business scenarios:

- Asynchronous order processing during communication outages
- Distribution of price lists, customer lists, vendor lists, etc.
- Removal of MIS activities from the OLTP environment
- Establishment of Executive Information Systems

One of the most important aspects of the central publisher scenario is the ability to move data to a separate SQL Server. This ability allows the primary server to continue to handle on-line transaction processing (OLTP) duties without having to absorb the impact of ad-hoc queries generally found in the Management Information Systems (MIS) departments.

FIGURE 8.1: Central publisher model

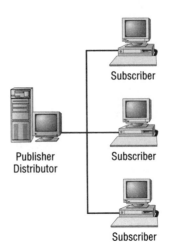

Subscriber

Publisher
Distributor

Subscriber

Subscriber

Central Publisher with a Remote Distributor

As shown in Figure 8.2, the distribution process has been separated from the publishing server. This detachment further removes overhead from the publishing server which may be involved with extremely high OLTP usage.

Publishing Subscriber

Figure 8.3 denotes the publishing subscriber model. In this case, the subscription server also acts as a publishing server. It will subscribe to the main publisher and then in turn publish the same data to other subscription servers.

This model is most useful in the following scenarios:

- Reduction of network traffic
- Reduction in communications costs over a slow or expensive link

F I G U R E 8.2:   Central publisher with a remote distributor

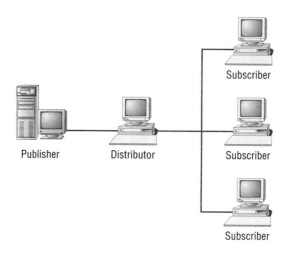

F I G U R E 8.3:   Publishing subscriber

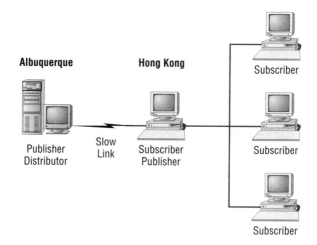

This model can be most useful for a situation in which there is an expensive or slow communications link. Transmitting data over phone lines for any length of time is not very cost effective. With a publishing subscriber scenario, you can replicate data several times per day to a single subscriber. That subscriber can then in turn republish the same information to other SQL Servers. If you have offices in Albuquerque and Hong Kong, you can reduce communications expenses by utilizing a publishing subscriber scenario.

Central Subscriber

The central subscriber model shown in Figure 8.4 is very useful in the following situations:

- Roll-up reporting

- Local warehouse inventory management

- Local customer order processing

FIGURE 8.4: Central subscriber

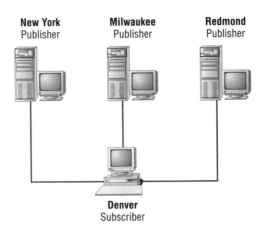

You need to keep several things in mind when you attempt to use this model. Because multiple publishers are writing to a single table in the database, you must take some precautions to ensure that referential integrity is maintained. What would happen if your New York office sends an order with a key of 1000 and your Milwaukee office also sends an order with a key of 1000? You would have two records with the same primary key in them. You could get bad data in your database as a primary key is used to guarantee a unique record. Only one of those records will post. To make sure this doesn't become a problem, implement a composite primary key. As part of that key, you should use the original order ID number along with a location-specific code. To expand on the example, you could give New York a location code of NY and give the Milwaukee branch a location code of MW. This way, the new composite keys would be NY1000 and MW1000.

Multiple Publishers of One Table

The model shown in Figure 8.5 is used when a single table needs to be maintained on multiple servers. Each server subscribes to the table and also publishes the table to other servers. This model can be particularly useful in the following business scenarios:

- Reservations systems

- Regional order-processing systems

- Multiple warehouse implementations

The same location code recommendations are advised for this model that were advised for the central subscriber scenario.

Exam Essentials

The exam stresses different replication scenarios and the business models to which they are best suited. Make sure you can recognize the different replication scenarios and match them up with a particular business situation.

FIGURE 8.5: Multiple publishers of one table

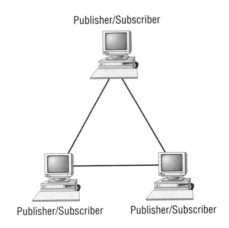

Publisher/Subscriber

Publisher/Subscriber   Publisher/Subscriber

Know the different replication scenarios and in what business situations they are most effective. Based on a particular business situation, you must choose the appropriate replication scenario. Remember that slow and expensive links are best suited to a publishing subscriber scenario. Roll-up reporting and a centralized warehouse strategy are best suited to the central subscriber scenario. Reservation systems can best be modeled with multiple publishers of one table. Finally, the central publisher scenario is useful to remove the impact of MIS usage from the OLTP environment.

Key Terms and Concepts

Distribution: The database that captures publication transactions and passes them along to subscription databases

Publisher: The database that is publishing transactions for use by subscription databases

Subscriber: The database that subscribes to the published information from the publishing database

Sample Questions

1. Which replication scenario is best suited to a business model in which a long-distance phone line is used to replicate data?

   A. Central subscriber

   B. Central publisher

   C. Publishing subscriber

   D. Central publisher with a remote distributor

   Answer: C is correct. This is an example of using a slow link.

2. Which replication scenario is best suited to a business model in which several different order processing systems need to send their orders to a warehouse for shipping?

   A. Central subscriber

   B. Central publisher

   C. Publishing subscriber

   D. Central publisher with a remote distributor

   Answer: A is correct. Remember that in the central subscriber scenario you should also include a location-specific component as part of the composite primary key. This helps ensure referential integrity.

3. Which replication scenario is "best" suited to a business model in which you have a high volume of traffic in your OLTP environment and you want to give your MIS department access to database information?

   A. Central subscriber

   B. Central publisher

   C. Publishing subscriber

   D. Central publisher with a remote distributor

   Answer: D is correct. Although you can use a central publisher scenario in this situation, removing the distribution process from the publishing server would be better because there is high volume of OLTP traffic.

Identify the functionality of dynamic backup.

This test objective is essentially a vocabulary word. You need to know what a dynamic backup is and a little bit about how a dynamic backup is accomplished.

Critical Information

SQL Server allows you to back up your databases dynamically (while they are in use), so that users can stay connected to the server while a backup is being run. When a database backup is started, SQL Server will first do a checkpoint of the database, thereby bringing the database up to date by copying all completed transactions from memory to the hard disks. SQL Server then "snapshots" the database and backs up the entire database. If users are trying to update pages, they will be temporarily blocked by SQL Server as it jumps from its current location to the pages the user wants to modify and quickly backs up those pages. Once they have been backed up, the dynamic backup returns to its current location and continues its backup process.

Any transactions that were not completed when the backup started will not be in the backup. They cannot be recovered if the database needs to be restored. Because of this, even though backups can be done during normal work hours, you will probably want to schedule some backups outside regular work hours. Then you will have a better idea of what is in the backup and what didn't make it to the backup.

NOTE Transactions that have not committed when the backup begins will be available for the next backup.

Exam Essentials

You must understand what makes a backup a dynamic backup.

Know what makes a dynamic backup "dynamic." Remember that a dynamic backup means that you can back up your database while the database is still in use. When the backup occurs it takes a snapshot of the database at that point in time. If other users are in the database and they attempt to change the data, the backup process will quickly back up the records that will be affected before they are changed and then continue the backup process normally.

Key Terms and Concepts

Snapshot: When you take a snapshot of a database, you are backing up information at that particular point in time. Any changes to the data that occur during the backup process will not be included. Only the data as it stands when the backup is initiated will become part of the backup.

Sample Questions

1. Which of the following are true about dynamic backups?

   A. All changes made to the data during the backup are included in the backup.

   B. No changes made to the data during the backup are included in the backup.

   C. The database can be in use during the backup process.

   D. The database cannot be in use during the backup process.

   Answer: B and C are correct. When you begin the backup process, you will get a snapshot of the data at that point in time. Any changes to the data during the backup will not be included in the backup; therefore, users can access the database while the backup process runs.

Identify how automatic recovery works.

This is a relatively straightforward process that you must know for the exam. In addition to understanding what automatic recovery is, you must also know what the "recovery flags" and "recovery interval" configuration options do.

Critical Information

Every time SQL Server is started, it runs automatic recovery. This feature is built into the SQL Server and cannot be disabled. Automatic recovery ensures that all transactions completed before a system crash are physically written to the database, and any uncommitted transactions are rolled back or removed from the database.

Basically, the automatic recovery checks each database's transaction log and looks for committed and uncommitted transactions. Committed transactions are rolled forward and uncommitted transactions are rolled back.

Automatic recovery recovers databases in the following order:

- Master
- Model
- Clear tempdb
- MSDB
- Pubs
- Distribution (if it exists)
- User databases

Two configuration options can be used to modify the behavior of automatic recovery:

Recovery flags: Determine what information SQL Server displays during recoveries. This flag allows you to turn on or turn off recovery messages. The default is off.

Recovery interval: Controls the maximum amount of time required to recover a database. If the time is exceeded, SQL Server will write a checkpoint to the log and continue processing.

You can change these using the sp_configure stored procedure or through the Configuration screens in SQL Enterprise Manager.

Exam Essentials

The automatic recovery process is essential to ensuring the integrity of your databases. You should know what the process accomplishes and the configuration options you can set.

Know what automatic recovery accomplishes. Remember that automatic recovery checks each databases transaction log and rolls forward committed transactions and rolls back uncommitted transactions. It does this in an orderly fashion beginning with the system databases and finishing with the user databases.

Remember what the automatic recovery configuration options accomplish. The two configuration options are recovery flags and recovery interval. The recovery flags allows you to specify whether or not you want to see messages during the recovery process. The recovery interval specifies the length of time the recovery process will run before SQL Server automatically checkpoints the database.

Key Terms and Concepts

Checkpoint: The mechanism by which SQL Server periodically writes modified data to a database. When a checkpoint is placed into a transaction log, all completed transactions residing in memory will be written to disk. Checkpoints run automatically in SQL Server; however, the SA or a DBO can force a checkpoint in a particular database.

Recovery flags: This configuration option allows you to specify whether or not you want to see messages during the automatic recovery process.

Recovery interval: A configuration option that allows you to specify the length of time recovery will continue before a checkpoint is written to a database.

Sample Questions

1. Which of the following are true about automatic recovery?

    A. Occurs every time SQL Server is started

    B. Will display recovery messages if the recovery flags option is set to true

    C. Can be disabled

    D. Begins with the system databases and then moves to the user databases

    Answer: A, B, and D are correct. You cannot disable automatic recovery.

Perform a database dump.

This exam objective focuses on the process involved in backing up a database. Several steps need to be taken to successfully back up your database.

Critical Information

When a database backup is started, SQL Server will first do a check-point of the database, thereby bringing the database up-to-date with all of the completed transactions. SQL Server then "snapshots" the database and backs up the entire database. If users are trying to update pages, they will be temporarily blocked by SQL Server, as it jumps ahead of the updates.

Any transactions that were not completed when the backup started will not be in the backup. Even though backups can be done during normal business hours, you will help to ensure a clean understanding of what is in the backup and what didn't make it to the backup by backing up databases at night.

In order to back up a database, you must perform several steps. The first step is to create a backup device. The second step is to back up your data. Use the DBCC commands to ensure your data integrity prior to backing up your data. These DBCC commands include the DBCC CHECKDB, DBCC NEWALLOC, and DBCC CHECKCATALOG.

You can use either the SQL Enterprise Manager or SQL to perform your backups.

Necessary Procedures

The exam focuses on the use of T-SQL to perform many of the tasks that you can use SQL Enterprise Manager for. Dumping a database is no exception. Here is the syntax required to dump a database:

```
DUMP <dbname> TO <device1> [,device2...] [WITH INIT]
```

As you can see from the syntax, you can dump a database to a single device or multiple devices. When you dump to multiple devices, you are performing a striped backup.

The WITH INIT keyword forces the device(s) being backed up to be initialized. Any data that is in those devices before the backup begins is removed. If you do not use the WITH INIT keyword, you can store multiple database dumps in the same dump device.

Exam Essentials

When you back up a database, you must back it up to a database dump device. You can accomplish this task by using the SQL Enterprise Manager or by using SQL statements. The exam focuses on the use of SQL statements.

Know the statements required to dump a database.   Remember that you use the DUMP statement to back up a database.

Key Terms and Concepts

DUMP: The DUMP command is used to back up a database to a dump device.

Sample Questions

1. Which of the following statements will back up a database called Frogger to the LilyPad backup device and make Frogger the only database in the backup device?

   A. BACKUP Frogger To LilyPad

   B. BACKUP TO LilyPad "Frogger" WITH INIT

   C. DUMP Frogger TO LilyPad WITH INIT

   D. DUMP TO LilyPad "Frogger"

   Answer: C is correct. The other choices will generate a syntax error.

Perform a striped backup.

This exam objective is more of a vocabulary word than an actual process. You must understand what a striped backup is.

Critical Information

The actual process of backing up the database is relatively straightforward. SQL Server allows a database to be backed up to a single device or to multiple devices. When you back up to multiple devices, you are performing a striped backup. If those devices can be accessed simultaneously (i.e., you have multiple hard disks or multiple tape drives), you are performing a *parallel striped backup*.

For example, a database that is backed up to tape may take an hour to back up. If there are three tape drives in the SQL Server box, and you simultaneously back up to all three devices, the backup would take approximately 20 minutes.

Another feature of striped backups is that they don't need to be restored simultaneously. In the previous example with three different tape devices, you could restore it onto a SQL Server that had only one tape drive. You would first restore Tape 1, then Tape 2, and then the last tape.

Necessary Procedures

To perform a striped backup, you must specify multiple backup devices when you perform your backup. You can accomplish this with the SQL Enterprise Manager, as well as through code. As with most topics on the exam, you must know how to perform these tasks using code.

Here is an example of using the DUMP statement to back up a database called Frogger to the backup devices LilyPad1, LilyPad2, and LilyPad3:

```
DUMP Frogger TO LilyPad1, LilyPad2, LilyPad3 WITH INIT
```

Frogger is the only database in those three dump devices.

Exam Essentials

Striped backups can greatly increase the speed at which your backup process occurs. Keep the following points in mind when you are studying for the exam.

Remember what a striped backup is. A striped backup occurs when you dump a database to multiple dump devices.

Key Terms and Concepts

Striped backup: A striped backup allows SQL Server to dump a database to multiple dump devices simultaneously. These dump devices can be on a local hard drive, a networked location, or even multiple tape devices.

Sample Questions

1. Which of the following statements will back up a database called Frogger to the LilyPad1 and LilyPad2 backup devices and make Frogger the only database in the backup devices?

   A. BACKUP Frogger To LilyPad1, LilyPad2

   B. BACKUP TO LilyPad1, LilyPad2 "Frogger" WITH INIT

   C. DUMP Frogger TO LilyPad1, LilyPad2 WITH INIT

   D. DUMP TO LilyPad1, LilyPad2 "Frogger"

   Answer: C is correct. The other choices will generate a syntax error.

Create a dump device.

Before you can dump a database, you must first create a dump device on which the database is to reside.

Critical Information

SQL Server backs up databases to an object called a backup or dump device. SQL has no built-in backup devices. You will need to create all of your backup devices and configure your backups in order to have databases that are backed up regularly.

WARNING Because SQL Server keeps the database devices (files) open while SQL Server is running, the databases aren't backed up during regular Windows NT backups. You need to configure SQL Server's backups because the default settings will not back up any of your databases! Once a backup has been made to a backup device, the device is closed and will be backed up normally during Windows NT backups.

You can use the Enterprise Manager or the *sp_addumpdevice* stored procedure to create your dump devices. You should be familiar with the sp_addumpdevice stored procedure for the exam.

You can create backup devices with the sp_addumpdevice command. The syntax for the command specifies the logical name for the device and the path to the file that will be created after the backup is completed.

One important feature of dump devices is that they do not have to be local. All other database devices must be located on the same machine where SQL Server is running. Dump devices can be located anywhere on your network.

NOTE A backup device is basically a pointer that SQL Server remembers so it knows where to put the backup file when the backup is actually done. Because of this, files are not created when a backup device is defined, but when the backup is actually performed. In addition, a dump device will automatically grow and shrink as needed.

Necessary Procedures

Use this sp_addumpdevice syntax to create your database dump devices anywhere on your network:

```
sp_addumpdevice 'type', 'logical name', 'path'
```

The type parameter specifies whether you are backing up to disk or tape. The 'logical name' is how you will refer to the device in SQL Server, and the 'path' is the path to the physical file where the device will be located.

You can follow these steps to create the LilyPad1, LilyPad2, and LilyPad3 dump devices:

1. Start ISQL/W.

2. Issue the command:

```
EXEC sp_addumpdevice
'disk', 'LilyPad1', 'C:\MSSQl\Backup\LilyPad1.bak'
EXEC sp_addumpdevice
'disk', 'LilyPad2', 'C:\MSSQL\Backup\LilyPad2.bak'
EXEC sp_addumpdevice
'disk', 'LilyPad3', 'C:\MSSQL\Backup\LilyPad3.bak'
```

3. The results returned should say 'Disk' device created.

Exam Essentials

You must first create a dump device before you can perform a backup. The exam focuses on the stored procedures necessary to do so.

Remember how to create a dump device using the sp_addump-device stored procedure. Use the sp_addumpdevice stored procedure to create a dump device. Unlike regular database devices, dump devices can be anywhere on your network, and they can grow and shrink automatically.

Key Terms and Concepts

Dump device: A dump device is used to store backups of databases and transactions logs. A dump device can store multiple database and log dumps in it.

Dynamic sizing: Dump devices are 0 bytes in length when they are first created. They automatically resize themselves as backup information is loaded into them.

Sample Questions

1. Which of the following statements will create a dump device called LilyPad on the computer named BKPServer?

A. sp_addumpdevice 'disk', 'LilyPad',
   '\\BKPServer\Dumps\LilyPad.bak'

B. sp_createdumpdevice 'disk', 'LilyPad',
   '\\BKPServer\Dumps\LilyPad.bak'

C. sp_addumpdevice 'LilyPad',
   '\\BKPServer\Dumps\LilyPad.bak'

D. sp_createdumpdevice 'LilyPad',
   '\\BKPServer\Dumps\LilyPad.bak'

Answer: A is correct. The other choices will generate a syntax error.

Dump a transaction log.

The transaction log for a database is a running total of all of the transactions that have occurred in that particular database. This test objective stresses your ability to dump a transaction log and to use various dump options in the appropriate situation.

Critical Information

One of the features of SQL Server is that the transaction log is truncated (cleaned out) only after a successful backup of the log. Many companies run SQL Server for two or three months with no problems until suddenly no new transactions can be recorded because the transaction log has filled up.

The good news is that the transaction log will be cleaned out by SQL Server as part of a normal transaction log backup. The bad news is that SQL Server doesn't do this by default. All backups (and thus the cleaning or truncating of the log) must be configured by the administrator.

Another advantage of backing up the transaction log is that it can be restored up to a certain point in time. For example, if you have a backup of the transaction log for Wednesday, and you discover a major error that occurred at 4:05, you can restore the data up to 4:00.

Necessary Procedures

The transaction log can be backed up by issuing a DUMP TRANSACTION statement. This command not only backs up the log, it also truncates it. Here is the syntax of the DUMP TRANSACTION statement:

```
DUMP TRANSACTION <db_name> to <device>
```

Various switches can be added to the command to change the way the backup works.

TRUNCATE_ONLY

This switch is used only to truncate (clean out) the log. This switch may be used if the database is backed up in its entirety every night. Maintaining a backup of the log would be redundant, yet the log still needs to be cleaned out.

NO_LOG

This switch can be used as a last resort. Normal backups of the log first make an entry to record that the log has been backed up, and then the log is cleared out. If the log is completely full, the record of the backup can't be made, so the backup fails, along with the truncating of the log. You should immediately back up the database after you use this command because there will be no record of the transactions since the last backup occurred.

NO_TRUNCATE

This switch does the opposite of the truncate_only switch—it backs up the log without truncating or cleaning it out. The main purpose for this switch is to make a new backup of the transaction log when the database itself is either too damaged to work or is completely gone.

Here are a couple of examples using the DUMP TRANSACTION commands. The first example will dump a log without cleaning it out:

```
DUMP TRANSACTION Frogger TO LilyPadLog WITH NO_TRUNCATE
```

This example will clean out the transaction log without saving it:

```
DUMP TRANSACTION Frogger TO LilyPadLog WITH
TRUNCATE_ONLY
```

Exam Essentials

Keep the following things in mind about using the DUMP TRANS-ACTION statements to back up a transaction log.

Remember what the NO_LOG option does and when to use it. The NO_LOG option is used with the DUMP TRANSACTION command to specify that the backup is to clean out the transaction log without logging the fact that it has just performed a backup. You should immediately back up the database after performing a non-logged operation such as this.

Remember what the NO_TRUNCATE option does and when to use it. The NO_TRUNCATE option is used with the DUMP TRANSACTION command to specify that the backup should not clean out the transaction log. You should use this option when your database has been corrupted, but the transaction log is still intact. This will allow you to restore your database, and then apply your "orphaned" transaction log. This will give you up-to-the-second recovery of your database.

Remember what the TRUNCATE_ONLY option does and when to use it. The TRUNCATE_ONLY option is used with the DUMP TRANSACTION command to specify that the backup is to clean out the transaction log without backing it up. This is useful in situations where you don't want to make a backup of the transaction log, but you want to clean it out. This command is useful in the database development stage.

Key Terms and Concepts

DUMP TRANSACTION: Used to dump a transaction log. Three specific options (TRUNCATE_ONLY, NO_TRUNCATE, and NO_LOG) affect what happens to the transaction log. Be sure that you are familiar with them and know when they are appropriate.

Sample Questions

1. Your database has been corrupted, but your transaction log is still intact. Which DUMP TRANSACTION option should you use to make a backup of your orphaned transaction log?

   A. NO_TRUNCATE

   B. TRUNCATE_ONLY

   C. NO_LOG

   D. BACKUP_ONLY

   Answer: A is correct. You can apply your transaction log to the restored database and then continue processing as normal.

2. You are currently developing a database and doing a lot of testing. Which of the following DUMP TRANSACTION options would you use to clear the transaction log without saving it?

   A. NO_TRUNCATE

   B. TRUNCATE_ONLY

   C. NO_LOG

   D. BACKUP_ONLY

   Answer: B is correct. The TRUNCATE_ONLY option will remove the inactive part of your transaction log without saving it.

3. You are receiving error messages stating that you can longer make changes to your database. The likely cause is that the transaction log has filled up. Which DUMP TRANSACTION option will clear the transaction log so that you can continue working?

   A. NO_TRUNCATE

   B. TRUNCATE_ONLY

   C. NO_LOG

   D. BACKUP_ONLY

   Answer: C is correct. Dumping a transaction log is a logged transaction. Because the log is full, you can't perform a logged dump. You should immediately make a backup of your database after you perform a nonlogged operation such as this.

Load a database dump.

This exam objective focuses not only on the LOAD statement, but on the process that must be performed before and after a load has occurred.

Critical Information

Restoring SQL databases requires several steps:

1. Find and fix the cause of the failure.

2. Drop all of the affected devices.

3. Drop all of the affected databases.

4. Re-create the affected devices.

5. Re-create the affected databases.

6. Set the database to single-user mode.

7. Restore the database from a database backup.

8. Restore (or reapply) the transaction log from a log backup.

9. Change the database from "DBO use only" mode.

Find and Fix the Cause of the Failure

This step involves troubleshooting NT and/or SQL Server to determine the cause of the failure. There are two basic reasons for determining the cause:

- To fix the problem

- To (hopefully) prevent it from happening in the future

Dropping the Affected Devices

After a hardware failure or corruption of a device, the device must be dropped before it can be re-created. The sp_dropdevice command or Enterprise Manager can be used to drop a device.

Dropping the Affected Databases

Before the database can be re-created, it must first be dropped. The normal procedure, sp_dropdatabase, expects to find the database before it drops it. This expectation can cause problems when the database is completely gone because the command will not execute properly. SQL Server 6.5 adds the DBCC DROPDB command that will drop the affected database even if the database is gone or corrupted beyond repair.

Re-create the Affected Devices

SQL Server tracks databases by the number of pages allocated on each device, and whether the pages are for data or the transaction log. Therefore, when you re-create devices to be used for the database, you need to make the devices as close to the originals as possible. For instance, if the original database is contained on the payroll.dat device file with a size of 100MB and on the device called payroll2.dat with a size of 150MB and the log is contained on payroll_log.dat with a size of 50MB, you should re-create these three devices with the same sizes.

You may want to use the "Create for Load" option when you make your devices. Initializing the devices will be faster, and the devices can be used only to load backups. After the loading is complete, the database will be marked for "DBO use only" until you change it.

Re-create the Affected Databases

For the backup to be restored to the exact condition it was in, you need to re-create the database with the same devices and sizes that were originally used.

Set the Database to Single-User Mode

SQL Server requires the database to be in single-user mode before a restoration can take place. If you use Enterprise Manager, this is done automatically. If you use T-SQL commands to restore the database, you will need to set the option manually. The command is:

```
sp_dboption 'single user', TRUE
```

Restore the Database

Enterprise Manager can be used to quickly restore databases. Simply highlight the database to be restored, choose the backup, and choose to restore. For the exam, however, you must be able to recognize the LOAD statements.

To load a database called Frogger from dump device LilyPad1 and LilyPad2, run the following code:

```
LOAD DATABASE Frogger FROM LilyPad1, LilyPad2
```

Remember that you must first put the database into single-user mode. Once your load has completed, your database will be in DBO-use-only mode. You should run the sp_dboption stored procedure again to disable this option.

Exam Essentials

As a database administrator, you must be able to restore a database. A database may need to be restored for numerous reasons. The exam stresses the LOAD statement and tests your knowledge of what must take place before a load can occur.

Remember the LOAD statement.   The LOAD DATABASE statement is used to load a database from one or more dump devices.

Remember the database options required for a load.   Your database must be in single-user only mode before you perform a load. Once the load has completed, your database will be in DBO-use-only mode. You should disable this option so that other users can again access the newly restored database.

Remember the rules. A corrupted database must be dropped along with all affected devices before a restoration can occur. When you re-create your devices and databases, it is imperative that you re-create them in the same order and with the same sizes as you initially created the database. You must then alter the databases in the same size and manner as well. If you don't, there is no guarantee that your backup will restore properly.

Key Terms and Concepts

DBO use only: This option will be set after you perform a restoration of your database. You should turn this option off to allow users access to the newly restored database.

Sequence is important: Remember that the sequence in which you created your devices and databases (as well as how you expanded them) is critical to ensuring a valid restoration. You must re-create all of your affected devices and databases in the same order that you initially created them to ensure a valid recovery.

Sample Questions

1. Which statement will load a database named Frogger from the LilyPad backup device?

   A. LOAD Frogger FROM LilyPad

   B. LOAD DATABASE Frogger FROM LilyPad

   C. LOAD Frogger, LilyPad

   D. LOAD DATABASE Frogger, LilyPad

   Answer: B is correct. The other three choices will generate syntax errors.

CHAPTER

9

Replication

Microsoft Exam Objectives Covered in This Chapter:

▶ **Identify prerequisites for replication.** *(pages 284 – 287)*

▶ **Configure the servers used for setting up replication.** *(pages 288 – 289)*

▶ **Set up various replication scenarios.** *(pages 290 – 295)*

▶ **Implement replication.** *(pages 295 – 296)*

▶ **Schedule a replication event.** *(pages 297 – 299)*

▶ **Recognize the situations in which you must perform manual synchronization.** *(pages 300 – 301)*

▶ **Identify the system tables that are used in replication.** *(pages 301 – 302)*

▶ **Resolve setup problems.** *(pages 303 – 304)*

▶ **Resolve fault-tolerance problems and recovery problems.** *(pages 304 – 309)*

The objectives for this portion of the exam are designed to test your ability to work with the replication features available in SQL Server 6.5. These topics are stressed heavily on the exam. If you decide to "overkill on the studying" in any particular area, make it replication.

Identify prerequisites for replication.

This exam objective covers exactly what it says. It covers the hardware and software requirements necessary to implement replication.

Critical Information

Several requirements must be met in order to make replication work. They are:

- The publishing server must have at least 8MB of RAM dedicated to SQL Server.

- The subscribing server must have at least 8MB of RAM dedicated to SQL Server.

- The distribution server must have at least 16MB of RAM dedicated to SQL server.

- All servers must be registered in Enterprise Manager on the computer where replication will be set up. The servers can be registered during the installation and configuration of publishing.

- The publishing server must be SQL Server version 6.0 or later, although version 6.5 is highly recommended.

- The subscribing servers must be ODBC-compliant. (Compatible servers include SQL Server, Access, Oracle, and DB2.)

- The tables to be published must have a primary key in place.

- SQL Executive must be configured and running on the publication and distribution servers.

- The distribution server must have a new database created for the sole purpose of tracking replication. The default name of the database is Distribution, although any name can be chosen.

- Because the SQL Executive makes secured connections between SQL Servers, either named pipes or multi-protocol support must be installed (to enable a trusted connection).

- System databases (Master, Model, tempdb, MSDB) cannot be replicated; only user databases can.

- SA rights are required to set up replication.

Exam Essentials

Replication plays a major role on the exam. You should know all of the replication scenarios presented in Chapter 8 (and when to use them), as well as all of the topics covered in this chapter.

Know the minimum amounts of RAM necessary to run replication for each database.   Both the publishing server and subscription server must have at least 8MB of RAM allocated for SQL Server. The distribution server must have at least 16MB of RAM allocated for SQL Server. The distribution database can be located on the publishing server, the subscription server, or on its own separate SQL Server.

Know which types of machines can use replication.   The publishing and distribution servers must be Microsoft SQL Servers, but the subscription servers can be Microsoft SQL Servers or an ODBC database (like Access, Oracle, and DB2).

Remember the attributes necessary to publish information.   The information to be published must contain a primary key.

Know what the ramifications of replication are on the SQL Executive service.   The SQL Executive service controls and operates replication. Because the SQL Executive needs to have a trusted connection to the different servers, you must have named pipes or multiprotocol installed.

Key Terms and Concepts

Publisher/subscriber metaphor: Replication uses a publisher/subscriber metaphor. One server publishes information. There is a store-and-forward service called *distribution*. You also have subscribers who receive the replicated information. This is similar to a newspaper in which a paper is published and sent to a delivery person who delivers it to you, the subscriber.

Sample Questions

1. Which of the following are true of replication?

   A. The publishing server must have at least 16MB of RAM dedicated to SQL Server.

   B. The subscription server must have at least 8MB of RAM dedicated to SQL Server.

   C. The distribution server must have at least 8MB of RAM dedicated to SQL Server.

   D. The distribution server must have at least 16MB of RAM dedicated to SQL Server.

   Answer: B and D are correct. Publishing and subscription servers require only 8MB of RAM to be dedicated, while the distribution server must have 16MB.

2. Which of the following servers can publish data?

   A. Microsoft SQL Server 6.0

   B. Microsoft SQL Server 6.5

   C. Microsoft Access through ODBC

   D. Oracle through ODBC

   Answer: A and B are correct. The publishing server must be a Windows NT-based machine running SQL Server 6.0 or later. Any of the choices could be subscribers.

3. The SQL Executive service operates replication and needs to use trusted connections in order to accomplish its tasks. Which of the following must be true?

   A. You must be running IPX/SPX protocol.

   B. You must be running TCP/IP protocol.

   C. You must be running named pipes and/or multi-protocol.

   D. None of the above.

   Answer: C is correct. In order to establish a trusted connection, you must be running either named pipes or multi-protocol.

▶ Configure the servers used for setting up replication.

This test objective examines the necessary setup of your servers before replication can begin.

Critical Information

The main thing you need to remember here is that the SQL Executive service will use trusted connections to perform replication tasks. This means that your servers must be configured to use integrated security (or mixed). To use integrated security, you must have the named pipes and/or multi-protocol installed.

To avoid possible conflicts with passwords and security, Microsoft suggests that you create a single SQL Executive account on a central server and then have all SQL Servers in the enterprise use that single SQL Executive account.

Refer to Chapter 1 for information on how to configure your security options.

Exam Essentials

Before replication can begin, the SQL Executive service must be able to access all servers involved through a trusted connection. Trusted connections in SQL Server require named pipes and/or multi-protocol to be installed.

Remember that the SQL Executive uses trusted connections.
The SQL Executive service controls and operates replication. Because
the SQL Executive needs to have a trusted connection to the different
servers, you must have named pipes and/or multi-protocol installed,
as well as integrated or mixed security.

Key Terms and Concepts

Trusted connection: In order to use a trusted connection in SQL
Server, either named pipes or multi-protocol must be installed. In
a trusted connection, NT Server validates the user accounts rather
than the SQL Server. You must also have the integrated security
option set.

Sample Questions

1. Which of the following are true about the SQL Executive service?

   A. You can use the SQL Executive account across multiple
   servers in the enterprise.

   B. You cannot use the SQL Executive account across multiple
   servers in the enterprise.

   C. The SQL Executive account requires integrated or mixed security to accomplish replication.

   D. The SQL Executive account can use only standard security to
   accomplish replication.

   Answer: A and C are correct. Microsoft suggests that you use a
   single SQL Executive account for your SQL Servers. Replication
   requires trusted connections, which in turn means integrated security, which in turn means that named pipes and/or multi-protocol
   must be installed.

Set up various replication scenarios.

This exam objective is a reiteration of the scenarios discussed in Chapter 8. You should take a second look at the scenarios presented. Pay attention to where the distribution database is located.

Critical Information

Let's quickly revisit the replication models.

In the central publisher scenario shown in Figure 9.1, notice that the distribution database is on the publication server. The publishing database is doing all of the regular work of a database, and it is also using valuable CPU cycles to maintain the distribution database.

FIGURE 9.1: Central publisher model

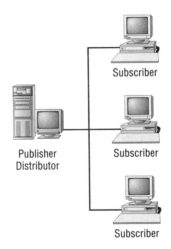

Subscriber

Publisher
Distributor

Subscriber

Subscriber

In the scenario shown in Figure 9.2, the distribution database's impact on the publishing server is reduced. This gives the publishing server more CPU cycles and memory resources.

F I G U R E 9.2: Central publisher with a remote distributor

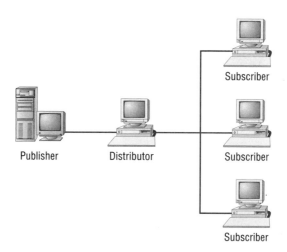

In the publishing subscriber scenario in Figure 9.3, the problems of low bandwidth are alleviated. This configuration is ideal for situations in which there is an expensive or slow communications link.

In the central subscriber scenario in Figure 9.4, satellite offices perform roll-up reporting. Notice that there are multiple publishers and only a single subscriber. Keep in mind that you should use some type of location code as part of your primary key to ensure referential integrity.

Finally, information is replicated in both directions in the multiple publishers of one table scenario depicted in Figure 9.5. Each machine acts as both a publisher and a subscriber. You should use location codes here as well.

FIGURE 9.3: Publishing subscriber

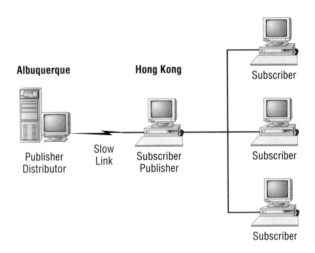

FIGURE 9.4: Central subscriber

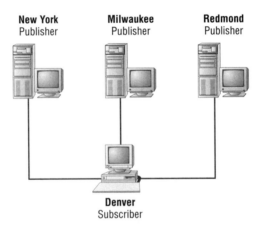

FIGURE 9.5: Multiple publishers of one table

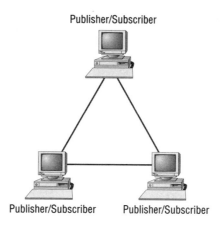

Publisher/Subscriber

Publisher/Subscriber   Publisher/Subscriber

Exam Essentials

The exam stresses the different replication scenarios and the business models for which they are best suited. Make sure that you can recognize the different replication scenarios and match them up with a particular business situation.

Know the different replication scenarios and in what business situations they are most effective. Based on a particular business situation, you must choose the appropriate replication scenario. Remember that slow and expensive links are best suited to a publishing subscriber scenario. Roll-up reporting and centralized warehouse strategies are best suited to the central subscriber scenario. Reservation systems can best be modeled with multiple publishers of one table. The central publisher scenario is useful to remove the impact of MIS usage from the OLTP environment.

Key Terms and Concepts

Replication: Replication uses a publisher/subscriber metaphor to send specific pieces of data (called *articles*) to various subscribers of the information. You should consider the data sent to a subscriber as read-only because the information will not be sent back to the publisher if it is modified. Do not mark the database as read-only; this will not allow replicated articles to be inserted on the subscription databases.

Sample Questions

1. Which replication scenario is best suited to a business model in which a long-distance phone line is used to replicate data?

   A. Central subscriber

   B. Central publisher

   C. Publishing subscriber

   D. Central publisher with a remote distributor

   Answer: C is correct. This is an example of using a slow link.

2. Which replication scenario is best suited to a business model in which several different order processing systems need to send their orders to a warehouse for shipping?

   A. Central subscriber

   B. Central publisher

   C. Publishing subscriber

   D. Central publisher with a remote distributor

   Answer: A is correct. Remember that in the central subscriber scenario you should also include a location-specific component as part of the composite primary key. This is done to help ensure referential integrity.

3. Which replication scenario is "best" suited to a business model in which you have an extreme amount of traffic in your OLTP environment and you want to give your MIS department access to database information?

   A. Central subscriber

   B. Central publisher

   C. Publishing subscriber

   D. Central publisher with a remote distributor

   Answer: D is correct. Although you can use a central publisher scenario in this situation, removing the distribution process from the publishing server would be better because there is heavy OLTP traffic.

Implement replication.

This objective tests your familiarity with the different steps involved in implementing replication.

Critical Information

You should follow these steps to implement replication on your system.

1. Decide on a replication model.

2. Choose a distribution server (local or remote) as per the model.

3. Register all SQL Server machines in the Enterprise Manager or create ODBC definitions (for non-SQL Server subscribers).

4. Install named pipes and/or multi-protocol, and set the security to integrated or mixed.

5. Install and configure publishing support (one-time installation).

6. Create publications and articles (ongoing).

7. Subscribe to the articles and publications.

Exam Essentials

You should be familiar with the steps involved to implement replication.

Remember the steps needed to implement replication. Basically, decide on a model, register computers, ensure trusted connections, install publishing, publish information, and subscribe.

Key Terms and Concepts

Design: As with most things, a database's *design* is the most important component for success. Make sure you spend some time deciding on the proper design for your replication needs.

Sample Questions

1. Which of the following are steps used in the setup of replication?

   A. Decide on a replication model

   B. Install standard security

   C. Install TCP/IP protocol

   D. Install Publishing

   Answer: A and D are correct. Replication requires integrated or mixed security. The TCP/IP protocol is not necessary to implement integrated security, but named pipes or multi-protocol is.

Schedule a replication event.

This objective focuses on your ability to use the Enterprise Manager to schedule a replication event.

Critical Information

By default, data will be published continuously, in batches of no more than 100 transactions. Using the Enterprise Manager, you can schedule data to be published every x number of minutes so that you can publish at your convenience.

Necessary Procedures

Use the following steps to schedule a replication event. This procedure assumes that you have already created some publications and articles.

1. From the Enterprise Manager, select Manage ➤ Replication ➤ Publications. The Manage Publications window will appear.

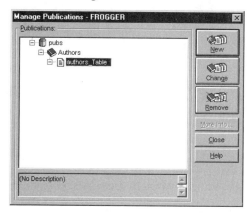

2. Double-click on an article in the publishing screen. You should see the Edit Publications dialog box.

3. Click the Synchronization tab.

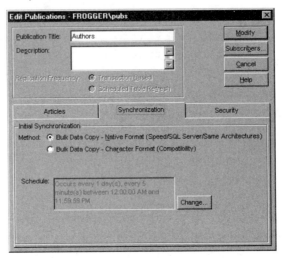

4. Click the Change button next to the schedule box. This will open the Task Schedule box.

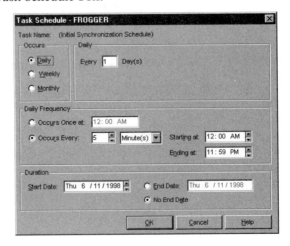

5. Make your changes in the task scheduler, and then click OK.

6. Click Modify in the Edit Publication windows.

7. Close the Manage Publications dialog box.

Exam Essentials

You can schedule replication to run continuously or on a custom schedule that you devise.

Remember that you can schedule replication tasks. To schedule a replication task, you must work with the Synchronization tab in the Edit Publications dialog box.

Key Terms and Concepts

Scheduling: The task scheduler is an extremely valuable tool that allows you to proactively administer your database system. With it, you can schedule replication tasks, create tasks to automatically back up databases, clear transaction logs, and perform many other administrative tasks.

Sample Questions

1. Which of the following is true about replication?

A. You can schedule a replication task to fire automatically at a predetermined interval.

B. You can schedule a subscriber to replicate information back to the distributor.

C. Replication can be used to perform database backups.

D. Replication can be forced every 100 transactions.

Answer: A and D are correct. Replication can be scheduled to fire whenever you want. Replication events fire every 100 transactions by default. However, this option can be modified.

Recognize the situations in which you must perform manual synchronization.

This topic focuses on your ability to recognize situations in which a manual synchronization must be performed rather than letting scheduled transactions be applied.

Critical Information

There are not many situations in which you must perform a manual synchronization. A synchronization process copies the data and schema from the publishing database to the subscription database.

Synchronization needs to be performed for every publication and applies to new subscribers only. You may want to perform a manual synchronization when there are extremely large tables to be synchronized or when you are working over a slow and expensive link.

Exam Essentials

Manual synchronization is a user-initiated process. Keep the following point in mind when you are studying for the exam.

Know when to use manual synchronization. Remember that manual synchronization can be beneficial when you have a slow and expensive link, or when the tables to be synchronized are very large.

Key Terms and Concepts

Manual synchronization: Manual synchronization is beneficial when you have a slow and expensive link or when the tables to be synchronized are very large. You can implement a manual synchronization through the replication screen in Enterprise Manager, or you can apply a current database backup to your subscription database.

Sample Questions

1. Which of the following are good reasons to manually synchronize a table?

    A. When you are applying a backup to the subscription tables

    B. When you are subscribing over a slow link

    C. When the tables are very large

    D. When the tables are very small

    Answer: B and C are correct. If you apply a backup to the subscription tables, you may not need to perform a synchronization.

Identify the system tables that are used in replication.

This exam objective is a simple matter of memorization. You must know which tables are on which server.

Critical Information

Table 9.1 lists the servers and the tables in each of them. Remember that any table beginning with "sys" is a publication table. Remember that mslast_job_info is the *only* table on the subscriber. Everything else is a distribution table.

TABLE 9.1: Tables Used for Replication and Their Locations

Publishing	Distribution	Subscription
syspublications	msjobs	mslast_job_info
syssubscriptions	msjob_commands	
sysarticles	mssubscriber_jobs	

Exam Essentials

These types of questions are almost "gimmes" on the exam. Make sure you memorize the items in Table 9.1.

Know which tables are in which database.   Remember that if it begins with "sys," it is a publishing table. If it's mslast_job_info, it's the subscription table. Everything else is a distribution table.

Key Terms and Concepts

Replication tables: Replication tables are used by SQL Server to track replicated information, when it is to be replicated, where it is to be replicated, and if the replication is successful.

Sample Questions

1. Which of the following are tables in the publication database?

A. syssubscriptions

B. mssubscriber_jobs

C. syspublishers

D. msjobs

Answer: A and C are correct.

Resolve setup problems.

This topic is very similar to the prerequisites topic. If you have the prerequisites, then replication should work.

Critical Information

If replication doesn't work initially, you should check all of your prerequisites and ensure that everything has been set up correctly. This includes named pipes and/or multi-protocol, integrated security, SQL Executive account, all SQL Servers, and minimum RAM requirements.

Exam Essentials

Replication setup problems stem from incorrect configurations. Make sure that the prerequisites listed earlier in this chapter are all met.

Remember the replication prerequisites.   Ensure that you have configured your SQL Server properly before you attempt to use replication.

Key Terms and Concepts

Integrated security: Replication requires integrated security to be installed. Integrated security forces Windows NT to authenticate users rather than SQL Server.

Sample Questions

1. Which of the following would you check when troubleshooting replication?

   A. Security settings

   B. SQL Server Net-Libraries (protocols installed)

   C. SQL Executive account

   D. SQL Executive service is running

Answer: A, B, C, and D are correct. You can check all of these things while troubleshooting replication.

Resolve fault-tolerance problems and recovery problems.

This topic covers several essential areas of replication troubleshooting. This topic is also stressed on the exam.

Critical Information

Several different things can go wrong with replication. The sources for potential problems are in the logreader process and in the distribution process. Let's look at a couple of scenarios and then see how to troubleshoot them.

No Subscribers Are Receiving Transactions

If no subscribers are receiving transactions, it is unlikely that the distribution process is corrupted because none of the subscribers are receiving changes. It is much more likely that the logreader process is not working properly.

First, you need to determine whether or not the logreader or the distribution process is failing. The easiest way to check this is to look at the command column in the msjob_commands table, which is stored in the Distribution database. As SA, you can run the following Transact-SQL commands using the Distribution database:

```
SELECT command
FROM MSjob_commands
```

If no transactions are stored here, you know the problem exists with the logreader process. If transactions are stored here, you know that the distribution task has errors. If a logreader or distribution task does not appear to be running, you should edit the scheduling information for that particular task.

One Subscriber of Many Is Not Receiving Changes

If only one subscriber is not receiving the changes and others are receiving the changes, you know that the logreader process is working properly. Check for the following problems:

- The distribution process for that particular subscriber is not working properly.

- The subscribing database is unavailable (because it is in DBO Use Only mode, in single-user mode, marked suspect, or for some other reason).

- The subscribing server is unavailable (because it is shut down, in single-user mode, or for some other reason).

- The replication login ID has been removed from the subscribing server.

- The distribution task is waiting for a manual synchronization event.

Initial Synchronization Jobs Not Applied to the Subscriber

If initial synchronization jobs are not being applied to the subscribing database, it is likely that either the synchronization task or distribution task is failing. Check the command column of the msjob_commands table to determine whether or not Sync commands have been stored there. If no Sync commands are stored there, you know the synchronization process is failing; otherwise, the distribution process is failing.

If the logreader or distribution tasks do not appear to be running, you should edit the scheduling information for that particular task.

Replication Recovery Problems

Due to its replication design, SQL Server can normally recover automatically after a disaster. However, there are a few considerations to keep in mind regarding the publishing server, distribution server, and the subscribing servers.

Publishing Server Recovery

The distribution server keeps a pointer to mark where it stops when reading a published database. The marker makes recovery simple if the publishing server is offline for some reason. When the publishing database is online again, the logreader will continue where it left off.

If the publishing database is rebuilt and reloaded from backups, you should resynchronize with the subscribers.

Distribution Server Recovery

Distribution servers keep track of where they stop replicating to the subscribers. When a distribution server is offline and then comes back online, it will continue processing where it left off. You should have a coordinated backup scheme to guarantee that distribution server backups match up with publishing server backups. In this way, information from the logreader process will be synchronized and automatic recovery can take place.

If the synchronization fails for some reason (you restore an old backup of the distribution database and the logreader pointers are off), the logreader process will log errors. The easiest way to fix this problem is to unsubscribe the subscribers and then resubscribe and resynchronize.

Subscribing Server Recovery

Subscribing servers are the easiest of the three servers to recover. Because transactions are stored in the Distribution database, when the subscribing server comes back online, the stored transactions will be processed.

If the subscribing server is down for an extended period of time, you don't want the transactions stored in the Distribution database to age out and, therefore, not be applied. To help ensure that aging does not take place, you can disable the scheduled cleanup task associated with the subscriber in the Distribution database.

In the event you must restore a subscribing database and the transactions have aged out from the distributor, it is easiest to just resynchronize the databases.

Exam Essentials

You should keep the following things in mind regarding replication troubleshooting.

Remember that most replication problems stem from the logreader process or the distribution process.   You should use the Manage Scheduled Tasks window as your first line of inquiry into potential problems.

Know what to look for when a problem occurs and what you can do about it.   What to look for is very dependent upon what scenario is in place. For example, all of your subscribers are receiving replication normally except one. What is most likely the problem? Answer: Well, the logreader is working because everyone else is receiving correctly, so it must be a problem with the distribution process or the subscription server.

Key Terms and Concepts

Troubleshooting: Troubleshooting is an art form. You need to practice in order to get better at it. Replication troubleshooting is no exception. A good understanding of what is supposed to be happening will allow you to do a better job of troubleshooting. Keep the previous items in mind when troubleshooting your systems.

Sample Questions

1. If no subscribers are receiving replicated transactions, what is probably the problem?

   A. The logreader process is dead.

   B. The distribution is dead.

   C. The subscription process is dead.

   D. The problem is internal to SQL Server and has nothing to do with replication.

   Answer: A is correct. The logreader process is the most likely candidate because no machine is receiving. If the logreader were working properly, then you might go after the distribution process.

2. If only one subscriber of many suddenly quits receiving replication transactions, what is the most likely problem?

   A. The logreader process.

   B. The distribution process.

   C. The subscription process.

   D. The problem is internal to SQL Server and has nothing to do with replication.

   Answer: B is correct. Because the other subscribers are receiving, your problem is with the distribution process or the individual subscriber.

3. If you are having problems with replication, where is the easiest location to begin gathering information to troubleshoot the problem?

  A. The Manage Alerts window

  B. The Current Activity window

  C. The Publication window

  D. The Manage Tasks window

  Answer: D is correct. You can check in the Tasks window to be sure that the replication tasks are being performed on a regular basis and no errors are occurring.

CHAPTER

10

Connectivity and
Network Support

▶ **Set up support for network clients by using various network protocols.** *(pages 312 – 316)*

▶ **Install an extended stored procedure.** *(pages 316 – 318)*

The objectives for this portion of the exam focus on your ability to support network clients and add functionality to your SQL Server in the form of extended stored procedures.

Set up support for network clients by using various network protocols.

This exam objective focuses on knowing how to install additional network protocols for client support.

Critical Information

You can use the SQL Client Configuration Utility to configure client network libraries and to report on which version of the DB Library the client is using. You must match up your client protocols and libraries with those that are supported by your SQL Server.

Necessary Procedures

To use the SQL Client Configuration Utility, select Start ➤ Programs ➤ Microsoft SQL Server 6.5 ➤ SQL Client Configuration Utility. This window has three tabs with the following options:

- DB Library options

- Net Library options
- Advanced options

DB Library Options

The DBLibrary tab (shown in Figure 10.1) offers only two DB Library Configuration options:

Automatic ANSI to OEM: Automatically converts ANSI characters to OEM characters. Although most clients will use the ANSI character set, there are some that will use their own OEM character sets.

Use International Settings: Allows your client to take advantage of international settings. This option includes support for the money datatype and date/time datatypes.

The Version Statistics section reports the DB Library version, DB DLL version, location, date, and size.

F I G U R E 10.1: The DBLibrary tab in the SQL Server Client Configuration Utility window

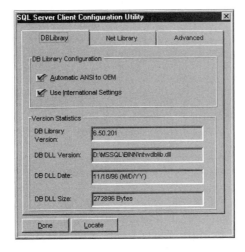

Net Library Options

The Net Library tab (shown in Figure 10.2) displays the current default network library configuration. In the figure, you can see that Named Pipes is listed as the Default Network. The network libraries on both the client and server must match for them to communicate. The Version Statistics section reports the Net Library version, location, date, and size.

FIGURE 10.2: The Net Library tab in the SQL Server Client Configuration Utility window

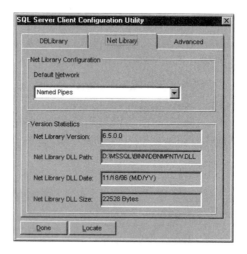

Advanced Options

In the Advanced tab, you can add new libraries to your client's configuration. This option allows you to set up support for various network protocols for your network clients.

To make modifications to your client configuration, you need to add information into the Client Configuration section. You can specify a server (your client machine) and the DLL you want to load. In the example shown in Figure 10.3, the computer name is Gizmo, the DLL name is Named Pipes, and the Connection String field is left blank. If you need remote connections, you can enter a login string with your user ID and password in this field.

F I G U R E 10.3: Adding client configuration information to the Advanced tab in the SQL Server Client Configuration Utility window

If you do not know where the DLL you want to use is stored, click the Locate button. This brings up the Locate Libraries dialog box, which lists where your network and database libraries are located on that machine.

When you are finished filling in the information, click the Add/Modify button. Your new library will now be listed in the Current Entries field.

Exam Essentials

The main issue here is not "how to install the libraries." The main issue is "picking the correct libraries and determining the most appropriate tool to do it."

Know why you use the SQL Client Configuration Utility. Use this utility to report and to modify network library settings for an individual client. Your client and server need to use the same net-library in order to communicate.

Key Terms and Concepts

Network Library: Installing the appropriate network library is imperative for clients who want to communicate with the SQL Server. Both the SQL Server and the client must be using the same protocols in order to communicate.

Sample Questions

1. The SQL Client Configuration Utility can be used to do which of the following?

   A. Add network libraries

   B. Add database libraries

   C. Configure languages

   D. Rebuild the Master database

Answer: A and B are correct. To configure languages or rebuild the master database, you should use the SQL Setup Utility.

Install an extended stored procedure.

This test objective focuses both on what an extended stored procedure is and how you install it on your SQL Server.

Critical Information

Extended stored procedures are generally created in C or C++ and then compiled into a DLL file. You should then place the DLL in the same folder as the stored procedure sp_addextendedproc, which registers the function with the function and name of the DLL. The information will be stored in the *syscomments* and *sysobjects* tables as an extended stored procedure, with X as the object type. You must do this for each extended stored procedure within the DLL.

Necessary Procedures

In this example, if you have an extended procedure DLL called FROGGER.DLL, which has a function called Leap in it, you would execute the following stored procedure to register and install the extended procedure:

```
EXEC sp_addextendedproc 'Leap', 'FROGGER.DLL'
```

Exam Essentials

Extended stored procedures can greatly enhance the functionality of your database. Keep these things in mind when you are dealing with extended stored procedures.

Remember that only the SA can register an XP.   Only the SA has permission to register an extended stored procedure. The XP resides outside of SQL Server and, as you recall, anything that passes outside of SQL Server is the domain of the SA.

Know how extended stored procedures are stored.   Extended stored procedures are stored as functions in a DLL.

Key Terms and Concepts

Extended stored procedure: An extended stored procedure is a function in a DLL that has been mapped into SQL Server. This allows SQL Server to implement functionality that cannot be programmed directly into the server itself. For example, xp_sendmail is a popular stored procedure which will generate e-mail from SQL Server.

Sample Questions

1. Which of the following accurately installs an extended stored procedure called Swim from the FROGGER DLL file?

   A. EXEC sp_addextendedproc 'Swim', 'FROGGER.DLL'

   B. EXEC sp_addextendedproc 'FROGGER.DLL', 'Swim'

   C. EXEC xp_addextproc 'Swim', 'FROGGER.DLL'

   D. EXEC xp_addextproc 'FROGGER.DLL', 'Swim'

Answer: A is the correct answer. All other choices will generate a syntax error. You must also be the SA in order to run this command.

CHAPTER

11

Tuning and Monitoring

Microsoft Exam Objectives Covered in This Chapter:

▶ **Identify the benefits of installing the tempdb database in RAM.** *(pages 320 – 324)*

▶ **Configure the number of worker threads.** *(pages 325 – 327)*

▶ **Select the appropriate settings for read ahead.** *(pages 327 – 329)*

▶ **Select the appropriate settings for locks.** *(pages 329 – 332)*

▶ **Monitor log size.** *(pages 333 – 336)*

▶ **Tune and monitor physical and logical I/O.** *(pages 336 – 342)*

▶ **Tune and monitor memory use.** *(pages 342 – 344)*

▶ **Set database options.** *(pages 344 – 348)*

▶ **Update statistics.** *(pages 349 – 352)*

The objectives for this portion of the exam cover your ability to monitor and tune your SQL Server. You must be able to work with tempdb, worker threads, read-ahead settings, and locks. You must also be familiar with monitoring input and output and memory usage.

Identify the benefits of installing the tempdb database in RAM.

This exam objective focuses on your ability to identify the benefits and potential disadvantages of installing tempdb in RAM.

Critical Information

During installation of SQL Server 6.5, the tempdb database is created on the Master device with a size of 2MB. There is only one tempdb database on the server, and it is shared by all the other databases on the server. Without tempdb, many of the most basic functions of SQL Server would not be possible. Tempdb has three major functions:

- Storing interim results from system functions

- Storing user-created temporary data sets

- Maintaining pointers and overhead for server-side cursors

Tempdb can sometimes be one of the biggest mysteries of SQL Server tuning. The tempdb size you need and its location will depend on a number of factors including:

- The developer's use of explicitly created temporary tables

- Lack of proper indexing on tables (which forces the system to create worktables in tempdb)

- The number of server-side cursors used

- The number of users accessing the server

Two megabytes is rarely enough tempdb space to accommodate your users' needs, especially if you have a large number of users or an application that is written to be tempdb-intensive. If you need to increase tempdb size while tempdb is located in the Master device, you have three primary options.

- You can expand the Master device and increase the size of tempdb in that location.

- You can also create a new device for tempdb and move tempdb to the new device.

- Your last option is to use RAM to house your tempdb.

Although the last option looks very attractive at first, placing tempdb in RAM has benefits and dangers all of its own. Let's take a closer look at these benefits and dangers.

Many application developers use temporary tables to store result sets, lookup tables, intermediate results, and other critical data. It should be obvious that the speed of access to this data is critical to the performance of the application. One way you can speed up this access is to place your tempdb device on the fastest physical disk; however, another way is to place the tempdb database in RAM. This configuration can be set by using the Enterprise Manager Server Configurations window or using the stored procedure *sp_configure*.

The benefits can be significant. If temporary data is accessed from RAM rather than disk, it can be retrieved much faster. In addition, temporary tables can be created as global objects, giving them the ability to service multiple connections. If the performance benefit can be so astounding, then why not make this a standard priority when configuring a server? Unfortunately it is not that simple. As with most performance tuning actions, there is an equally negative reaction. In this case, the downside is memory starvation.

WARNING   When placing tempdb in RAM, the memory that you are requesting is not taken from the preallocated memory reserved for SQL Server that was set from the "memory" configuration option. The memory given to tempdb in RAM is taken from what you have left for Windows NT. If you are not careful when placing tempdb in RAM, you can starve the OS and perhaps even prevent the SQL Server from starting due to insufficient memory.

When tempdb is placed in RAM, it indirectly affects the size of the data cache. If you want to place tempdb in RAM without adding more memory to the computer, you must reduce the amount of memory allocated to SQL Server so that your operating system is not starved for memory resources. Reducing allocated memory will directly affect both procedure and data caching; however, data caching will take the majority of the hit. This can bring your server down to a crawl if there is not enough memory to cache the data so that it can be effectively accessed in RAM, rather than from disk.

Microsoft recommends that your system have at least 64–128MB of RAM before you place tempdb in RAM. However, the amount of memory in the computer is irrelevant. What really matters is how that memory is being used. Because tempdb cannot be split between RAM and disk, your RAM device must be large enough to satisfy your entire tempdb needs. Again, these needs depend on the number of users and how the applications are written.

If you have enough memory in your computer to place a fully functioning tempdb in RAM and also have enough data cache to provide buffers for all of your frequently accessed data, then placing tempdb in RAM may be a good move. On the other hand, given a choice between a RAM-resident tempdb and more data cache, the cache will usually give better performance. Test it for yourself, and take the appropriate action based on the results of your test.

Exam Essentials

Tempdb is used by all of your databases to handle certain types of processing. It is a working storage location that can be configured locally on a device or in RAM. When you place tempdb in RAM, you should be aware of the benefits and dangers.

Know the benefits of placing tempdb in RAM.   Placing tempdb in RAM can give certain types of applications a performance boost. MIS applications in which there are a large number of ad hoc queries and heavy sorting use tempdb and would, therefore, benefit. OLTP-type applications that are more data-modification intensive (inserting, deleting, and modifying records) don't use as many tempdb resources and would benefit more by having additional memory for the data cache.

Key Terms and Concepts

Ad hoc query: An ad hoc query is a nonstandard query in which you join information from many different tables. These are generally what-if scenarios that are created on-the-fly rather than at design time. Ad hoc queries are commonly used for MIS reporting. For example, you want to know how many widgets between 2 and 3 inches were sold to males between the ages of 40 and 45 in Los Angeles County from the 1st of June through the 15th of May.

Data cache: The area of SQL Server memory used to store data from queries. The data cache and the procedure cache share what memory is left after all other SQL Server objects have been served. You cannot configure the amount of data cache or procedure cache, but you can specify what percentage of remaining memory each should have.

Procedure cache: The area of SQL Server memory where stored procedures are loaded after they have been run. Because they stay resident in memory, they can be quickly accessed for repeated use.

Sample Questions

1. Which of the following are benefits of placing the tempdb database in RAM?

   A. Significant performance boost for OLTP applications

   B. Significant performance boost for MIS applications

   C. Leaves more RAM for NT

   D. Leaves more RAM for SQL Server

   Answer: B is correct. There would probably be a performance loss for OLTP applications because they don't use tempdb very often. When you place tempdb in RAM, it leaves less memory for Windows NT and it doesn't affect how much memory you have allocated to SQL Server.

Configure the number of worker threads.

This exam objective tests your knowledge of what worker threads are and how they are used.

Critical Information

SQL Server is a single process (program) with many threads. The SQL Server is most efficient when a single thread is responsible for a single task. When the task list becomes larger than the number of threads available, some tasks will have to share threads in what is called *thread pooling*. Thread pooling decreases the efficiency of your SQL Server.

Every user connection gets a thread from this pool of threads. When a connection makes a request to the server, it is assigned a worker thread that performs that function on the server.

To avoid thread pooling, you can configure SQL Server to use a higher value for its maximum worker threads configuration. As you might expect, this also has its drawbacks. When a thread is created for a user connection, additional memory (about 20KB) is allocated for threading resources. If the maximum worker threads value is configured too high, unnecessary resources may be consumed because a new thread is automatically created for every user connection.

When determining the number of worker threads that should be configured, once again you must walk that thin line between resource consumption and system responsiveness. Too few threads will make the system unresponsive; too many threads will waste precious resources.

Fortunately, thread pooling is not always a bad thing. Every connection is not always active. Sometimes, connections made by a client application lie dormant while a user inputs data, prints a report, or engages in other activities. If this is the case, that thread can be used by another connection without causing any delay. The secret is to configure the maximum number of worker threads to represent the value of average active connections. You can check the Current Activity window in the SQL Enterprise Manager (Server ➤ Current Activity) to evaluate the current connection activity.

To change the size of the thread pool, you can use the sp_configure stored procedure or the Server Configuration screen in Enterprise Manager.

Exam Essentials

Worker threads are used to carry out SQL Server tasks. Remember the following points about worker threads when you are studying for your exam.

Know what worker threads are. Worker threads are stacks of tasks that the SQL Server must carry out. A new thread is assigned to each user connection. You may want to add additional threads as users spawn subprocesses that require additional threads.

Know what thread pooling is. Thread pooling occurs when the maximum number of tasks exceeds the maximum number of worker threads configured. When this occurs, one task will have to wait until another task is finished before it can use one of the threads.

Key Terms and Concepts

Thread pooling: Occurs when the maximum number of tasks exceeds the maximum number of worker threads configured. When this occurs, one task will have to wait until another task is finished before it can use one of the threads.

Worker thread: Stacks of tasks that the SQL Server must perform. A new thread is assigned to each user connection.

Sample Questions

1. Which of the following is true about worker threads?

   A. The number of worker threads available can be configured.

   B. If there are more tasks than worker threads, thread pooling occurs and performance may decrease.

   C. Every user connection is assigned a thread.

   D. Worker threads are used only when tempdb is in RAM.

Answer: A, B, and C are true. Worker threads are always used whether or not tempdb is in RAM.

Select the appropriate settings for read ahead.

This exam objective focuses on your understanding of what read ahead accomplishes in your SQL Server.

Critical Information

When data is accessed from a SQL Server, the query optimizer will usually select an index that will make this process more efficient. Sometimes, however, the optimizer determines that less I/O will result from reading every record of the table sequentially than from using an index that is not optimal for the task. When the optimizer makes this choice, it performs a *table scan*. A table scan is sometimes referred to as a *horizontal operation* because performing a table scan is a bit like reading a book from cover to cover to find a certain group of facts. The action intuitively progresses from page to page in a horizontal fashion from beginning to end.

You can make horizontal operations more efficient. One way is to *read ahead*. Read ahead is the process by which SQL Server pulls pages from disk to cache before a query actually needs them, thereby reducing the amount of time needed to process the query as the needed pages are already in RAM.

Read-ahead threads can place the necessary pieces of data in front of the query worker thread so that the query can be processed much faster. This procedure only works with horizontal operations because they are the only operations during which the read-ahead threads can predict exactly which page will be needed next. When an index is used, the next needed page is not known until the next index entry is accessed.

Exam Essentials

When you have the read-ahead configuration options configured properly, you can gain a significant improvement in horizontal operations. Keep these points in mind when you are studying for the exam.

Know the purpose of the read-ahead configuration options. The read-ahead configuration options allow SQL Server to fetch data more efficiently during a horizontal operation.

Key Terms and Concepts

Horizontal operations: These operations occur when you perform a table scan of some type. A table scan simply means that SQL Server reads a table from top to bottom without using an index. The query optimizer determines whether or not to use a index if it is available.

Sample Questions

1. Which of the following operations can be improved by correctly managing the RA (read-ahead) configuration options?

A. Vertical operation

B. Horizontal operations

C. Z-Hold operations

D. Queries that utilize indexes

Answer: B is correct. Horizontal operations are table scans in which the SQL Server reads data in the table from beginning to end. Horizontal operations are used with queries that do not take advantage of indexes.

Select the appropriate settings for locks.

This test objective focuses on your understanding of the LE thresholds (lock escalation thresholds). You should know what happens when an LE threshold is met and what their default values are.

Critical Information

One of the primary responsibilities of the server in a client/server scenario is managing *concurrency.* Because multiple clients can access the same data at the same time, ensuring data integrity and managing concurrency are critical tasks of the server. SQL Server manages concurrency by placing locks on data when it is being accessed by a client application.

> **NOTE** Concurrency is defined as the ability of the SQL Server to support multiple users at the same time, even if these users want the same data.

Appropriate locks can prevent two users from changing data at the same time. Locking can also be used to prevent a user from reading data that another transaction has changed, but not yet committed. Without locking, SQL Server would be of no use at all—there would be no way to determine what data was changed, when it was changed, where it was changed, or by whom. There are several different types of locks in SQL Server. The two we are concerned with are *page locks* and *table locks*. Page locks lock one 2KB data page at a time. SQL Server uses table locks when there are so many page locks on a table that it makes more sense to lock the entire table.

The LE threshold configuration options are values that allow you to specify when the page locks are escalated to a table lock. There are three settings for lock escalation: LE Threshold Maximum, LE Threshold Minimum, and LE Threshold Percent.

> **NOTE** LE threshold values are server-level. You cannot have alternate escalation values on different databases on the same server.

LE Threshold Maximum

The LE Threshold Maximum value sets the total number of pages of a table that an individual transaction can hold before the page locks are escalated to a single table lock. The default value is 200 pages.

LE Threshold Percent

The LE Threshold Percent value indicates the percentage of a table that can be locked at the page level before escalation to a table lock occurs. This is helpful for smaller tables. The default value for this setting is 0, which disables the percentage escalation.

LE Threshold Minimum

This setting allows an override of the LE percentage for smaller tables. For example, if you have a very small table consisting of only 30 pages and the LE threshold is set to 50%, the locks on that table would escalate as soon as 15 page locks were held by a single transaction. For a small table, this may be too small and the overhead too insignificant to make it worth escalating at 15 page locks. For this scenario, the LE Threshold Minimum will specify the minimum number of page locks to hold before the locks are escalated. The default for this value is 20.

WARNING   LE Threshold Minimum is an advanced option. You will not see this option in the Server Configurations window unless you set "Show Advanced Options" to 1.

Determining the proper settings for lock escalation requires you to know your data very well. You must know your user base and the level of concurrency required by the users. Allowing liberal lock escalation reduces resource consumption by allowing you to reduce the configured number of locks. This reduction comes at the expense of concurrency as more connections will want locks on larger objects.

Exam Essentials

Lock escalation can be used to improve the overall concurrency performance of your database. Keep the following in mind when you are studying for the exam.

Know what the different LE configuration options are used for, and know their default values.   The lock escalation threshold options are used to determine when a set of page locks are escalated to a table-level lock. The LE Threshold Maximum is used to specify the maximum number of pages that must be locked before the table lock occurs. The default value is 200. The LE Threshold Percent is used to specify the percentage of pages locked before escalation. The default value is 0, or disabled. The LE Threshold Minimum is an advanced configuration option that allows you to specify a minimum number of pages to be locked before an escalation can occur. This is useful for small tables with few pages. The default value is 20 pages.

Key Terms and Concepts

Lock escalation: When a process locks pages in a table, other users cannot access them. As a single process gains more locks on a table (such as during a table-wide data modification), eventually the LE Threshold is met. At that point the entire table is locked and the process holding the locks can complete more quickly because it doesn't have to wait for other process locks to release.

Sample Questions

1. Which of the following are true about the LE Threshold Maximum?

    A. This is a percentage of pages to be locked before a table lock occurs.

    B. This is the number of pages to be locked before a table lock occurs.

    C. This setting has a default value of 50 percent.

    D. This setting has a default value of 200 pages.

    Answer: B and D are correct. The LE Percentage is used for Answer A and has a default value of 0, or disabled.

Monitor log size.

One of the most important components of any SQL Server database is the transaction log. You need to be familiar with how to monitor the size of your transaction log.

Critical Information

The transaction log provides fault tolerance, a mechanism for reliable backups, automatic recovery functionality, replication functionality, and much more. These advantages can be realized only when the transaction log is working. When the log fills to capacity, you will no longer be able to use your database. For this reason, you need to keep a close eye on your log sizes and clean them out appropriately.

You must continually monitor the transaction log to ensure that there is enough space remaining for the users of the database to perform their tasks. The easiest way to watch this is through the Performance Monitor, as shown in Figure 11.1. By selecting the SQL Server - Log object, you can select counters to watch log sizes and percentages for all of your databases. Tracking these over time will allow you to find the right balance between log size, transaction activity, and backup strategy.

Necessary Procedures

You can use the SQL Performance Monitor to gather information about your transaction logs. Remember that when a transaction log fills to capacity, you can no longer use the database.

FIGURE 11.1: Transaction Log tracking using the SQL Performance Monitor

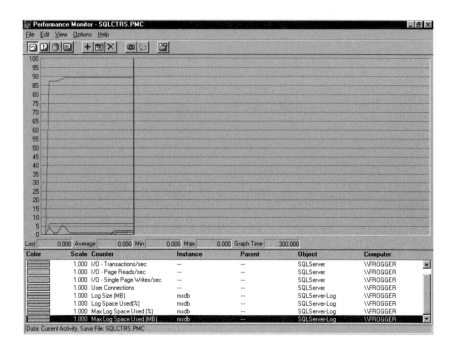

Follow these steps to monitor the contents of a transaction log:

1. Start the Windows NT Performance Monitor. If necessary, start a new chart by selecting File ➤ New Chart from the menu.

2. Add a new counter by selecting Edit ➤ Add to Chart. Select SQL Server - Log from the Object drop-down list. Select Log Space Used(%) from the Counter List Box. Select msdb from the Instance list box. Click Add and then Done to close the dialog.

3. The line will probably be flatlined at 0. However, watching this over time will give you the status of the transaction log.

4. Save the chart if desired. Exit the Performance Monitor.

NOTE The percent of log counters can only be monitored when a database has been created with its transaction log residing on a separate device.

Exam Essentials

Monitoring the amount of space used in your transaction logs is critical to maintaining your databases. If a log fills to capacity, you can no longer use the database.

Remember that you can use the Performance Monitor to monitor a transaction log. The Performance Monitor can be used to monitor the transaction log, but only if the log has been placed on a separate device from the database.

Key Terms and Concepts

Transaction log: Transactions logs contain all of the modifications to your data. If a transaction log becomes full, you can no longer make changes to your database. In order to avoid this problem, you must be careful when you manage your transaction logs.

Sample Questions

1. Which of the following are true about monitoring the transaction log?

    A. The transaction log can be monitored when it is on the same device as your database.

    B. The transaction log can be monitored with the SQL Performance Monitor utility.

    C. The transaction log can be monitored only when it resides on a device other than its database.

D. The transaction log can be monitored with the SQL Server TranMon utility.

Answer: B and C are correct. There is no such thing as a TranMon utility.

▶ Tune and monitor physical and logical I/O.

This exam objective focuses on your ability to properly configure physical and logical I/O. The monitoring portion of this exam objective can be done with the SQL Performance Monitor. The tuning is accomplished by properly managing configuration options like the data cache percentage, RA configurations, indexing, etc.

Critical Information

The performance bottleneck in almost every SQL Server database application is the I/O subsystem. This operating system component always seems to be working overtime to accommodate all of the users' requests for data. Fortunately, you can reduce the I/O on your server before it becomes a serious bottleneck.

I/O is the process of reading or writing from a database. The smallest unit of I/O in SQL Server is the 2KB page. All data is read in pages, and all data is written in pages. All I/O in SQL Server is logical I/O, but some I/O is physical I/O. Logical I/O is defined as a data read or write operation that is made to a cache or disk. Physical I/O is subclassified as a data read or write that is made to disk only.

When configuring I/O, your ultimate goal is to reduce logical I/O as much as possible. However, you can take additional steps to reduce physical I/O specifically.

Configuring Physical I/O

You can take several approaches to tuning physical I/O. Because all the effects of a reduction in physical I/O are cumulative (i.e., they will likewise reduce logical I/O), physical I/O seems to be a good place to start. I/O can be caused by either a data read or write activity. You need to understand how these activities use the I/O subsystem and how you can reduce this drain on resources.

Increasing Memory for Data Cache

As stated earlier, physical I/O is caused by data reads and writes to and from disk. The best way to reduce the amount of data accessed from disk is to increase your data cache so that the data can be in cache when it is needed, instead of sitting on disk. The best way to reduce the volume of physical I/O is to add more memory and increase the configured allocation of memory to SQL Server.

NOTE   If you increase the memory configuration to allocate more memory to SQL Server, this will split this memory between the data cache and procedure cache. If you want to allocate all of this new memory to a data cache, you must reduce the procedure cache configuration because this setting specifies the percentage of remaining memory allocated to procedure caching.

Using Read Ahead

We previously discussed the advantages that read ahead could have for reducing physical I/O. In reality, it does not reduce physical I/O, it simply shifts responsibility for physical I/O from the query thread to read-ahead threads. This shift allows the query to view these reads as logical reads, rather than physical reads.

NOTE   Remember that read ahead was only a factor for those operations which were horizontal in execution.

Setting Recovery Interval

When a transaction modifies a record in the database, that change is made to the page sitting in cache. If the page is not in cache already, the query reads the page into cache from disk, resulting in a physical read. After the modification is made to the page in cache, it is not immediately written to disk. The page stays in cache until it is flushed out by the system. Two system processes have the primary responsibility to flush a page from cache: the *checkpoint* and the *lazywriter.*

The checkpoint is a sleeping system process that wakes up about every minute and evaluates how much work has been done on each database since it went to sleep. When evaluating a database, it may choose to perform a checkpoint operation on that database if enough work has built up since the last time it actually performed a checkpoint. The amount of accumulated work that can build up before the database checkpoints is called the *recovery interval.* This option can be set in the Server Configurations window. The default value is 5 minutes.

NOTE Although the recovery interval is a server-level configuration, the value is used at the database level. The default of 5 minutes specifies that the dirty cached pages of an individual database will be flushed to disk as soon as 5 minutes of work accumulates for that database.

If the checkpoint process finds that the recovery interval has been reached, the database will be checkpointed. A checkpoint is the process of copying all dirty pages in cache to disk, both data pages and transaction log pages as well as pages representing uncommitted transactions. A page is defined as dirty if it has been changed since it was brought into cache. If the recovery interval has not been reached, the checkpoint process will skip that database and move on to the next database. When it has finished evaluating all of the databases on the server, it will go back to sleep.

NOTE In order to maintain data integrity, transaction log pages are always flushed to disk as soon as the transaction commits. This allows any committed transactions which may be waiting to checkpoint to be rolled forward during SQL Server auto recovery.

This approach is used rather than simply writing data modifications directly to disk because the longer the page can remain in cache, the greater the likelihood that the page may be modified more than once. Because the smallest unit of I/O is the page, the more of these that can be logical rather than physical, the better off you are. Changing a page in cache is logical I/O, and writing a page to disk is physical I/O. A page can be forced to stay in cache longer by increasing the recovery interval configuration. If more work is required to accumulate before the database is flushed, then the physical act of flushing will occur less often. This will reduce physical I/O.

Managing Logical I/O

In our discussion of physical I/O, our focus was on turning physical I/O into logical I/O. When you read and write from a database, you want the activity to occur in cache rather than on disk. When tuning logical I/O, you need to concentrate on ways to eliminate page access, whether those pages lie in cache or on disk. Of course it is impossible to eliminate page I/O completely. After all, that is the very work that the server is designed to perform. You can reduce page I/O significantly, however. This is done mainly through proper index usage and efficient application development techniques.

The reality is that much of the work involved in tuning logical I/O is beyond your control as an administrator. The database developer has much of the control over logical I/O. Some application development techniques are more efficient than others. If the developer uses efficient coding techniques, he or she can significantly reduce I/O. The method you use to ask for data does matter.

Using Indexes

A DBA can use one specific technique to reduce logical I/O. This technique is the proper use of indexes. By adding new indexes or restructuring existing ones, you may be able to reduce logical I/O. Be careful here. Indexes, although beneficial to extracting data, are very costly to maintain if you have too many of them. Every time that you add, delete, or modify a record, some or all of the indexes on that table may need to be updated. The more indexes you have, the longer this process will take.

Exam Essentials

Tuning and managing logical and physical I/O is a major task you must perform as an administrator. Keep the following points in mind when you are studying for the exam.

You should be familiar with what is stored in the procedure cache and the data cache and know how to configure them. Remember that the data cache consists of all data pages that have been read into memory. The procedure cache is used to store the query plans for procedures that you have executed. You can use the Server Configuration screen to make changes to the percentage of remaining memory that the procedure cache shares with the data cache.

Remember other tuning options at your disposal. You can configure the RA settings to shift the impact of physical I/O. Proper use of the recovery interval and the checkpointing process can reduce physical I/O. Proper use of indexes can also help to reduce your I/O needs.

Key Terms and Concepts

Logical I/O: All input and output operations performed in SQL Server are considered logical I/O.

Physical I/O: Physical I/O is a subset of logical I/O and occurs when you are actually moving data from disk to cache or vice versa.

Sample Questions

1. If you have 64MB of RAM on your Windows NT Server and you want to allocate 26MB to SQL Server and 14MB to the procedure cache, what should you do?

   A. Allocate 26MB to SQL Server, and set the procedure cache to 22%.

   B. Allocate 40MB to SQL Server, and set the procedure cache to 80%.

   C. Allocate 26MB to SQL Server, and set the procedure cache to 14MB.

   D. You cannot directly set the amount of RAM allocated to the procedure cache.

   Answer: D is correct. You cannot set the amount of RAM allocated to the procedure cache. You can only allocate memory to SQL Server. Once all of the database objects have been allocated RAM, the remaining RAM in SQL Server is divided between the procedure cache and the data cache. You can set the procedure cache percentage. This will allocate x percent of the remaining RAM to the procedure cache and the rest to the data cache.

2. Which of the following could you use to tune the physical and logical I/O in SQL Server?

   A. Proper use of indexes

   B. Proper use of the recovery interval

   C. Proper use of the read-ahead options

   D. Proper use of the procedure cache percentage

Answer: A, B, C, and D are correct. You can make changes to all of these configuration options to directly affect the amount of logical and physical I/O.

3. A checkpoint does which of the following? Select all that apply.

   A. Writes dirty pages to disk every minute

   B. Evaluates the option of writing dirty pages to disk every minute

   C. Writes dirty pages to disk whenever a recovery interval has been reached

   D. Reads pages from disk before a query will need them

   Answer: B and C are correct. Answer D refers to read-ahead options.

Tune and monitor memory use.

This exam objective focuses on how to determine the amount of memory to allocate to SQL Server and how to determine when your SQL Server has enough memory.

Critical Information

Determining how much memory to allocate to SQL Server is a relatively straightforward process. Chapter 1 discussed how much memory to initially give to SQL Server. As you may recall, a balance must be struck between SQL Server and Windows NT. If Windows NT does not have enough memory, its performance drops and, therefore, SQL Server's performance drops as well. If SQL Server doesn't have enough memory, its performance degrades.

To determine whether or not SQL Server has enough memory, you can look at several different performance counters in the SQL Performance Monitor, and you can use T-SQL.

Determining If Memory Is Too Low

One of the most important performance counters to look at in the Performance Monitor is the cache hit ratio. The cache hit ratio determines how often data is found in cache, rather than being read from hard disk. This value should be as close to 100% as possible. If it is low, you should think about moving your tempdb database into RAM, allocating more RAM to SQL Server, or adding more RAM to the computer and then allocating more RAM to SQL Server.

Determining If Memory Is Too High

It is possible to have too much memory allocated to SQL Server. Again, if you look at your cache hit ratio and it is continually very high (which is good), then you might want to investigate the objects that are stored in your caches. The easiest way to do this is to run the T-SQL command: DBCC SQLPERF(LRUStats).

This command will return the 20 oldest objects stored in cache in the form of a list of statistics. If you find many T-SQL commands and stored procedures that are used only once, then you may have more RAM allocated to SQL Server than is strictly needed.

Exam Essentials

Tuning memory can have one of the greatest impacts on your SQL Server. Too little memory can seriously hamper the overall performance of your databases. Too much memory (while not a horrible problem) can be better allocated to other services that your NT Server supports.

Remember what the cache hit ratio represents.   The cache hit ratio tells you how often data is found in data caches rather than in RAM. This value should be as close to 100% as possible. If it is low, you may want to allocate more RAM to SQL Server, or move tempdb into RAM.

Key Terms and Concepts

Tempdb: Your applications use tempdb as a work area. It is used primarily by ad hoc queries, queries in which you join many tables and for sorting.

Sample Questions

1. Which performance monitor counter relates most directly to memory use in SQL Server?

A. RA Threads

B. Cache hit ratio

C. MemStat

D. Page reads/sec

Answer: B is correct. The cache hit ratio determines the percentage of time that data was found in cache rather than being read from disk.

Set database options.

This test objective focuses on the standard database options that can be set. You can use the sp_dboption stored procedure or the Enterprise Manager to set these options. You need to know what the different options mean.

Critical Information

Database options can be set using the stored procedure *sp_dboption*. You may also use the Enterprise Manager shown in Figure 11.2. The options listed here are all dynamic. There is no need to shut down and restart the server in order for these options to take effect.

FIGURE 11.2: Database options

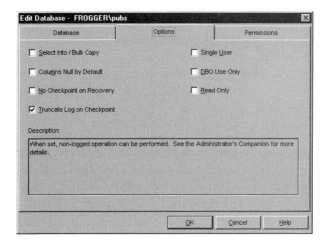

Select Into/Bulk Copy: You cannot turn off transaction logging in SQL Server; however, some operations are not logged by design. Two of these are Fast BCP and Select Into. Turning on this switch will allow a BCP into a table to proceed nonlogged. Select Into is a SQL command that creates a new table and populates that table with data in a single statement. Select Into is also a nonlogged operation. This switch must be engaged for this statement to be allowed.

WARNING   Immediately after any nonlogged operation you should perform a full database backup. Because the data was not placed into the transaction log, your database is not recoverable until you perform a database backup.

Columns Null by Default: When you create a table in SQL Server, you specify for each column whether it will allow null values. If you do not specify explicitly, this default is used. The default status of this checkbox is cleared. If you want your application to be compatible with ANSI standard behavior, you must select this checkbox.

No Checkpoint on Recovery: When the SQL Server service is restarted, the server goes into a state of recovery where transactions are committed or rolled back depending on the status of the transaction and the data that has been flushed to disk. This can be a lengthy process. To prevent the same recovery from being needed again, a checkpoint is normally performed on each database after the recovery of that database. If you have another system failure before the completion of the entire recovery, the checkpoint will enable the server to simply continue where it left off. Selecting this option allows the recovery to happen a little faster, but eliminates the benefits provided by this checkpoint.

Truncate Log on Checkpoint: When a checkpoint occurs, it marks a portion of the transaction as inactive. The inactive portion of the transaction log is that portion which lists all completed transactions up to the point of the first open transaction. When this option is selected, the transaction log is automatically cleared of this inactive portion without making a backup. This switch makes all transactions since the last full database backup completely unrecoverable. While very helpful in development to keep the transaction log from filling during testing, this option should be used with great caution on a production server. The default state of this checkbox is clear.

TIP The SA has the authority to call a checkpoint on any database by using the T-SQL CHECKPOINT command. If the Truncate Log on Checkpoint option is set, this action by the SA will *not* cause the transaction log to truncate. Truncation will occur only during a system-initiated checkpoint.

Single User: This switch prevents more than one user from having an open connection to the database at any point in time. This switch does not specify what position on the user hierarchy this user must be. When the database is placed in single-user mode, no users can have open connections to the database (other than the user performing the change to the setting). If this is not the case, the request to change this setting will fail. Some operations require a database to be in single user-mode. DBCC ShrinkDB is an example.

WARNING   Do not get the single-user database option confused with the ability to start the server in single-user mode. The database setting impacts only that database. Starting the server in single-user mode means that only one user will be able to access the entire server.

DBO Use Only: When this checkbox is selected, only the database owner or other logins aliased as DBO can access the database. When a database is created using the For Load option, this option is automatically set and must be cleared before your users will have access to the database.

Read Only: When this option is selected, the database is explicitly marked as read only. No data modifications to the database may be made. If your database application is truly a data warehouse with no data modifications being made, you may want to consider setting the read-only option to on. This will significantly improve performance. When a database is marked as read only, SQL Server completely disengages all locking on that database.

WARNING   If you will be replicating to a database using SQL Server replication, the subscriber cannot be marked as read only even if your users will be making no changes to the data. This prevents the distribution server from issuing replicated transactions on the subscribing database.

Exam Essentials

Appropriate use of the database options enhances your ability to manage your databases. You should keep the following in mind while studying for the exam.

You should be able to recognize the different database options available in SQL Server.   Remember when the following database options are appropriate: Select Into/Bulk Copy, Columns Null by Default, No Checkpoint on Recovery, Truncate Log on Checkpoint, Single User, DBO Use Only, and Read Only.

Key Terms and Concepts

Database options: Used to control access to your database, as well as some of the databases default behavior. For example, you can mark a database as read only and have it truncate the transaction log on every checkpoint.

Sample Questions

1. Which of the following statements is useful in a design-time environment (where you don't care about database backups)?

   A. Truncate Log on Checkpoint

   B. DBO Use Only

   C. Single User

   D. No Checkpoint on Recovery

   Answer: A is correct. Because you are in a testing and design phase, you don't care about backing up your data. In this case, you don't want your transaction log to fill up either. By choosing Truncate Log on Checkpoint, your log will be cleared after every checkpoint.

Update statistics.

This exam objective tests your ability to recognize when you need to update distribution statistics and choose the T-SQL command used to accomplish this task.

Critical Information

There are many ways that most queries can be performed. Sometimes there is a choice of indexes that can be used, and there is always the option of performing a table scan. The best option will be the one that results in the lowest amount of logical I/O. With all of these different options, how do you make the best choice?

The *Query Optimizer* determines which index, or none at all, will result in the lowest amount of logical I/O. It evaluates the data and the restrictions that the query is requesting. With this information, the optimizer estimates how many pages will be read for each possible scenario and chooses the scenario with the lowest estimated page I/O. Distribution statistics are used to make this estimation.

An index is based on keys that define the order of the index. Along with the pages that hold the index levels, every index also stores a page of distribution statistics that holds information about how the index keys are distributed throughout the index. This distribution statistics page is used by the optimizer in its estimation of page I/O. Without good distribution statistics, the optimizer would continuously make the wrong selections pertaining to which index to use to satisfy a query.

These distribution statistics pages are completely static. They are never updated unless you ask for the update. There are two ways to perform an update on the distribution statistics of an index.

- You can use the Enterprise Manager.
- You can use the SQL statement UPDATE STATISTICS.

You should update distribution statistics whenever data distribution for an index key changes significantly. When you add or delete a significant amount of records in a table, the indexes will also change significantly. After a major modification to your index, you should update the statistics as soon as possible.

Performing an Update Statistics is a horizontal operation and probably will require a significant amount of I/O in order to execute. This task should be scheduled for the evening or sometime when users will not be trying to access the same data.

Necessary Procedures

This example assumes that you have added several hundred new authors to the Authors table in the Pubs database. Because you will also be running many queries involving this table, you should update the statistics. Follow these steps to update statistics on the Authors table.

1. Open ISQL/W, and log in as the SA user.

2. Enter and execute the following query. (This will update the statistics for all of the indexes on the Authors table.)

    ```
    USE pubs
    UPDATE STATISTICS authors
    go
    ```

3. The result should read This command did not return data, and it did not return any rows. Close ISQL/W.

TIP The syntax of the UPDATE STATISTICS statement used in the previous example is intended to update the statistics of all of the indexes on the Authors table. If you only want to update the statistics for a single index, follow the table name with a comma and the index name.

Exam Essentials

You need to know when you should update the statistics in your database. Keep these points in mind when you are studying for the exam.

Know when you should run the UPDATE STATISTICS statement.
The query optimizer uses static statistic pages to decide when to use a particular index. These pages are updated only when you specifically ask for them to be updated. If a significant number of modifications has been made to your data (and therefore your index), your statistics page will not accurately reflect your index. You should use the UPDATE STATISTICS statement at this point to put your statistics page back in synch with your index.

Key Terms and Concepts

Statistics: Created when you initially create an index. The query optimizer uses these statistics to determine whether or not to use that index in the query itself. If you modify your data, the statistics in the index may, over time, become skewed. To correct the statistics, you can run the UPDATE STATISTICS command.

Sample Questions

1. Which of the following are appropriate situations to use the UPDATE STATISTICS statement?

    A. When you have added several hundred new rows to a table

    B. When you have deleted several hundred rows from a table

    C. When you have modified data in nonindex fields in several hundred rows of your table

    D. When you have modified data in index fields in several hundred rows of your table

Answer: A, B, and D are correct. Activities that significantly alter your index should be followed with an UPDATE STATISTICS command to keep them in synch.

CHAPTER

12

Troubleshooting

Microsoft Exam Objectives Covered in This Chapter:

▶ **Locate information relevant to diagnosing a problem.** *(pages 354 – 358)*

▶ **Resolve network error messages.** *(pages 358 – 361)*

▶ **Check object integrity.** *(pages 361 – 364)*

▶ **Investigate a database that is marked suspect.** *(pages 365 – 368)*

▶ **Restore a corrupted database.** *(pages 368 – 373)*

▶ **Re-create a lost device.** *(pages 373 – 374)*

▶ **Cancel a sleeping process.** *(pages 375 – 376)*

The objectives for this portion of the exam cover your abilities to correctly identify problems, determine where those problems originate, and decide what actions to take to alleviate those problems. As with any kind of troubleshooting, there are no hard and fast rules about what to do. Every situation is a little bit different. This section attempts to address the best practices. Troubleshooting is one of the toughest areas on the exam if you do not have any real-world experience. To gain some simulated experience, you can work through the exercises presented in *MCSE: SQL Server 6.5 Administration Study Guide* by Sybex. Let's now focus on the topics presented for the examination.

Locate information relevant to diagnosing a problem.

This exam objective focuses on your ability to gather information about a problem. It is interrelated with the exam topic that discusses how Windows NT and SQL Server are integrated in that you take advantage of the NT Event Viewer to gather information. You should also know a little bit about what an error message's different components represent.

Critical Information

One of the best ways to gather information about problems in your system is to look at the different logs associated with SQL Server. You can use the SQL Server Error Log and the Windows NT Event Log. Let's take a closer look at each of these logs and the components of an error message.

The SQL Server Error Log

The SQL Server Error Log is a group of ASCII text files located in the \MSSQL\Log folder. The most recent log file is called ERROR-LOG (with no extension). As each new log is created, the old log file is renamed to ERRORLOG.1, the existing ERRORLOG.1 file is renamed to ERRORLOG.2, and so on for up to six history logs. The oldest log file ERRORLOG.6 is not renamed but is overwritten by ERRORLOG.5.

Because the error logs are in ASCII format, you can use any text editor (e.g., Notepad or MS-DOS Edit) to view them. Word processing programs that are capable of reading ASCII files (sometimes referred to as MS-DOS text), such as Microsoft Word and Corel's WordPerfect, can also be used to view the information. You can also use the SQL Server Error Log viewer shown in Figure 12.1. To open the viewer, start the SQL Enterprise Manager, connect to your server by double-clicking on it, and then choose Error Log from the Server menu.

The NT Event Viewer

As you've learned in previous chapters, Windows NT also logs SQL Server events and errors, and you can view these with the NT Event Viewer. For SQL Server administrators, the disadvantage of using the NT Event Viewer is that it not only logs SQL Server events, but it also logs events from other applications running in Windows NT.

F I G U R E 12.1: The SQL Server Error Log

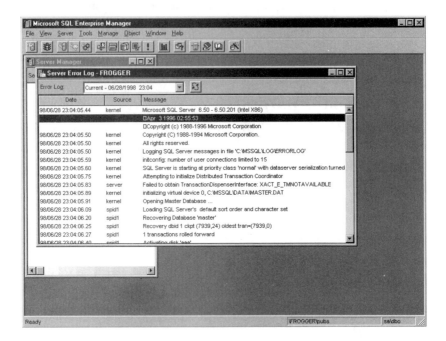

Error Message Components

You probably don't need to memorize the following list of error message components and severity levels for the exam. However, familiarity with the components may help you better understand what a question is asking.

An error message has the following components:

- The error number uniquely identifies the error message.

- The severity level tells you what type of problem has occurred in the SQL Server. Severity levels range from 0 to 25. In a nutshell:

  - Errors from 0–10 are informational.

  - Errors 11–16 are user errors.

- Errors 17 and 18 are resource problems. (A user's session is not normally interrupted when one of these errors occur.)

- Errors 19–25 are fatal errors in the program code. (Fatal errors are very rare and should be investigated as quickly as possible.)

- Errors with a severity of 20 and higher will terminate a user's connection to SQL Server.

- The error state identifies the source of the error. This can be especially useful if the same error occurs in several locations.

- The error message text tells you what the error is. Sometimes the text also includes a possible solution. For example, you might get an error message that tells you incorrect syntax near FOO. This could indicate that you forgot a comma, that you forgot to insert quote marks, or that you made some other such syntactical error.

To view the different severity levels and what they mean, refer to *MSCE: SQL Server 6.5 Administration Study Guide* by Sybex, or take a look at the SQL Server Books Online.

Exam Essentials

Troubleshooting is, indeed, an art form. As with any art form, you must practice to be good at it. You should attempt to work with all of the different troubleshooting techniques presented here before taking the exam. The more experience you have with this product, the easier the exam will be. Keep the following troubleshooting tips in mind while studying for the exam.

Know where to find troubleshooting information. Error messages in SQL Server are generated to several places. They can be generated and sent to the screen, but by default these errors are sent to different log files. In general, an error message is sent to both the SQL Server Error Log and the Windows NT Event Log.

Key Terms and Concepts

SQL Server Error Log: The SQL Server Error Log tracks errors and other messages on a per SQL Server session basis. When SQL Server is shut down and restarted, the error logs are rotated out in a six-log history.

Windows NT Event Log: The Windows NT Event Log tracks errors and status information for many different programs. The NT Event Log is broken down into several different segments. SQL Server writes events to the Application Log segment.

Sample Questions

1. Which of the following can be used to gather information about SQL Server error messages?

   A. SQL Server Error Log

   B. SQL Server Transaction Log

   C. Windows NT Event Log

   D. Windows NT Server Manager

   Answer: A and C are correct. SQL Server tracks errors in both the SQL Server Error Log and the Windows NT Event Log.

Resolve network error messages.

This objective tests your ability to interpret network problems and take appropriate action to resolve those problems. When you have a network problem, it is at the front-end, the network, the SQL Server, or any combination of these three items.

Critical Information

The first step in handling network problems is to isolate where the problem is occurring. Errors can come from SQL Server, the network, the front-end application, or any combination of these three items. Here is a list of some of the most useful practices for troubleshooting networking problems with SQL Server:

- Check your local connection to the SQL Server first. From the server machine, go to a command prompt and run the ISQL utility without the /S parameter. This will verify that you *do* have access to SQL Server and that named pipes is working on the local machine.

- Verify that you have network connectivity by running a NET VIEW statement from a command prompt or by double-clicking on the Entire Network icon in Network Neighborhood. If something shows up in Network Neighborhood other than your own computer, then you know that you can see the rest of the network.

- Check your remote connection to SQL Server over named pipes. You can do this by using the MAKEPIPE and READPIPE utilities.

- If named pipes comes up successfully, but you still cannot connect, you probably have a DB-Library problem. Verify that you have the same network library and DB-Libraries on both the server and the client computer. This can be done with the Setup program or with the Client Configuration utility.

Exam Essentials

Real-world skills will be helpful on the exam, but they are not an absolute requirement. Keep the following points in mind when you are studying for the exam.

Be able to recognize what the apparent problem may be given a scenario, the steps taken, and their results. In other words, know the steps listed previously in the bulleted list. For example, what steps can you take to verify that named pipes is working across the network? Use the MAKEPIPE and READPIPE utilities.

Key Terms and Concepts

Named-pipes utilities: The MAKEPIPE and READPIPE utilities come bundled with SQL Server and allow you to verify that the named-pipes protocol is working across the network and the local computer.

Sample Questions

1. Which tools would you use to verify that the named pipes protocol is loaded?

   A. SQL Server Setup utility

   B. SQL Server Client Configuration utility

   C. MAKEPIPE/READPIPE

   D. ChkPipe.EXE

   Answer: A, B, and C are correct. You can use the SQL Server Setup utility to verify that named pipes has been installed on the server or a client. You can use the client configuration utility as well. Finally, you can use the MAKEPIPE and READPIPE utilities to verify that named pipes is working properly, which in turn means that it has been loaded. What command can you use to verify that you have local access to SQL Server over a named pipe?

2. What command can you use to verify that you have local access to SQL Server over a named pipe?

   A. NET START MSSQLServer

   B. NET USE MSSQLServer

   C. makepipe and readpipe

   D. ISQL /Usa /P

Answer: C and D are correct. You can use the MAKEPIPE and READPIPE commands without the /S parameter to test local access over named pipes. You can also start the ISQL utility which communicates with SQL Server over a named pipe.

Check object integrity.

This exam objective focuses on your ability to properly detect which statements to use to verify the integrity of your database objects. You can use the various DBCC commands to check object integrity.

Critical Information

You can check the integrity of database objects by using the DBCC commands. There are several commands you should know for the exam, and several more that you may need to use to be a good administrator.

If these commands generate errors, you can try to recover data, or you can drop and rebuild the individual database objects in question. For example, if your system has a Severity 22 (SQL Server Fatal Error Table Integrity Suspect) or Severity 23 (SQL Server Fatal Error Database Integrity Suspect) error, DBCC commands may help you track down the problem. You can use the DBCC CHECKTABLE, DBCC CHECKDB, and DBCC NEWALLOC commands to investigate the consistency of your database. If you find that only one object is corrupted, you might try dropping and re-creating that object. If multiple objects are corrupted, there is still a chance that the error is in cache and not on the hard disk. Try stopping and restarting the SQL Server service or reboot Window NT, and then run the DBCC commands again. If this does not fix the problem, then the errors have migrated to your hard disk, and you should start your recovery procedures.

Table 12.1 provides a quick overview of some of the most common DBCC commands.

TABLE 12.1: Common DBCC Commands

DBCC Command	Function
DBCC CHECKTABLE	Verifies that index and data pages are correctly linked and that your indexes are sorted properly. It will also verify that the data stored on each page is reasonable and that the page offsets are reasonable.
DBCC CHECKDB	Same as DBCC CHECKTABLE, but it does the verification for every table in a database.
DBCC CHECKCATALOG	Checks for consistency in and between system tables. For example, if there is an entry in the sysobjects table for a table, there should be a matching entry (or entries) in the syscolumns table.
DBCC NEWALLOC	Verifies that extents are being used properly and that there is no overlap between objects that reside in their own separate extents.
DBCC TEXTALLOC / TEXTALL	Checks the allocation of text and image columns in a table or a database. The command has two options: FULL generates a report, and FAST does not generate a report.

Exam Essentials

The DBCC commands are used to verify object integrity. You should be familiar with what each of the DBCC commands in Table 12.1 reports.

Know the DBCC commands listed in Table 12.1. DBCC commands are used to check the consistency of your database and your database objects. You should be very familiar with the following three DBCC commands: CHECKDB, CHECKCATALOG, and NEWALLOC.

Key Terms and Concepts

Database objects: Items stored in a database. This includes tables, indexes, stored procedures, triggers, defaults, rules, etc.

Sample Questions

1. Which command can you run to verify that index and data pages are correctly linked, your indexes are sorted properly, the data stored on each page is reasonable, and the page offsets are reasonable for an entire database?

   A. DBCC CHECKTABLE

   B. DBCC CHECKDB

   C. DBCC CHECKCATALOG

   D. DBCC NEWALLOC

   Answer: B is correct. The CHECKTABLE command would only verify this information on the specified table.

2. Which command can you run to verify that index and data pages are correctly linked, your indexes are sorted properly, the data stored on each page is reasonable, and the page offsets are reasonable for a single table in a database?

   A. DBCC CHECKTABLE

   B. DBCC CHECKDB

   C. DBCC CHECKCATALOG

   D. DBCC NEWALLOC

   Answer: A is correct. If you want to check the integrity of the entire database, you should use the CHECKDB command.

3. Which command can you use to verify that extents are being used properly and that there is no overlap between objects that reside in their own separate extents?

   A. DBCC CHECKTABLE

   B. DBCC CHECKDB

   C. DBCC CHECKCATALOG

   D. DBCC NEWALLOC

   Answer: D is correct. NEWALLOC replaces the old CHECK-ALLOC command. Its advantage is that it doesn't stop running when an error is found.

4. Which command could you use to check for consistency in and between system tables?

   A. DBCC CHECKTABLE

   B. DBCC CHECKDB

   C. DBCC CHECKCATALOG

   D. DBCC NEWALLOC

   Answer: C is correct. You should run the CHECKDB and CHECKCATALOG commands before each database backup, otherwise you may back up bad data.

Investigate a database that is marked suspect.

This test objective is designed to investigate the problems that can occur that will mark a database as suspect. You should be familiar with these different causes.

Critical Information

A database can be marked as suspect for a number of reasons. You need to discover why a particular database was marked suspect before you can troubleshoot the problem. A suspect database will be grayed out in Enterprise Manager and will have the work (suspect) next to it as shown in Figure 12.2.

If a database device is offline, then all of the databases that have allocations on that device will be marked suspect. To resolve this problem, find out why the device is offline and bring it back online. Stop and restart the SQL Server service. The automatic recovery should unmark the suspect databases.

If a database device has been moved or renamed, or if it doesn't exist, you can bet that the error log will contain "Error 822 severity 21 Could not start I/O for request 2212." If the database device has been renamed, you should name it back to the original name and stop and restart the SQL Server service or investigate the sp_movedevice stored procedure in the Books Online. If the database device is missing, you should start your recovery procedures.

Another possible reason for a database to be suspect is a lack of permissions. This can happen only if you are using NTFS and the device is on the NTFS partition. You can fix this problem by making the administrator the owner of the device file and making sure that the SQL Server service has read/write permissions on the file as well.

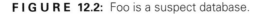

F I G U R E 12.2: Foo is a suspect database.

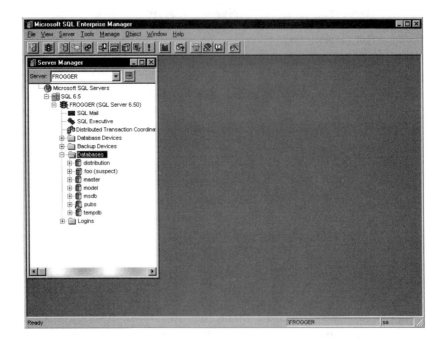

If the database appears to be fine, but you cannot remove the suspect status, you can run some T-SQL commands to manually reset the status of your database.

Necessary Procedures

You can run the following Transact-SQL script to manually reset the status of a database that has been marked suspect. For this script to work, you must first verify that the suspect database has allocations on devices that haven't been renamed and that are currently on-line. If this is the case, then try the following script:

```
sp_configure 'allow updates', 1
GO
```

```
RECONFIGURE WITH OVERRIDE
GO
USE master
GO
BEGIN TRAN
GO
UPDATE sysdatabases
set status=0 where name='your database name'
GO
```

If more than one row is affected by the UPDATE statement, issue a ROLLBACK statement and investigate further. Otherwise, continue with the rest of these statements:

```
COMMIT TRAN
GO
sp_configure 'allow updates', 0
GO
RECONFIGURE WITH OVERRIDE
GO
CHECKPOINT
GO
SHUTDOWN
GO
```

Exam Essentials

A database can be marked suspect for a number of reasons. Being a suspect is never much fun and SQL Server appreciates it even less than you might. You should resolve suspect databases as soon as possible.

Know what can cause a database to be marked suspect. Generally, a database is marked suspect when one of the devices that it has fragments on is no longer valid. An invalid device can be caused by a corrupted hard disk, being taken offline, or renaming the device.

Key Terms and Concepts

Suspect: If SQL Server detects problems with your database or the devices on which the database lives, it may mark your database as suspect. When a database is marked suspect, you can no longer use the database until the suspect status has been resolved.

Sample Questions

1. Which of the following can cause a database to be marked suspect? (Choose all that apply.)

   A. The database device is offline.

   B. The database device is in DBO Use Only mode.

   C. The database device is on an NTFS partition on which SQL Server does not have rights.

   D. The database device has been renamed.

Answer: A, C, and D are correct. Any of these could cause your database to be marked suspect.

Restore a corrupted database.

This exam objective stresses your need to understand the process of restoring databases in your system. You should focus on the major steps involved in the restoration process.

Critical Information

There are several steps to restoring SQL databases. The restoration process can be summed up in the following steps:

- Find and fix the cause of the failure.

- Drop all of the affected devices.

- Drop all of the affected databases.

- Re-create the affected devices.

- Re-create the affected databases.

- Set the database to single-user mode.

- Restore the database from a database backup.

- Restore (or reapply) the transaction log from a log backup.

- Change the database from DBO Use Only mode.

Find and Fix the Cause of the Failure

This step involves troubleshooting NT and/or SQL Server to determine the cause of the failure. There are two basic reasons for determining the cause:

1. To fix the problem

2. To prevent it from happening in the future

Drop All of the Affected Devices

After a hardware failure or corruption of a device, the device must be dropped before it can be re-created. You can use either the sp_dropdevice command or Enterprise Manager to drop a device. The syntax for the sp_dropdevice command is:

```
sp_dropdevice Device1, Device2, etc.
```

Drop All of the Affected Databases

Before the database can be re-created, it must be dropped. The normal procedure, sp_dropdatabase, expects to find the database before it drops it. This expectation can cause problems when the database is completely gone because the command will not execute properly. SQL Server 6.5 adds a DBCC command that will drop the affected database even if the database is gone or corrupted beyond repair.

Re-create the Affected Devices

SQL Server tracks databases by the amount of pages allocated on each device, and whether the pages are for data or the transaction log. Because of this, when you re-create devices to be used for the database, you need to make the devices as much like the originals as possible. For instance, if the original database was contained on the payroll.dat device file with a size of 100MB, and on the device called payroll2.dat with a size of 150MB, with the log on payroll_log.dat at 50MB, you should re-create these three devices with the same sizes.

You may want to use the Create for Load option when making your devices. Not only will it be faster to initialize the devices, but the devices can only be used to load backups. After loading is complete, the database will be marked DBO Use Only until you change it.

Re-create the Affected Databases

In order for the backup to be restored to the exact condition it was in, you will need to re-create the database with the same devices and sizes that were originally used.

Set the Database to Single-User Mode

SQL Server requires the database be in single-user mode before a restoration can take place. If you use Enterprise Manager, this is done automatically. If you use T-SQL commands to restore the database, you will need to set the option manually. The command is:

```
Set db_option "single user", TRUE
```

Restore the Database

Enterprise Manager can be used to quickly restore databases. Simply highlight the database to be restored, choose the backup, and choose to restore. You can also use the LOAD DATABASE command.

WARNING   SQL Server wipes out the old database when you restore a backup of a database—there is no merging of data.

Restore the Log

Enterprise Manager can be used to restore transaction logs. Restoring transaction logs can be thought of as reapplying all of the transactions just as they occurred.

NOTE   Unlike restoring the entire database, restoring transaction logs literally reapplies all of the transactions that took place between the time of the full database backup and the time of the backup of the transaction log.

To restore transaction logs using Enterprise Manager, highlight the database you want to restore and choose "Backup and Restore." You can also use the LOAD TRANSACTION command.

Change the Database from DBO Use Only Mode

If the database was originally created with the Create for Load option, after the database is loaded from a backup it will be marked as "DBO use only." In order for ordinary users to access the database, you will need to change it back to an ordinary database. You can use the sp_dboption stored procedure to accomplish this task.

Exam Essentials

Restoring a corrupted database is a series of steps. You should keep these steps in mind when you are restoring your databases.

Remember that you must re-create affected devices and databases in the same order in which you initially created them.
Because of the way that SQL Server stores its data, you must re-create and expand your databases and devices in the same order and size increments that you used initially.

Remember what transaction logs do. Transaction logs are a series of modifications written to your database. Once you have restored the data, you can apply your transaction logs from the time the backup was done through the latest transaction log backup. This can give you up-to-the-second recovery.

Key Terms and Concepts

Database backup: A database backup stores the data in the database. It does not store the transaction log unless the log and the database are on the same device.

Transaction log backup: A transaction log backup stores only the applied database transactions. It can be used for point-in-time recovery.

Sample Questions

1. What is the command to restore a database?

   A. RESTORE DATABASE

   B. RUN DATABASE

   C. LOAD DATABASE

   D. UNDO DATABASE

   Answer: C is correct. Use the LOAD DATABASE command to restore a database.

2. What is the command to restore a log?

   A. RESTORE LOG

   B. LOAD LOG

   C. RESTORE TRANSACTION

   D. LOAD TRANSACTION

   Answer: D is correct. To restore a transaction log, you use the LOAD TRANSACTION statement.

Re-create a lost device.

This exam objective focuses on two commands used to re-create a lost device: the DISK REINIT and DISK REFIT commands.

Critical Information

If your database device has been lost, but you still have valid backups, you can use the DISK REINIT and DISK REFIT commands to re-create the affected device and restore the database fragments that are on it.

The DISK REINIT statement adds the information previously stored in your *sysdevices* table back. The DISK REFIT command is used to re-create the information in your sysdatabases and sysusages tables.

These two commands should be treated as a single command. If you do not immediately follow the DISK REINIT command with a DISK REFIT command, you will be unable to use the DISK REFIT statement.

Exam Essentials

Re-creating a lost device involves dropping the device (if it hasn't been dropped already) and then re-creating the device by adding the proper entries to the appropriate system tables.

Keep the following in mind when you re-create a device.   You can use the DISK REINIT and DISK REFIT commands to place the appropriate information back into the system tables. Keep in mind that these two commands should be treated as two parts of a single statement.

Key Terms and Concepts

System tables: Tables in a relational database that are used for administrative purposes. For example, sysdevices, sysusages and sysdatabases are system tables in the Master database that track device names, size and location, database names, and which portions of a database live on which device fragments.

Sample Questions

1. Which of the following commands can be used to re-create a lost device?

A. RESTORE DEVICE

B. CREATE DEVICE

C. DISK REINIT and DISK REFIT

D. DISK INIT and DISK REFIT

Answer: C is correct. The other choices will generate a syntax error.

Cancel a sleeping process.

This exam objective resembles a vocabulary test. A *sleeping process* is a process that is waiting for a while before continuing to work. To cancel a process, you use the KILL statement.

Critical Information

Every process in SQL Server is assigned an SPID (system process ID) when the process is started. The SPID is stored in the sysprocesses table in the Master database, along with the following:

- Information on the process status (running, runnable, sleeping, and so on)

- A login ID

- A hostname, which is usually a computer name but can be an application name

- A block, which will contain the SPID of the blocking process

- The database name to which the process is attached

- A command that is running or waiting

You can view process information and cancel processes in two ways. As you might have guessed, you can view it from SQL Enterprise Manager or by using Transact-SQL statements. The KILL <procid> statement is used to kill a process.

There are a few rules to keep in mind when you are using the KILL statement:

- Only the SA can kill a process.

- System processes (MIRROR HANDLER, LAZY WRITER, CHECKPOINT SLEEP, RA MANAGER) cannot be killed.

- Processes running extended stored procedures (ones that begin with **xp**) cannot be killed.

Exam Essentials

The KILL statement is useful for killing processes that are hung, are blocking other activities, or are sleeping. Keep the following in mind when you are studying for the exam.

Remember who can use the KILL statement.   Only the SA can use the KILL statement.

Remember what processes cannot be killed.   Keep in mind that you cannot kill a system process or any extended stored procedures.

Key Terms and Concepts

KILL: The KILL statement is used by an SA who wants to cancel a process. You cannot kill a system process or a process that is using an extended stored procedure.

Sample Questions

1. Which of the following statements will cancel the Frogger sleeping process with a process ID of 7?

    A. WAKE Frogger, 7

    B. WAKE 7

    C. KILL Frogger 7

    D. KILL 7

    Answer: D is correct. The other choices will generate a syntax error.

Index

NOTE: Page numbers in *italics* refer to figures and tables; page numbers in **bold** refer to primary discussions of the topic

S

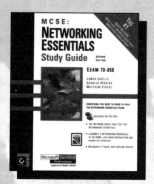

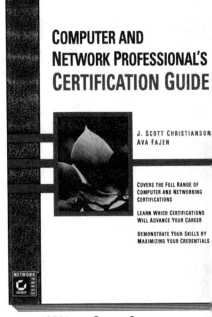